IMPLEMENTING

ISO 9001:2000

The Journey from Conformance to Performance

Tom Taormina
Productivity Resources, LLC

with

Keith Brewer
Dell Computer Corporation

Prentice Hall PTR
Upper Saddle River, NJ 07458
www.phptr.com

ISBN 0-13-061909-4

90000

Library of Congress cataloging-in-publication data available.

Editorial/Production Supervision: *Vincent Janoski*
Acquisitions Editor: *Bernard Goodwin*
Marketing Manager: *Dan DePasquale*
Manufacturing Buyer: *Alexis Heydt-Long*
Editorial Assistant: *Michelle Vincente*
Cover Design Director: *Jerry Votta*

© 2002 by Prentice Hall PTR
Published by Prentice-Hall PTR
Prentice-Hall, Inc.
Upper Saddle River, NJ 07458

Prentice Hall books are widely used by corporations and government agencies for training, marketing, and resale. The publisher offers discounts on this book when ordered in bulk quantities. For more information, contact Corporate Sales Department, Phone: 800-382-3419; FAX: 201-236-7141; email: corpsales@prenhall.com; or write Corporate Sales Department, Prentice Hall PTR, One Lake Street, Upper Saddle River, NJ 07458.

All products or services mentioned in this book are the trademarks or service marks of their respective companies or organizations.

Printed in the United States of America

10 9 8 7 6 5 4 3 2 1

ISBN 0-13-061909-4

Pearson Education LTD
Pearson Education Australia PTY, Limited
Pearson Education Singapore, Pte, Ltd.
Pearson Education North Asia Ltd.
Pearson Education Canada. Ltd.
Pearson Education de Mexico, S.A. de C.V.
Pearson Education—Japan
Pearson Education Malaysia, Pte, Ltd.

This book is dedicated to "My Three Sons" whose life experiences model the journey of continual process improvement.

CONTENTS

Foreword ....*xi*

Introduction ....*xv*

1

The ISO 9001 Imperative

1

ISO 9001:2000: What It Is and What It Isn't...3
Write Down What You Do 4
Do What You Write Down 5
Verify That You Are Doing It...8
Training Is Critical 10
ISO 9001 Makes Creative Processes More Efficient 11
ISO 9001 Is a Launch Pad for Success 11
The Language of ISO 9000 13
Why Does It Prevail?...14
Results of Certification 17
Why Achieve Certification?...18
When Certification Is Not Appropriate...20
Why Us and Why Now? 21
Is It an Investment or an Expense?...24

2

A History of ISO 9000

27

3

A Case Study at the Dell Computer
Asset Recovery Business

31

Phase 1 32
Phase 2 36
Summary 46

4

The 2000 Revision

47

5

The Relationship Among ISO 9000:2000,
ISO 9001:2000, and ISO 9004:2000

59

6

The Five Clauses of ISO 9001:2000

63

4 Quality Management System 64
5 Management Responsibility 78
6 Resource Management 101
7 Product Realization 113
8 Measurement, Analysis, and Improvement 145

7

ISO 9001 Implementation and Transition Strategy

169

Small Companies..169
Medium-Sized Companies..173
Larger and More Mature Companies...175
Organizations Transitioning from Earlier ISO Standards 177

8

Strategic and Tactical Planning

181

The Plan Outline 182
The Tactical Plan...186

9

The Implementers and Internal Audits

189

Successful Internal Auditing..191

10

Selecting a Registrar

199

11

Customer Focus and Results Measurement

203

What Is a Customer? 203
Measuring Results..206
Continual Process Improvement...209

12

Concurrent and Industry Segment Standards

213

13

Key Success Strategies

217

Write Down What You Do 218
Implementing the Processes 224
A Review of Other Key Strategies 225

14

ISO 9001 as a Profit Center

231

15

The Teachable Business Model

239

The Teachable Business Model 239

Appendix A

ISO-Babble and Audit-Babble: A Glossary of ISO 9000 Terms

249

Appendix B

Sample Quality Manual

257

Appendix C

Crosswalks Between ISO 9001:
1994 and ISO 9001:2000

281

Appendix D

An Audit Checklist for ISO 9001:2000

287

Appendix E

Functions Within a Quality Management System

311

Index

315

About the Authors

321

FOREWORD

Rarely does one have an opportunity to completely transform a large operating component of a highly successful company. This type of career opportunity usually comes from an unprofitable subsidiary of a major corporation, or a small young company being pushed by its backers to become profitable.

The Asset Recovery Business (ARB) is a division of Dell Computer chartered with managing product returns resulting from a 30-day, no questions-asked return policy. In July 1999, the organization was a microcosm of the parent company, including a manufacturing operation, marketing, telesales, and a retail outlet. It was previously run independently and therefore did not fully benefit from the best-in-class capabilities existing in the other divisions within Dell Computer. Additionally, the ARB managed returns across every Dell product line and for third party accessories, requiring an extensive knowledge of each product family. With Dell's unit shipments growing at a multiple of industry rates a transformation of the ARB business model was in order.

It has been my experience that the most successful approach for a general manager to undertake in moving an operating business to a new level is the introduction of a Total Quality Business Management system, based on the tenets of ISO 9000, backed by an investment in supporting Information Technology (IT) infrastructure. If the general manager can assemble a team of believers and zealots of this process, success is inevitable. This was the case for the Dell Computer ARB. In assessing the ARB capabilities in August 1999, five strategic development areas were identified.

- Infrastructure development
- Sales channel development/consolidation
- Increased manufacturing capability
- Metrics and reporting
- Quality

The first order of business was to build the leadership team to drive the necessary changes. Directors and senior managers were recruited for quality, manufacturing, sales and marketing, IT, engineering, and human resources. Each of these leaders recruited key individuals into their organizations, developing a management team with a renewed focus on process, business metrics, and financial results.

From the beginning, the leadership team focused on developing a Business Management Interactive System (BMIS) as an enabling technology for the business. Business processes were mapped, refined and documented in the system. Financial metrics and results were integrated into the BMIS, along with a communications tool to permit real time feedback at all levels of the organization. The BMIS quickly became the foundation for the transformation, acting as the system of record, the document control function and a Web based training and instruction tool.

Emphasis was placed on strategic planning and two-way communication across the division. Goals and objectives were established for all managers and communicated down through the organization. Weekly business planning sessions were established, including all functions within ARB and support organizations from within the parent company. The key was to communicate and over communicate strategic initiatives, quarterly business objectives, and financial results across the organization. Quarterly employee recognition events were utilized to celebrate successes, communicate and reinforce a focus on results, and drive morale.

Operationally, the existing manufacturing organization required a major restructuring to accommodate explosive growth. Goals were established and centered in three areas: increasing existing volume and capacity on the production line to meet growth projections, meeting product quality levels of Dell new product factories, and inventory management and financial controls. Six Sigma training was initiated for first- and second-level managers to achieve a common process language across the business functions.

Quality and safety organizations were established within the manufacturing team. Parent company metrics were adopted, with the focus placed on building infrastructure and feedback mechanisms into the production lines. A baseline was established against the metrics, and stretch goals were set and communicated. Training programs were launched, including an eight-hour new employee introduction seminar, hands-on production line training, and Web-enabled instructional training through BMIS. A Corrective Actions Board was incorporated into the business philosophy, providing a rigorous testing of process changes, formal communication of changes, and a documented system of record.

In parallel with these activities, an assessment of existing sales channels and future requirements was initiated. The hypothesis was that refurbished system customers were not first-time buyers, so they didn't need to touch and feel the product, and primarily needed a sales-person for knowledge about what was available to sell. A second hypothesis was that with an efficient sales channel, all products that could be moved into finished goods could be sold. The existing sales channel consisted of a consumer telesales operation, a commercial telesales operation, and a retail outlet. The most efficient sales channel was an e-commerce channel. The issue was that unlike other e-commerce web sites, ARB inventory was made up of unique systems. Dell is a build-to-order manufacturer and returns were originally built to unique customer specifications. The numbers were clear, however. It was not cost-effective to scale the retail outlet for projected growth and increasing the telesales capability was very expensive.

A program was launched in May 2000 to exit the retail space and temporarily absorb the sales volume in the telesales channels. In the following fiscal quarter, an e-commerce development was launched, including an inventory tracking system to populate a finished goods database. The system was on-line two quarters later, during the Christmas 2000 sales season. All processes were defined, documented and trained through the BMIS.

The result of this effort is a renewed business that within 18 months could be measured and compared with the best in Dell. The key business metrics tell the story. Sales volume increased nearly 150% with the e-commerce channel absorbing 70% of Consumer sales and 40% of Commercial sales. Marketing and sales costs were reduced significantly with an additional reduction forecasted for 2001. Manufacturing capacity increased three-fold through productivity increases, and quality increased four-fold. Inventory accuracy hit an all time high, and the safety record exceeded industry norms and became the best reported in Dell. Overall productivity increased dramatically as measured by revenue per employee.

We entered the next stage in the evolution of ARB, in February 2001. Loaded with an on-line management tool, a highly efficient e-commerce channel, and a strong manufacturing capability, a plan was developed to turn the ARB into a center of competency for returned system management. The plan centered on moving sales responsibility into existing Dell sales organizations and reporting the manufacturing facilities into the parent organization. The new role of the ARB is to manage the e-commerce site, provide daily visibility into system returns to the various Dell business segments and manage pricing and promotion activities for all segments. The enabling technology is the BMIS.

I am a business manager who is a student of quality. When the opportunity arose to document our success story as part of a book that promotes my value and belief system, I gave it my full endorsement. As you read the philosophy of "Quality as a Profit Center," hear more about the methodology implemented by Tom Taormina and Keith Brewer, and gain more insight into the successes it has brought to Dell ARB, you will discover compelling reasons to look toward totally integrating your business management system, as we have done. If you are a business professional who thinks that quality and ISO 9000 are overhead expenses and necessary evils, look again at the performance gains we have realized in a very short period of time. Don't put this book down until you have mapped a strategy to make quality everyone's job in your organization.

Michael P. Gagliardi
former Director and General Manager, Asset Recovery Business,
Dell Computer Corporation

INTRODUCTION

Most of us who were trained in traditional quality control and quality assurance tools have been on an ongoing journey to find a way to communicate quality concepts to other members of our organizations. Unfortunately we were, typically, ensnared in autocratic and bureaucratic national, industry, and military standards based on conformance, inspection, and detection. These models manifested themselves as prescriptive and adversarial tools to be used "against" those who were trying to deliver a product or service to the customer. With little positive information to offer to our coworkers, our efforts to "help" were seen as outside meddling.

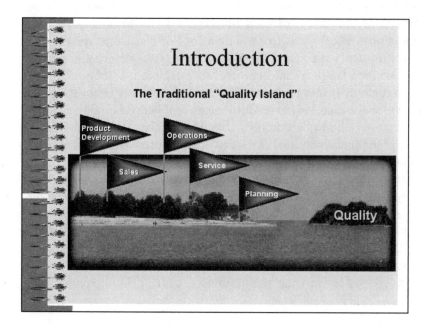

Over the last 30 years, the quality profession has grown substantially from its early legacy of "Write 'em up and shoot 'em down." We have developed amazing tools of proactive problem avoidance and factual decision making. To this day, however, quality professionals are often included in business processes only by brute force, when required by edict or by disaster control. We seldom find a sympathetic ear to our cries to incorporate quality tools into processes rather than establish inspection tollgates to find problems after the fact.

ISO 9000:1987[1] was fashioned after many of our classic quality standards. Within it, however, a few of us saw a new wrinkle that was the first glimmer of truly proactive quality. It contained elements instead of requirements. It implied that organizations should document the procedures that made them successful, operate to those procedures, and regularly audit the processes for conformance. That was a significant departure from generating volumes of prescriptive standards that were only read by the authors, followed only by edict, and inspected to death, after all costs were built into the product or service. We saw elegance in its simplicity and adaptability across industries and cultures. It offered the concept of proactive process auditing that we saw leading to the dismantling of tollgates and the removal of barriers to cooperation.

As with so many explosive concepts of the last few decades, I doubt that the founding fathers of ISO 9000 could have visualized the scope and breadth of the impact of their brainchild on traditional quality models. Its innocuous concept was to provide a tool of consistent quality to suppliers and customers within the European Union. It was advertised as an instrument that bridged language and cultures to establish a baseline for supply chain management. It met its expectations, but like many innovations discovered in the "space race," it led to unforeseen and yet to be realized spin-offs.

I would like to delude myself and boast that the worldwide acceptance of ISO 9000 is a result of the lofty goals of proactive quality management. In rare instances this might have been, but the truth is that a number of industries seized it as a "supply chain management" tool. As its adoption was more widely publicized, industries such as oil and gas exploration found it invaluable in reducing costly two-party quality system audits. Instead of maintaining staffs of auditors to evaluate their suppliers and staffs of hosts for their customers' auditors, it became clear that requiring suppliers to be independently audited and certified to ISO 9001 or ISO 9002 was much more cost-effective than maintaining a cadre of audit personnel. There's

---

[1]*Since the inception of the ISO 9000 family of standards in 1987, it has been customary to refer to the entire series as ISO 9000. With the release of the 2000 revision, there is now only one requirements document, ISO 9001 (retiring ISO 9002 and ISO 9003), so the new convention is to refer only to that. ISO 9000 is now the "Fundamentals and Vocabulary" document and most references to ISO 9000 herein are in the context of the 1987 and 1994 versions.*

nothing more powerful than significant reductions in overhead costs to spark the success of a quality management program. As word spread from boardrooms to locker rooms, others jumped on the bandwagon and began requiring ISO 9000 certification as a prerequisite to bidding on proposals or being added to an approved supplier list. As capitalism always prevails in free-market countries, hosts of consulting and auditing firms soon popped up like spring flowers, and a cottage industry was born around a simple set of quality tenets. Eventually, spin-offs were developed within specific industries; QS 9000 is probably the most dramatic example as an automotive industry standard. Finally, we who preach enlightened quality management had a tool that was becoming universally accepted that we could bring to senior management without being immediately thrown out the door for wanting to create more overhead and bureaucracy.

Again, the brilliance of the founding fathers was revealed when they set up standing technical committees and advisory groups to continually evolve and revise ISO 9000. These international bodies of experts developed a methodology for actively listening to those who are implementing the standard. They built an evolutionary model for continually updating the standard as success models were proven and documented. The first revision was published in 1994, including corrections and clarifications of unclear terms and jargon. The technical committees were hesitant to make any radical changes, fearing that the growing acceptance of the standard would come to a halt if it became too complex or prescriptive or moved toward becoming an excellence model.[2]

There were two factions within the quality community that kept debate over the future of the standard lively. One group (them) wants to keep it at a very baseline level and allow companies to find their own process models and excellence models to move from conformance to continual improvement. In other words, this faction wants the standard to remain as just the ante to get in the poker game. The other faction (us) lobbies to slowly upgrade the standard to encourage continual improvement and discourage those who would use the standard for minimal compliance just to get on a bidder's list. This group recognizes the need to keep the standard universal and not move it toward competing with existing excellence models.

From my experience, working with most of the major registrars in the United States, the first faction is the most pervasive. The registrars often comment that most of their certification audits wind up as exercises to find

---

[2]*State quality awards, Malcolm Baldrige, and Six Sigma are some common excellence models.*

minimal compliance in a sea of dissociated and inconsistent processes and procedures. An unfortunate offshoot of capitalism is that many consulting firms and registrars sell ISO 9000 as a magic pill for those looking for a quick fix to their quality or supply chain management problems. It has been possible to use boilerplate procedures and coaching to achieve, at least, initial certification to ISO 9001 or 9002. There are enough registrars whose profit motives drive more relaxed approaches to certification audits, hoping that companies will take a subtle hint and begin the journey of continual improvement on their own. Registrars often operate on the razor's edge, balancing their credibility with not making the customer unhappy enough to change registrars or give up on ISO 9000 certification. Consultants often strive to make themselves invaluable and permanent fixtures in client companies, withholding transfer of knowledge to the client in the pursuit of ongoing fees. Neither of these scenarios encourages motivation beyond minimal compliance at the lowest overhead cost. The small numbers of us who are using ISO 9000 as a tool of proactive continual improvement have been finding opportunities only among the most enlightened of business owners and operators. When a registrar shows up for an initial audit at a company that has been at my effect, there is often surprise and amazement that the organization actually lives their quality management system and that they are using it to enhance process performance.

In early 2000, the draft of the proposed next revision to ISO 9000 began its circulation through the quality community. It was greeted with mixed reactions because it was a total rewrite of the 1987 and 1994 versions. It replaced 20 elements with five clauses. It advocated the use of "The Process Approach."[3] It required emphasis on continual process improvement and customer satisfaction. It proposed that companies must live their quality policy. By its design, it also closed most of the loopholes that allowed minimally compliant systems to achieve ongoing certification. Once again, the capitalists saw a profit motive and the purists saw a tool to spread the gospel of continual improvement. Courseware and publications hit the street immediately, distributed by those who warned of impending doom for organizations that did not upgrade immediately. It reminded me of software manufacturers that imply that your programs will self-destruct if you don't buy their latest upgrades. Being a purist (with ongoing capitalistic aspirations), I

---

[3] *The Process Approach implies that every activity in an organization has a defined start and finish and can be measured.*

held out, advising all who would listen to stay abreast of the new revision but not spend any money until the final standard was published.[4]

When the final draft was published in September 2000, there was an immediate flood of new publications and seminars claiming to enlighten everyone on the changes from the first draft. On December 13, 2000, the revised standard was published. There is now a third wave of material available (including mine) with the "real" story of ISO 9001:2000. It will now take months for registrars and companies to develop pragmatic guidelines for implementation and auditing. In fact, the ISO Implementation Committee has stated that the registrars and their client companies will wind up establishing realistic implementation standards, leading to a new, evolving body of knowledge for others to model. Because companies will have a three-year window after release to become compliant, a viable compilation of anecdotal and experiential data could be five years in the future. If you are planning to be minimally compliant with ISO 9001:2000, this is ammunition to procrastinate. If you want to be a quality pioneer instead of a quality spectator, why wait? The process methodology included in ISO 9001:2000 exists in this book, is validated (by the Dell ARB success story), and is available for pioneering leaders to implement today.

Since 1991, Productivity Resources, LLC has been helping organizations make the journey from conformance to performance with a process called "ISO 9000 as a Profit Center." Our exact methodology is proprietary, and our concepts are elegant in their simplicity but difficult to implement. We often share the process in public forums and it is contained in my trilogy of ISO 9000 books,[5] so we hope to encourage you to proactive implementation as opposed to procrastination.

Our journey is one of a very nontraditional approach to quality management. It is difficult to plan and even more difficult to implement because it takes visionary leaders with great courage to become quality pioneers and enable the cultural change necessary to move most organizations from conformance to performance. This methodology requires paradigm shifts in traditional companies and a foundation in process building for younger

---

[4]*Any books or articles published prior to 2001 may contain data from early drafts of ISO 9001:2000 that has subsequently been changed. If you have published material that has only Clauses 5 through 8 or makes reference to "permissible exclusions," it is probably out of date and not completely representative of the final standard.*
[5]*Virtual Leadership and the ISO 9000 Imperative, Prentice Hall, 1996; Successful Internal Auditing to ISO 9000, Prentice Hall, 1999; Assessing ISO 9000 for Your Business, ABS Government Institutes, 1999.*

entrepreneurships. The rewards are beyond comprehension for those who would challenge traditional methods and find in each tenet of quality an opportunity for a proactive center of profit. The success of global business in the new millennium will be based on the implementation of one profound concept. We must develop a business culture based on mutual trust and communities of healthy, learning entrepreneurs who are responsible for their own actions. All previous models have been based on manipulation of people and all have failed to achieve lasting success. Behavior modification has never, and will never, yield a high-performance business community.

Just as the model of manipulation of people[6] has failed, so has trying to *control* or *assure* quality. All previous models assumed that human error and variability were inevitable and that controls must exist to ensure compliance. The healthy learning communities of the 21st Century will return ownership of outcome to the people who perform the work. These entrepreneurs will have a clear vision and the power to execute and continually improve their processes. Process variability will be eradicated by personal craftsmanship and its effect will never reach internal and external customers. The craftsmen's rewards will be based on customer satisfaction. The word *quality* will disappear from our lexicons because the traditional concept of quality will become a state of mind, rather than an activity.

The world will not end with the demise of the "quality police." In fact, a world without quality will lead to the greatest increase in quality and productivity ever seen. This concept is as revolutionary as the invention of the silicon chip and as old as recorded time. When we finally embrace these truths, they will have just as profound an impact on global business as the personal computer.

The longest journey begins with a first step. This journey begins with the realization that we have collected sufficient anecdotal and experiential data to move to the next stage along the continuum of business maturity. That step is the theme of this book, moving from conformance to performance. Specifically, utilizing ISO 9001:2000, we will build a new paradigm that integrates the tools of quality and process improvement and share them with everyone in the value delivery system. We will show compelling reasons for dismantling adversarial, overhead inspection, detection, and assurance functions and replacing them with accountability for all who operate

---

[6]*Most colleges and universities teach the behavior modification method of management, in which business leaders are encouraged to manipulate the behavior of their people to achieve desired business results. Data is now being revealed that suggests that this approach does not work and will never work for long-term business success.*

the processes. We will reveal a framework for the cultural evolution that is required to ensure that organizations are postured to assume a leadership role in their industries. We will cite case studies where the transition from conformance to performance has proven to be one of the most profoundly beneficial activities ever undertaken. We will chart the path of converting overhead costs into opportunities for profit. The centerpiece case study featured will be the ARB of Dell Computer. The Dell case study will show how one enterprise has moved their baseline quality management system from conformance to performance. ISO 9001:2000 will help you move your ISO 9001 initiatives from simple conformance to continual improvement and from an overhead expense to a profit center. This book provides clear evidence that a quality management system based on ISO 9001 can be a system of continual business process improvement, instead of a tool of traditional (and costly) quality management.

1

The ISO 9001 Imperative

This chapter is a reality check that clearly defines the imperatives of becoming ISO 9001[1] literate. It gives business leaders enough information for them to know exactly why they need to implement ISO 9001 and what level of urgency they should exercise to deploy it in their organization. Further, it shows the leaders how to use ISO 9001 as a marketing tool. ISO 9001-certified companies are seen as leaders in their industries and that marketing advantage can be the difference in winning highly competitive contracts. This chapter also encourages companies to seek out new markets and new customers previously closed to them because they did not have the credentials to bid on jobs requiring quality management system certification.

The universal acceptance of ISO 9001 can be traced directly to the simple elegance of its fundamental tenets:

---

1. *Since the inception of the ISO 9000 family of standards in 1987, it has been customary to refer to the entire series as ISO 9000. With the release of the 2000 revision, there is now only one requirements document, ISO 9001, so the new convention is to refer only to it. ISO 9000 is now the "Fundamentals and Vocabulary" document and most references to ISO 9000 herein are in the context of the 1987 and 1994 versions.*

- Document what you do.
- Do what you documented.
- Verify that you are doing it.

More specifically, ISO 9001 encourages each company to distill what makes it successful and document the success formulae in the form of process procedures. It compels companies to systematically follow those procedures until the procedures no longer support their needs. As processes evolve and change, the process owners must continually change, delete and add procedures to reflect the newer methods. To verify that the documented procedures are being followed, ISO 9001 suggests that companies build a nonadversarial system of internally auditing those processes and procedures, regularly and forever.

Some critics of ISO 9001 claimed that the standard said nothing about customer satisfaction or continual improvement. The 2000 revision has taken care of those shortcomings and a few others. ISO 9001:2000 now includes requirements for the following:

- Effective operation and control of processes
- Continual process improvement
- Proving evidence of management commitment
- Addressing customer needs, expectations, and satisfaction
- Evaluating training effectiveness
- Managing the physical work environment
- Establishment of measurable quality objectives

In other words, ISO 9001:2000 has raised the bar from a quality assurance system of minimal compliance to a quality management system that will recognize an organization's commitment to quality and to the customer.

In this chapter we build on these tenets and explore the frequently asked questions about ISO 9001. We dispel the myths and rumors surrounding the standard and its implementation. We show how it can help your company's strategic quality initiative and continual improvement efforts and, ultimately, your business goals and profitability.

ISO 9001:2000: What It Is and What It Isn't

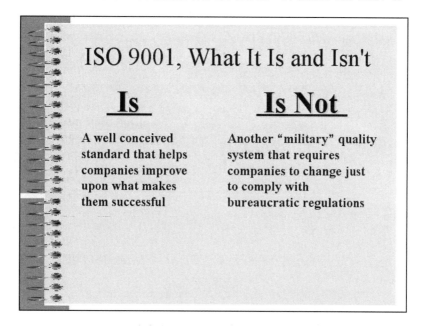

The downfall of most quality conformance systems is that they rely on a system of checks and balances, rules and remedies, prevention and detection, doers and checkers. There is almost always an action followed by a reaction. Traditional quality systems assume that the jobholder is going to make mistakes and it erects ever-growing walls to contain those defects. Within these walls are small doors, tended by learned individuals who can judge which avenue the defective material will travel. These guardians of quality pass judgment on which products are acceptable, which should be reworked, which must be repaired, and which are banished to the scrap heap.

Conventional quality wisdom assumes that workers are capable only of rote, repetitive actions and that more highly trained individuals downstream must ensure that all previous steps were accomplished successfully before products or services can move forward in the value delivery continuum. Each time a process is added, the bureaucracy to support it has to be added into the system.

If a company is held compliant to a rigid government or industry quality standard, there are usually specific prescriptive steps required for their quality system to be approved to the appropriate standard. Compliance often includes changing the way a company does business, adding detective and preventive steps to a process, and adding specific police functions to ensure compliance. I have seldom seen a prescriptive quality system that did not add cost to the product or service. I have also witnessed few that added any significant value to product or service quality. Inevitably, I have never seen a rigid quality system that didn't systematically reduce productivity and worker morale because of its adversarial nature.

WRITE DOWN WHAT YOU DO

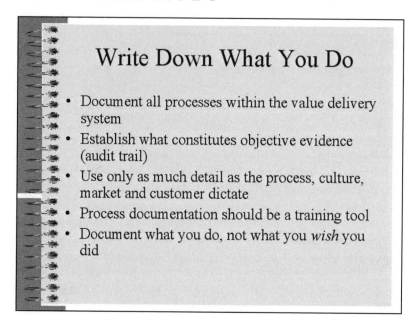

If you have an existing quality management system, ISO 9001 will not compel you to dismantle it. In fact, many companies have concurrent standards that exceed the basic requirements of ISO 9001. To achieve certification, these companies need only verify compliance with ISO 9001 and provide evidence that their system is compliant and effective through examination of quality records and compliance audits. If your quality management system is effective in producing consistent results, your journey to certification may be painless and inexpensive. In my experience, however, most companies fail to document their processes, have old and ineffective operational procedures, or do not follow what is documented. In these cases, ISO 9001 implementation becomes a value-added, cathartic process of systematically replacing ineffective procedures, adding new and productive ones, and streamlining operations. Here are a couple of quotes from ISO 9001 that summarize the nonprescriptive approach it offers to quality management:

> *This International Standard promotes the adoption of a process approach when developing, implementing and improving the effectiveness of a quality management system, to enhance customer satisfaction by meeting customer requirements.*[2]

> *All requirements of this International Standard are generic and are intended to be applicable to all organizations, regardless of type, size and product provided. Where any requirement(s) of this International Standard cannot be applied due to the nature of an organization and its product, this can be considered for exclusion.*[3]

Despite rumors that abound about the process of ISO 9001 implementation, there aren't any prescriptive elements that you will have to implement that do not make sense for your business culture! You need only address those elements that are germane to your business. If you have disdain for bureaucratic procedures that stifle creativity and productivity, then ISO 9001 is the quality system for you. If you would like to dismantle the walls of inspection and find more productive uses for those talented guardians of quality, please read on.

DO WHAT YOU WRITE DOWN

In most companies, quality engineering, manufacturing engineering, sustaining engineering, human resources, or all of these departments write operational procedures. The procedures are often written in a form that demonstrates the prosaic skills and furthers the technical writing career of the author. They are written in the most stylish form of the language of the discipline of the author. If quality engineering writes them, they are full of quality buzzwords. If human resources writes them, they are full of kinder and gentler rules of conduct that can be changed in a heartbeat. They are seldom written in a form that concisely communicates policy or establishes brief,

---

2. *ISO 9001:2000, Paragraph 0.2.*
3. *ISO 9001:2000, Paragraph 1.2.*

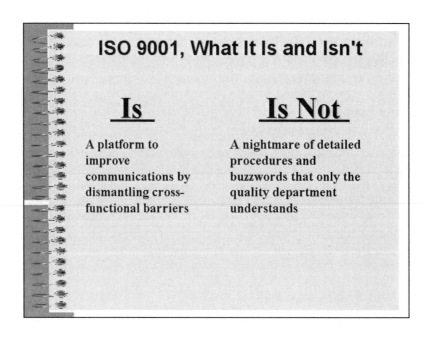

Do What You Write Down

- Follow the process procedures
- Make them dynamic, change as the business changes
- Don't develop "work-arounds"

definitive procedures. They are usually full of pseudo-legalistic terminology designed to cover every nuance. In fact, the more convoluted contingencies a procedure writer can cover, the higher his or her perceived worth may be.

ISO 9001, What It Is and Isn't

Is

A platform to improve communications by dismantling cross-functional barriers

Is Not

A nightmare of detailed procedures and buzzwords that only the quality department understands

Most procedures I have read establish clear boundaries and erect organizational silos. Some really verbose procedures actually dig moats around departments and isolate them from the rest of the world.

Another truism that I have found is that procedures are seldom read by anyone other than the author. They are reviewed for form, nit-picked for detail, approved in a vacuum, and filed away until something blows up. When there is a crisis, procedures are usually read by a "witch hunter" searching for evidence to support a case against some poor jobholder that will lead to a "burning at the stake."

If the documentation requirements of ISO 9001 are followed, the results will be a concise quality manual that establishes basic policies, supported by second- and, as required, third-tier job descriptions and process procedures that reflect, in few words, how things are actually done. The best procedures are the most brief: It took eight years to write the original ISO 9001, yet it was less than seven typed pages in length. As I help companies write procedures, I often share this quote with them:

> *I have made this letter rather long only because I have not taken the time to make it shorter.*
>
> — *Blaise Pascal, 1656*

ISO 9001 requires that operational procedures deal with how all the functions within the value delivery system interact. This mechanism is usually one of the most beneficial in the implementation process. By objectively looking at the association of processes and the functions of various departments, I often uncover duplication of activities, expensive crutches constructed to patch a crisis but never removed, and holes in the system for which no one is responsible. It is not unusual to find costly redundancies that are continually overlooked because the same people perform them, day in and day out, without ever questioning why.

My reality check for an effective ISO 9001 documentation system is this: Can you bring in a competent worker off the street and effectively and efficiently train him or her in a job and processes? I encourage the jobholders to write down the procedures they use.[4] This approach greatly simplifies procedures and gives ownership to the people who do the work (even if the author is the only one who reads it, the mission is accomplished!).

---

4. *This is explained in more detail in Chapters 6, 7, 8, and 12.*

VERIFY THAT YOU ARE DOING IT

The third step in the ISO 9001 tenets, "Verify that you are doing it," is accomplished through a methodical system of regular internal audits of processes compared to procedures. The internal auditing scheme ensures that the procedures are understandable and accurate. At the end of the day, the language of ISO 9001 becomes the language of your company, silos are dismantled, moats are filled in, and jobholders actually talk to one another about improving processes.

In most classic quality systems, ownership of processes is vested in managers and delegated to jobholders. Because accountability is usually delegated without adequate authority, the rules of ownership have to be strict and tollgates must be in place to ensure compliance with the canons of conduct. A typical scenario might involve a design draftsperson who is given a project by an engineer. He or she usually has strict rules from the engineer on how the project is to be documented. Although the draftsperson is expected to read the engineer's mind and correct subtle oversights, that person is often discouraged from including an opinion on how a design might be optimized. That creative work is reserved for the engineer, although the designer may have had many years of more practical experience. In most design cycles, the draftsperson has a formal checker besides the engineer. However, the engineer is seldom the subject of a reality check until the design is in its prototype stage.

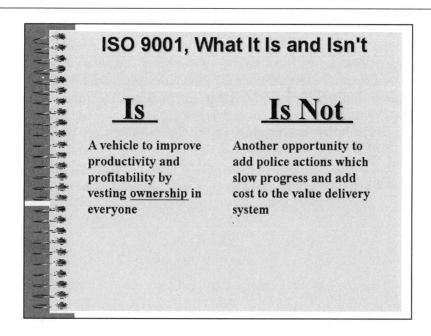

ISO 9001, What It Is and Isn't

Is

A vehicle to improve productivity and profitability by vesting ownership in everyone

Is Not

Another opportunity to add police actions which slow progress and add cost to the value delivery system

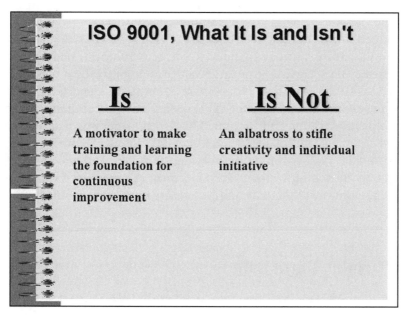

ISO 9001, What It Is and Isn't

Is

A motivator to make training and learning the foundation for continuous improvement

Is Not

An albatross to stifle creativity and individual initiative

In a well-executed implementation of ISO 9001, ownership of a job and its processes is vested in those who perform the job or process. In the last example, the engineer would have a clear set of requirements of what is expected of him or her before the detail work is turned over to the next process owner. Both the engineer and the designer would have distinct job descriptions with related proven process procedures. The designer would have clear boundaries and would be the internal customer of the engineer. Well-written procedures encourage the engineer and the designer to collaborate to improve both jobs and make the final product of their efforts the best it can be. There is no need for a checker for the draftsperson or an added-cost step for the engineer if the entire design process follows the tenets of ISO 9001. Unnecessary overhead is reduced, adversarial relationships are dismantled, and costly rework is all but eliminated in an effective ISO 9001 quality system.

Training Is Critical

Training is one of the key elements of ISO 9001. What an odd requirement to place in a quality management standard! "Of course we are all trained. We went to school and have been training on the job all of our careers! The big guy must have lied to us when he said ISO 9001 wasn't prescriptive, because now he's saying we have to do training! Anyway, we've been planning on training, but our development and production schedules have been so hectic that we haven't gotten around to it—but it's going to be in next quarter's budget. Besides, I just sent my secretary to school to learn letter writing."

ISO 9001 says that jobholders must be competent and trained, and that they must continually learn the skills needed to do their jobs. We so often neglect formal training and assume that process operators know what is expected of them. If jobholders are going to be responsible for their own work, they must be trained in the requirements. As technology advances, jobs change and processes change. Training must continue or the quality management system will stagnate and lose its effectiveness.

Keep Your Training Up-To-Date

Perhaps one of the reasons you are reading this book is because your management and quality training are a bit rusty. My practical experience has yielded the following hypothesis about technical training. Thirty years ago, training was good for 10 to 15 years. Twenty years ago it was good for 8 to 10 years. Fifteen years ago it was good for 5 to 8 years. Ten years ago, it was good for 3 to 5 years. Five years ago it was good for 2 to 3 years, and today it is good for 1 to 2 years. My assertion is that in each span of time specified, there have been quantum changes in technology that make it imperative to have additional training to be able to function in a technically based industry.

Look at the evolution of the personal computer. In its first ten years of existence, there were four quantum changes in platforms (the XT/AT, the 286/386, the 486, and the Pentium). Each change caused the previous technology to be virtually obsolete. Software is evolving on a daily basis. A major manufacturer of two-way radio equipment told me recently it was their design goal to evolve and add features to their products so that consumers would want to buy a new radio every 18 months! The point is that our society is changing too rapidly to put training on the back burner.

ISO 9001 MAKES CREATIVE PROCESSES MORE EFFICIENT

Much of the criticism of ISO 9001 comes from the engineering community, with claims that it stifles their creativity with cumbersome procedures. When closely analyzed, that translates to "I want to play with technology without a rule book" and "I don't want anyone to know how much of my R&D time is spent in reinventing the wheel." I have been involved in this arena most of my career and I have witnessed the geometric progression in technology causing engineers to resist discipline more than when they smoked briar pipes and kept hardcover laboratory notebooks! It is unreasonable not to have a formal system of design that involves everyone in the value delivery system. It is wasteful not to keep detailed design development and design review notes so that the wheel is not continually reinvented. It is suicide not to have configuration engineering and sustaining engineering keeping up with the evolution of current products. Rather than stifling creativity, ISO 9001 reduces wasted time and motion and keeps the design goals clear as technology changes halfway during product development.

ISO 9001 IS A LAUNCH PAD FOR SUCCESS

The bottom line is that ISO 9001 is an evolutionary step in the Industrial Revolution, not a revolutionary step to instant success. It is the platform from which to launch a new phase in business maturity through process control, internal auditing, customer focus, and continual improvement. It encourages a cultural shift away from adversarial management systems and

ISO 9001, What It Is and Isn't

It Is

- EVOLUTION not REVOLUTION
- A CULTURE not A PROGRAM
- STRUCTURE not CONTROL
- BOUNDARIES not ANARCHY

tollgate inspections. It is not the magic pill that will help you lose 60 pounds in six weeks. ISO 9001 offers a structure in which to work and continually improve. It is not a system of police actions that require many dollars of overhead to sustain. It provides boundaries that keep you out of the ditches with policies and a mission statement that reflect the path you have chosen to follow. It is not the anarchy of everyone traveling a different path looking for the Emerald City. ISO 9001 is discipline without bureaucracy. It provides a set of rules without requiring empires to enforce them. Properly done, it instills a sense of urgency in its process owners, replacing the panic of missed schedules, rejected orders, and lost profits. It replaces damage control management with management by fact. That is, it drives out the tradition of moving from grass fire to grass fire with operating a business by dealing with the issues that are of most importance first (I call it Pareto management[5]). It is all about achieving sustaining quality, not just meeting arbitrary objectives and bogeys. It is commitment by all who participate in the quality management system, not compliance to rules owned by the quality department. It is shielding customers from receiving defective products and ineffective services, rather than continually using the customer as an un-

---

5. *In Pareto analysis, events are identified in rank order from the most important to the least important.*

willing beta tester. It encourages you to get rid of vendors and peddlers and replace them with partners in the future of your company. At the end of the day, ISO 9001 is the platform to launch your future, not the end of your worries!

THE LANGUAGE OF ISO 9001

Have you ever tried to reach a consensus on the definition of a technical term with a group of professionals? How may times have you read the glossary in a technical document? Where did the definitions you hold near and dear come from? Here's a case in point.

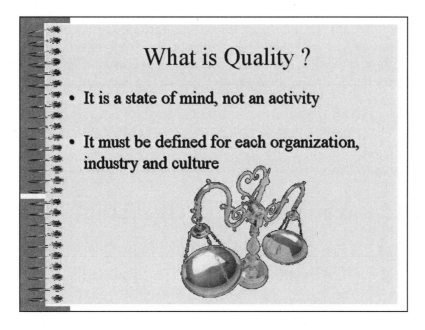

How do you define quality? Some frequently given answers include the following:

- Fitness for use
- Compliance to specification
- Excellence (Mercedes vs. Chevrolet)
- Goodness (reliability)
- Customer satisfaction

Take those five common answers from the American English vocabulary and culture, translate them into the languages and cultures of the more than 140 countries that have adopted ISO 9001, and consensus becomes just a dream.

Another insightful contribution of the effort of the European Union (EU) to implement a universal quality standard is the vocabulary in ISO 9000:2000. This standard complements ISO 9001 by defining the terminology of ISO 9001 in concise verbiage and translating it into French and Russian in a single document. As with ISO 9001, it is not the last word, nor will everyone agree with the definitions, but it does help level the playing field. For instance, ISO 9000:2000 defines quality as the degree to which a set of inherent characteristics fulfills requirements. Chances are, you will have to read that about ten times more to fully appreciate the definition and then you will file it away with the rest of the glossaries in your technical library (after all, we don't want to confuse our beliefs with new input). The significance of the ISO 9000:2000 definition is that, when it is used in the context of ISO 9001, quality can be universally translated from Brooklyn to Barstow and from the Rio Grande Valley to the Ruhr Valley.

WHY DOES IT PREVAIL?

Why Does ISO 9001 Prevail?

- It gives international credentials
- Companies are shopping for "qualified" suppliers
- It is required in some industries
- It is selection criteria in others
- It withstands the test of time and logic

We've discussed what ISO 9001 is, what it isn't, and some of its benefits. So far, we've created a lot of hype for a quality management system. Why has this European quality standard become the topic of discussion from boardrooms to locker rooms around the industrialized world? After all, it was originally supposed to be just a two-party certification system within the EU![6]

In my experience, the cream that rises to the top is that everyone is looking for qualified suppliers. In the past, every aspect of supplier selection was either a shot in the dark or a costly process of qualification, selection, and newlywed growing pains. ISO 9001 removes a variable from the equation. If a company is certified, it had, at least on a given day, demonstrated a viable baseline quality management system that meets a known set of tenets. With the 2000 revision, it also means that the company has demonstrated a dedication to customer service. Wouldn't it be comforting if, when you went to buy a car, you knew that each of the manufacturers had a compliant quality system? You could eliminate one of your selection criteria and concentrate on price, comfort, ride, and value without wondering if they even test their product or audit their assembly processes.

Be advised that there is no guarantee that you aren't going to buy a lemon from an ISO 9001-certified company, but chances of it are far less of a gamble than selection from a glitzy advertisement. Chances are better that an ISO 9001-certified company is going to have more focus on quality compliance than one chosen for you by your assistant purchasing agent. There are many published lists of ISO 9001 certified companies[7] and those lists are becoming a "yellow pages" for companies looking for new suppliers.

As I have implied, ISO 9001 has become the de facto quality standard in the United States and around the world. I regularly interview salespeople and ask how often it shows up as a requirement in bid packages and requests for quotation. A few years ago, it was just an informational question on a few bids. Now, it is mandatory for some companies, and larger companies ask if you are certified; if you are not, they ask when you plan to be.

---

6. *The original intent of ISO 9000 was a two-party system of companies within the EU certifying their suppliers. The current system of third-party audits is a mutation spawned by its universal acceptance.*

7. *One such list of certified companies can be found at www.QualityDigest.com.*

I have witnessed a number of ISO 9001 implementations that were championed by the sales staff and marketing groups because they were either not qualified to respond to certain bids, or they saw the handwriting on the wall that their customers were gradually cutting back their potential supplier pool to ISO 9001-certified companies. If you have not seen questions about ISO 9001 show up on bid requests, you may be in a domestic industry that has a limited customer base. I am headquartered in Nevada where the mining and gaming industries prevail. In mid-2000, there were 34,000 certified entities in the United States but only 78 in Nevada, where the dominant industries realize no immediate marketing benefit from ISO 9001 certification. Some cottage industries will never see ISO 9001 requirements. However, our globe is shrinking every day, customers are more demanding, and we are all looking for the most competitive advantage we can muster to keep our position and to capture our share of the marketplace.

It must be stated at this point that ISO 9001 is not an ironclad requirement in most environments. Any company that makes it a requirement does so to promote its own quality goals. Anyone who threatens you with "ISO 9001 or else" is feeding some self-serving interest. The one area where there has been a requirement is when selling certain "regulated products" to the EU. These products include toys, medical devices, personal protective equipment, and construction products. (Yes, the Lego® Toy Company is ISO 9001 certified!)

Before products are placed on specific lists in these groups and are qualified to be sold to the EU, they must have the CE mark on them, much as many devices in the United States must have the Underwriter's Labs (UL) mark and similar Canadian products must have the CSA mark. ISO 9001 certification in these companies is often a prerequisite[8] to exhaustive product testing by agencies that work for the EU. When testing is complete and the product is proven, the CE mark may be placed on the product (unlike the marks of ISO 9001 registration that are specifically prohibited from being displayed on products). To make the universe of companies required to be ISO 9001 certified even smaller, there have been very few directives released for certified products. This is a painfully slow process that is taking far longer than anyone in the ISO 9001 community imagined.

---

8. *ISO 9001 certification is supposed to be an absolute requirement for a company prior to obtaining the CE mark on its products. In practice, this may not always be enforced.*

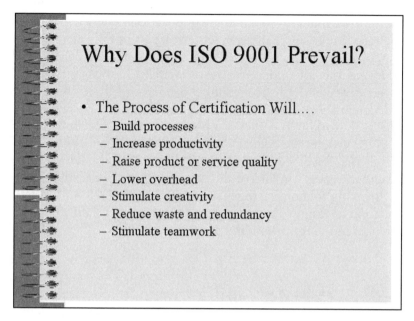

This lack of mandatory requirement is one of the reasons that ISO 9001 implementation is a hot topic in some areas and lukewarm in others. As you will discover, the best reason to become ISO 9001 certified is the improvement realized from the process of becoming certified.

Quality Management Encourages Teamwork

The process of ISO 9001 implementation, done well, is an incredibly cathartic undertaking. It roots out activities that are not producing results. As existing procedures are revised or developed, wasteful methods are identified. As internal audits are performed, holes in processes are recognized and fixed. As the process repeats itself, continual improvement is inevitable.

ISO 9001 involves virtually everyone in the organization in the quality management system.[9] As process operators are trained and quality awareness

---

9. *A quality management system is defined as all activities from initial customer contact through determination of customer satisfaction and all processes in between. It could more accurately be called a business process management system.*

is heightened, product quality improves. As groups work together to document and refine processes, they almost always find areas of productivity improvement and ways to eliminate duplication of effort. As jobholders become responsible for their own actions, layers of bureaucracy are dismantled, tollgate inspection is virtually eliminated, and overhead is reduced.

Having the jobholders revise or write their own procedures stimulates creativity and job ownership. Ad-hoc committees brought together to document a process often find new and better ways to operate that process because working together is a powerful tool of ingenuity. These cross-functional groups also reduce waste and redundancy because they identify crutches that have been built into processes by those who didn't take the time and the energy to look at the interaction of all operations within a system. Bringing jobholders together to make ISO 9001 work often lays the foundation of teamwork in companies that have had a difficult time getting ownership in the team-building process.

Why Achieve Certification?

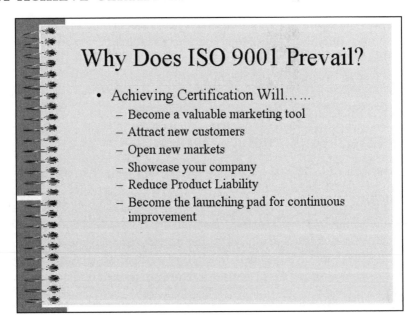

As a result of the process of ISO 9001 implementation, many companies cite improved documentation, positive cultural impact, higher perceived quality, and faster development time. Many use ISO 9001 implementation as the rationalization for continual improvement and a launching pad for strategic quality initiatives that will be sustained and not become another "program du jour." When you successfully complete initial certification, you will receive a handsome certificate to hang in the lobby. If you are like many companies, you will commission a banner or post a billboard outside your facility proclaiming your certification to ISO 9001. You may even throw a big celebration party for your company (don't forget to invite your suppliers and your customers). The process is the most valuable benefit of ISO 9001, and the certification party may be the most fun, but the result of ISO 9001 certification certainly is a big reason to make the journey. You can use the various marks[10] on your stationery, on your sales brochures, and in your advertising to attract new customers. You can use the marks in your marketing efforts (as long as you do not affix a mark to a product). You can use them to open new markets outside your traditional sphere of influence by approaching companies as an ISO 9001-certified addition to their supplier base. You can use them to showcase your company by opening up your processes for benchmarking by other companies. Some ISO 9001 companies even provide advisory and auditing services to their suppliers.

There have been a number of cases reported in trade journals where ISO 9001 has been used as part of the legal defense of companies involved in product liability suits. The premise is that a company that has an ISO 9001-certified quality system has a definable minimum quality standard. I don't see an entire new field of legal services starting based on ISO 9001. However, it is an interesting side note to add to the list of reasons for becoming ISO 9001 certified.

A more lofty reason for becoming certified is that the lengthy road to ISO 9001 certification fosters a "we can do anything" culture. Pioneering companies that matriculate from the initial certification begin to look to state and national quality award criteria[11] to see where their next challenge will come from. If ISO 9001 certification can be the impetus to achieving higher levels of excellence, it is worth the price of admission.

---

10. *Your registrar will provide logos of the various agencies that they use to validate certification, such as the RAB, RVA, or the NACCB.*
11. *Such as the Malcolm Baldrige Award or state quality awards.*

WHEN CERTIFICATION IS NOT APPROPRIATE

In this chapter, we've given a host of reasons to become ISO 9001 certified. We would be remiss if we didn't pause at this point and give some valid reasons why you should not pursue ISO 9001 certification.

If you are a local or regional business or cottage industry, there is little reason to actually seek certification. The model for an ISO 9001 quality management system is certainly valid. However, the formal certification process is a fairly expensive outlay for a small business.

Another reason not to seek certification is that you are content with the status quo, you are happy with your quality management system, and you are comfortable with your market share. Not every company wants to grow and some are content to stay with the tools that made them successful. Still others are what I call limited perpetuity companies. That is, their owners are planning to sell or they are ripe for a buyout. In those cases, spending money on anything new and changing cultures is contraindicated. (On the other hand, being ISO 9001 certified before a merger or acquisition might be a value addition for the seller.)

The best reasons not to seek certification include these:

- Someone said you had to.
- You are looking for a quick fix to some endemic or systemic problem.

If a customer or your senior management has waved a magic wand and ordered your facility to get certified and you have no vested ownership in the decision, it is the wrong thing to do. Unless the key players are convinced that ISO 9001 certification will help them in their journey toward productivity and quality improvement, it will be a horrendous waste of money and manpower, resulting in frustration and failure.

An unfortunate example is a company that I encountered a couple of years ago. They invited me to rush an ISO 9001 system into place for them in three months so that they could win a key contract. I declined because they were interested in a superficial effort just to satisfy a customer and they wanted it done in an unreasonably short amount of time.

I recently received word that they did not find anyone willing to work to their requirements and they struggled through a two-year implementation journey on their own. They implemented a "window dressing" system and were cited for 32 major nonconformities on their initial assessment audit (one or two major "findings" is considered excessive for the first formal audit). What a waste of time and money!

ISO 9001 Is Not a Quick Fix

Everyone in the quality management system must own his or her processes to be effective and to pass a certification audit. Objective evidence of conformance must exist and efficacy must be evident.

If you think implementation of ISO 9001 is a magic pill to cure your productivity or quality woes, it isn't. It will exacerbate existing cultural problems, unless you plan to deal with those problems first and make the needed changes.

Early in my career as a manufacturing manager, I was fortunate to meet a very wise salesperson who taught me the following lesson: When bar coding first came into vogue, I wanted to bar code everything in my inventory and every piece moving around the production floor. I saw it as a panacea to solve my inventory inaccuracies and my work-in-process tracking problems. I usually shun salespeople, but I solicited this one to show me his company's bar coding equipment so I could do a budgetary estimate and shake out the money to buy the equipment. Before he opened his catalogs, he asked if I would give him a tour of the manufacturing and inventory area. When we returned to my office, he started to pack his briefcase. In amazement, I asked why. He told me that, as much as he would like to sell me the equipment, I needed about six months to get my existing system cleaned up and operating correctly before I ever thought about adding another variable to the system. He said that unless the manual systems were working, bar coding would create an even bigger mess than I had already.

I have never forgotten that lesson and I give the same advice to potential clients when they want to use ISO 9001 as a tool to cover up a mess that should be fixed at its root cause. ISO 9001 is not a quick fix for anything. The process, by design, takes from six months to more than two years. It requires a gradual cultural change for most companies, not an overnight reengineering job.

Finally, there are no magic pills in the ISO 9001 medicine cabinet: It is just common sense and hard work. If your personality is one of instant success, or slash and burn, please close this book now and leave it in the library of your local business school.

WHY US AND WHY NOW?

In 2000, there were more than 350,000 ISO 9000 certifications worldwide in more than 140 countries. The numbers reinforce some of the reasons

Why Us and Why Now?

- Contractual Requirements
- Reduction of multiple assessments
- Be a pioneer in your industry
- Certification takes 6 months to 2 years
- What you don't know can hurt you

already stated to pursue ISO 9001 certification. The reasons to do it now include the following:

- The world is shrinking. Most industries now have global competitors where, just a few years ago, the major threat was regional or local.
- The marketplace is expanding. For the same reason that we have global competitors, reasonable transportation and the information superhighway give us access to an international marketplace.
- There is a growing demand for excellence. We are not accepting the hype that high-value products and services are throwaway items. As consumers, we place increasing emphasis on quality, reliability, and value.

The fiscal reasons for becoming ISO 9001 certified are clear. The need to keep and grow market share is also clear. To begin the journey, ISO 9001 provides the stimulus to start the long-awaited quality improvement initiatives or to restart existing efforts that stall every time there is a hiccup in the market. It helps launch the process of continual growth and improvement. It dismantles adversarial relationships and makes work more interesting and fun.

As we mentioned earlier, there only a few industries thus far in which ISO 9001 is a contractual or legal requirement. Because the process of becoming certified is lengthy, proactively implementing ISO 9001 is far less costly and painful than waiting until it is mandatory. A number of the more in-demand registrars may have backlogs and challenges meeting your timelines. Some quote lengthy lead times in scheduling certification audits, especially around year's end.

In industries such as petrochemical processing, ISO 9001 is being implemented now because it eliminates costly assessments that are historically performed by every major customer. Some process plants had full-time staffs to host audits and assessments. Since ISO 9001 has become widely accepted in this industry, companies are saving large sums of money by not having to perform quality audits and not having to host them.

Another good reason to begin the process of ISO 9001 certification now is that what you don't know can hurt you. There is a great deal of misinformation being spread by those who are casually familiar with ISO 9001 and yet hold themselves up as experts. There are also those who would exploit any opportunity for a profit. Several years ago I received a call from a client who had just begun the ISO 9001 journey. A salesperson had told the company that if it did not buy a particular product that he was peddling, the company would never be able to be ISO 9001 certified. The allegation was, of course, absurd. I wonder how many times he had used that threat on others and made a sale.

Why Us and Why Now?

- Strategic business advantage
- Ability to sell to the EU
- Launching pad for improvement
- Demand for excellence
- Listing in "The New Yellow Pages"
- Capture and build on successes
- Dismantles adversarial relationships and makes work fun

Be a Leader in Your Field

The final reason that I offer to begin your ISO 9001 implementation now is my favorite. Most of the companies I work with want to be the leaders in their industry or field. They want to be able to boast that they were the "first on their block" to achieve certification. It is exhilarating to work with folks who want to excel at what they do and it's fun to watch the ISO 9001 process enhance their productivity, quality, teamwork, market share, and profitability. With the release of the 2000 revision, there is truly an opportunity for your organization to be one of the first to be certified as having "demonstrated customer satisfaction."

Oh yes, one more thing. This is one of my favorite Texas euphemisms: When you ain't the lead dog, the view don't change much.

IS IT AN INVESTMENT OR AN EXPENSE?

One of the most frequently asked questions about the certification process is "How much will it cost?" The ISO 9001 champion is usually on his or her feet with "We will save more than it will cost," but that seldom gets by the folks who control the purse strings. As true as the assertion often is, the question is relevant and companies must start the process with their eyes open and their budgets established.

By far, the greatest cost is the internal expense of documenting procedures, training, and performing internal audits. Many implementers who are hesitant to point these costs out measure them at the onset. I firmly believe that if you don't know where you are, you likely don't know where you are headed. Spend some up-front time documenting the cost of quality, the cost of rework, productivity, and whatever metrics make sense for your environment. Establish a benchmark set of numbers at the time you start the ISO 9001 process and track them on a regular basis. Without a score, a football game is pointless. Without statistics, you can't make corrections during the game.

Develop a budget based on how many ad-hoc hours of work you anticipate and with what labor mix. Be sure that those who control the budget agree with the budget and with the benchmark.

If you have a viable quality group within your company, you may be able to launch your ISO 9001 efforts by sending representatives to seminars, workshops, and lead auditor training. Include these costs in your startup budget. Also include time for them to observe successes in other companies and to continually learn about ISO 9001, because the world of ISO 9001 is changing almost daily.

If time is of the essence and you want to implement ISO 9001 with a minimum of startup problems, then you will need a consultant who has a number of successful ISO 9001 implementations behind him or her. As a steering committee member asked me recently, "This isn't your first rodeo, is it?" An effective consultant will help you get launched on your own as quickly as possible and keep you from making costly startup mistakes. He or she will show you how to reduce costs and how consultants will pay for themselves many times over by demonstrating the most painless ways to develop your processes and procedures.

On the other hand, if you hire a consultant to do the entire implementation process for you, it will be an extremely expensive and frustrating effort. The expense will not just be in the consulting fees. The big cost will be in the fact that you will not, in all probability, achieve your goals because the consultant will own the processes, not the jobholders. If those who operate the processes are not "walking the talk," you will not pass an assessment audit.

I use and recommend the "yellow pad" approach. That is, I have the jobholders write their own procedures on a yellow tablet. The consultant can put their words into procedural format, but the people who do the work are the only ones who really know the processes. I also recommend that internal auditors come from the rank-and-file workers. When people own what they do, they will do it gladly and costs will be minimized.

A History of ISO 9000

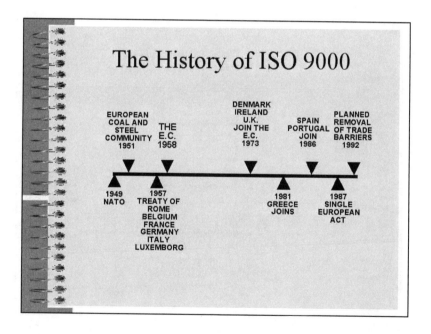

This chapter is a brief history of ISO 9000. It provides just enough information to help the reader understand the events leading to the release of the standard and why it has become globally accepted in such a brief time. It reinforces why the standard has been so widely accepted and why its implementation continues to grow despite its detractors.

After World War II, Europe was in ruins and the United States was retooling its war industries for peacetime purposes. Besides forming the North Atlantic Treaty Organization (NATO) as a precaution to another world war, leaders of many European countries realized that they would have to work together if they were to ever rebuild their infrastructure, become industrialized again, and compete with the United States. From its formation in 1958, The European Community (EC; now the European Union [EU]) strived to unify Europe into one customer and supplier base. Early on, they realized that manufacturing companies would have to appear to be compliant to a common set of standards, despite the language and cultural barriers that existed. To that end, they commissioned the International Organization for Standardization (IOS) in Geneva to write a set of nonbinding quality standards that companies could use to evaluate the quality management systems of potential suppliers. Over eight years, the organization wrote the ISO 9000 series of standards that the EU accepted as the single quality standard to be adopted by all member countries.

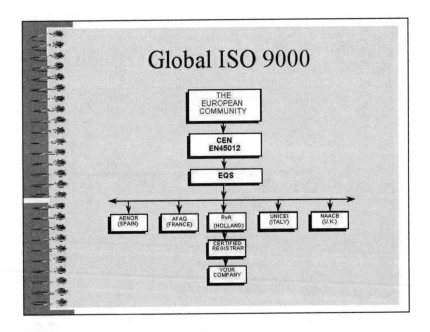

ISO 9000 was released in 1987. From the initial intent to create a two-party, nonbinding standard, it immediately became the focus of quality professionals worldwide because it simply and elegantly transcended barriers of culture and language, which no other quality standard had been able to do. It moved beyond nationalistic ownership issues and provided a nonpolitical baseline for quality.

The EU also contracted with the IOS to update the standard every five years, giving it, as it turns out, a life of its own. Soon, the IOS became ISO, which is actually from *isos*, the Greek word for equal (as in *isosceles* or *isometric*). "Notified bodies"[1] sprang up worldwide.

In the United States, the Registrar Accreditation Board (RAB), the American National Standards Institute (ANSI), and the ASQ are all working toward complete international recognition for the United States. The U.S. version of ISO 9000 is Q9000, which is identical to ISO 9000, save the American spellings of words. The first update, in 1994, was the result of suggestions from working groups worldwide for improving the standard. The second revision, released in December 2000, is the first complete rewrite of the standard, now referred to as ISO 9001:2000.

The EU did not achieve its target to have the standard fully accepted by 1992. The currency issue has since been resolved (the Euro will become the official currency as of January 2002) and the EU and the other countries of Europe are truly coming together as a single voice in international commerce. Their monumental reconstruction task now appears shadowed by their contribution of the ISO 9000 standard to Europe as a whole and to the world of quality.

---

1. *A notified body was originally the organization in each EU country that controlled and implemented their version of ISO 9000. Today, such bodies exist in more than 140 countries and they contribute to the Technical Committees and Working Groups that continually maintain the standard.*

3

A Case Study at The Dell Computer Asset Recovery Business

by Keith Brewer

The charter of Dell's Asset Recovery Business (ARB) is to manage products returned under Dell's 30 day, no-questions-asked return policy. The Asset Recovery Business was created as a separate entity in 1999 when the computer remanufacturing operation was moved out of the Dell Services organization. I joined the ARB as the new Senior Quality Manager November 1, 1999. The quality management system that was in place at that time was a derivative of the system that had been in place prior to becoming a stand-alone business. While that system had been effective when remanufacturing was a part of another business, it was clear to me that the inherited system would not be auditable in time for a surveillance audit scheduled for December 1999. When I informed the director of the ARB that we would not be auditable in December, I also committed to him that we *would* be auditable by May 2000.

Fortunately Mike Gagliardi, who was then the director and general manager of ARB, shared my vision of a Business Management System (BMS) that contained all the processes, procedures, work aids, metrics, and reports that were necessary for ARB to be a successful business. As shown in Figure 3.1, the BMS would encompass all functions of ARB, not just those addressed by ISO 9000. These functions included marketing, sales, finance, IT, and the product returns team.

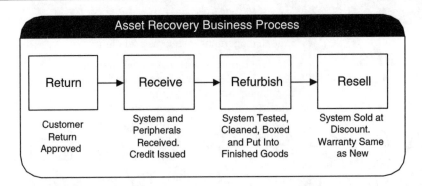

FIGURE 3.1. The ARB business process.

The transition began in February 2000 when I began looking for a consultant who shared the same vision of a BMS. Whoever joined this effort needed to bring to the job an understanding and commitment to challenge the existing models—to create a management system from scratch and do it quickly. There just wasn't time to philosophize or develop lengthy implementation plans. ARB needed to be ready in less than 90 days.

Tom Taormina of Productivity Resources proved to be the consultant I was looking for. Our initial phone conversation lasted well over an hour and by the end of that call he and I had agreed on a vision and a plan.

PHASE 1

The first step was a gap analysis of ARB to ISO 9002. As expected, the analysis proved what we already knew. We had to start at the very basic level and build a system from the ground up. While Taormina gathered a team to join him in Austin, I put in writing my philosophy for the ARB BMS, shown in Figure 3.2.

The initial draft of ISO 9000:2000 reinforced the value of a consistent management system across the business. The changing focus from operations involving the development, production, and delivery of products and services to the broader view of all business aspects exposed the shortfalls of the typical ISO 9000 Quality Management System. The BMS design criteria, shown in Figure 3.3, incorporated this forward view.

I eliminated the ISO reference to focus people on the needs of the business, not the acronym. Too often I had heard people say: "We have to do this because of ISO," or "We can't do that because ISO won't let us." Neither phrase is correct, but both are used as justification for an action or an

BMS Philosophy

- ARB will be successful only by focusing on the management system as a whole

- The ARB Business Management System will be designed to address current and future management system requirements by incorporating a continuous process improvement methodology across the enterprise

FIGURE 3.2. The BMS philosophy.

BMS Design Criteria

- All process, procedures and work instructions follow same model
- All ARB documentation developed for dissemination via the intranet
- Documents in native html format. Enabler applications will not be called to open documents
- Revision and version control will be accomplished by use of intranet publishing software and Dell control mechanisms
- All references to "ISO" are being eliminated from our business documents
    - ✓ **"If it isn't right for our business, we won't do it."**
- ARB senior managers are responsible and accountable for the content of the BMS

FIGURE 3.3. The BMS design criteria.

excuse for inaction. As we developed the ARB BMS, I wanted people to focus on what was necessary to run the business. The phrase, "if it isn't right for our business, we won't do it," became the frame of reference for all our processes and procedures. I also told people, "ISO is a four-letter word in my vocabulary," to reinforce the idea that we needed to focus on our business processes. It was my job as quality manager to make sure our processes met the requirements of the standard.

Senior manager accountability was also an essential ingredient. The BMS was to be owned by line management, not quality, and everything that went into BMS had to be with the full agreement, ownership, and accountability of the senior management team.

It was also clear that, in order to have processes and procedures disseminated on the intranet, an intranet design was needed. A high-level concept map, shown in Figure 3.4, was developed as a starting point.

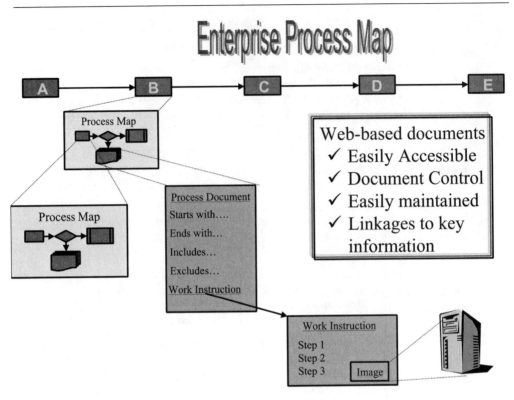

FIGURE 3.4. The BMS enterprise process map.

The model was designed to portray the concept of linked documents all relating to a distinct process, task or operation. These documents could be in the form of process maps, procedures, work instructions, or images. There were two ground rules for development of the pages:

- **All documents had to be converted to a native hypertext markup language (HTML) format for posting.** The system had to display documents quickly to meet the requirement for easy access. To achieve the best speed, no enabler applications were to be called to display information. The documents also had to be formatted for readability without the need for excessive scrolling. A production associate working in a build cell doesn't have time to wait for an application to open or to read through a lengthy document to find the piece of information she or he needs.

- **All information should be no more than three clicks away from the home page.** This proved to be easier said than done. It forced the team to look for innovative ways to arrange and display technical information in a clear manner. It also meant that the site would be easier to navigate because the user would never be deep into sub-menus or links.

In late March 2000, a small team of consultants and ARB employees began the work to get ARB to a point where it was auditable by the ISO registrar. The gap analysis performed by Taormina provided the road map.

Some process documentation and mapping existed in ARB as a result of an initiative begun in early 1999 to develop a process-oriented view of the business. Although process mapping training and some Dell internal consulting assistance was provided, there was wide variation in content and layout as the lessons were applied. One or two areas had extensive process maps that were very thorough but nearly impossible to follow for the daily tasks. Other areas had high level documents that provided an overview of the responsibilities and duties of a department or function but were not detailed enough to serve as work instructions or training tools.

We decided to focus the team on developing a series of high-level procedures that would address the 19 elements of ISO 9002. The goal was to clearly describe what ARB did in each of the areas to make certain we had the foundation for a comprehensive management system. Although the design goal was to have a BMS that covered all of ARB, the short-term emphasis had to be on the elements of the 1994 version of ISO 9000.

The team began the arduous task of developing what was to become the basis of the ARB Business Management Interactive System (BMIS). By the time of the ISO surveillance audit on May 24, 2000, the team, in partnership with the associates and area managers of ARB operations, had developed, documented, and approved 49 procedures. During this same period a BMS manual was created, a company-wide corrective action tracking tool was implemented, 22 ARB employees were trained as internal assessors by Taormina, and three Business Management Internal Assessments (BMIA) were conducted as part of new assessor training. All of the documentation was captured on the ARB BMIS site that went live on the Dell intranet May 22, 2000. ARB was auditable.

The surveillance audit conducted May 24, 2000 was a success. The auditors were aware that the organization had been declared "not auditable" six months earlier and were amazed at the progress that had been made in a short time. They were particularly impressed with the intranet application (BMIS) and our plans to expand the breadth and depth of the site. It also was obvious to all that ARB had only begun to become compliant with ISO 9002 and that much work remained. However, the auditors tested the high-level procedures and were satisfied that we were on the right track.

We had met the goal of being ready for a May audit and we had learned a lot in the process. The initial design and layout of the processes and procedures proved to be cumbersome and difficult to maintain. Unless we took an entirely new approach to the design of the system, the result would be unnecessarily complicated and ultimately not functional.

PHASE 2

During July 2000, Cynthia Miller joined ARB as the team leader for BMIS development. She had several years' experience as one of Dell's internal ISO 9000 consultants and had worked with all major Dell units in implementing quality systems. Her comprehensive knowledge of the ISO 9002 criteria and her wide-ranging experience within Dell brought an invaluable perspective to BMIS development. Most important, she recognized the power of BMIS to fundamentally change how ISO 9001 was integrated into a business.

Our next moment of truth would be in December 2000, when the next surveillance audit would be scheduled. In the intervening six months the team needed to take what was a very high level, mile-wide and inch-deep BMS and drive it to the most detailed level of the business. We needed to take the initial implementation of our model and develop the structure through which processes, procedures, work aids, reference material, and all other documents necessary to run the business could be displayed in a logical hierarchical design. We knew that in some areas only one or two levels of detail would be necessary. In others, such as manufacturing, more in-depth instructions had to be available. Because ARB handled each and every product made by Dell, procedures and instructions needed to handle product line differences were called for without sacrificing the basic process structure and workflow. It quickly became clear that what had worked in Phase 1 wouldn't work in Phase 2. The basic structure of our first forty-nine procedures did not give us the needed flexibility.

Miller and the team spent several weeks considering different approaches to the problem. They looked at how other production units of Dell created and posted their documents. Some were on the intranet; some were on departmental servers with restricted access. Some intranet sites had links that opened other lengthy documents created for a paper-based quality management system. In many of the units we surveyed, the functional organizations had different approaches to documentation, all of which were accessible from a common home page. The layout, look, and feel of the functional pages reflected the styles of the individuals who developed them.

All of the units satisfied the requirements for documenting a quality management system, but none of what we saw met the requirements of the ARB BMS philosophy and design criteria.

As the team studied what worked and what didn't work in ARB and in other businesses an idea began to take shape. What eventually emerged was a simple concept—the "box and bullet."

Figure 3.5 gives an example of the box-and-bullet format used as a template for creation of a procedure in ARB. *Box* refers to the simplified process flow that is on the left side of all processes, procedures, work instructions, and work aids. The intent is to demonstrate the sequence of events in a process or operation and to provide varying levels of detail, depending on the purpose of the document. The first box can represent the initial step in a process or procedure or the first task in a lower level procedure. Subsequent

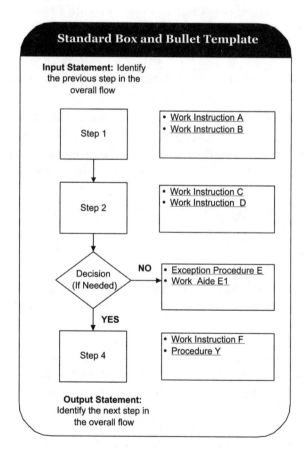

FIGURE 3.5. A standard box-and-bullet template.

boxes indicate a linear flow of steps until the process or procedure ends. The end is reached when the output of the process becomes the input of a subsequent process or at the end of a process or procedure.

Bullet refers to a series of statements to the right of each box. These statements can be links to procedures, work instructions or work aids pertinent to the process step identified in the box. The bullets can also be brief descriptions of the tasks involved in the process step identified in the box. The complexity of the process step determines the type of information to be conveyed by the bulleted text.

The success of any intranet site is very dependent on its usability. Numerous factors—from colors, fonts, and font size to placement of navigation aids and other design decisions affect how the site is perceived and determines its ultimate usefulness. The BMIS also needed to comply with Dell Web development guidelines. Once again, the team started with a set of high-level criteria and over time redesigned the web layout to make it more user-friendly, easy to navigate, and most of all, effective.

The high-level criteria were as follows:

- The user should be able to return directly to the home page from anywhere within the site with one click.
- Dell standard Web page links were to be at the top of each page
- A menu of major ARB functions should be on the left side of the page and each function should lead to lists of departments or operations within that function. This menu needed to be persistent on all pages.
- The right side of the page should contain links to work instructions, work aids, and reference material.
- There should also be links to metrics and to document ownership and revision information.
- The center portion of the page was reserved for display of processes, procedures, and work instructions in the box-and-bullet format.

Figure 3.6 presents screen shots from the BMIS Web page. The Dell standard Web links and a button bar that is customizable for BMIS content are placed at the top of the page. The ARB logo is positioned below the Web link and button bars.

The Web links, BMIS button bar, and ARB logo are persistent on all pages. The ARB logo is hyperlinked to return the user to the home page from anywhere on the site.

FIGURE 3.6. Screen shots of elements from the BMIS Web page.

FIGURE 3.7. The navigation menu
on the left side of the BMIS Web page.

Figure 3.7 shows the left navigation menu which includes each of the major functions in ARB. Clicking on the function titles opens sub-menus on which the user can select department or procedure links, depending on the function.

While the Web developers were creating the graphic elements and layout of the intranet structure the BMS team turned their focus to taking the box-and-bullet structure and applying it to all of ARB. The continuous flow manufacturing (CFM) area was selected as the pilot project. It is the most complex function in ARB operations and would present the most challenges to the creation of Web documentation.

The ARB of Dell refurbishes in the CFM lines all Dell-manufactured products, from Inspiron and Latitude portable computers to all models of Dimension and OptiPlex desktop computers. ARB also refurbishes workstations, servers, and storage products. In some cases, ARB receives products that are no longer in new-build production and our systems need to be able to retain and provide access to this information. Consequently, BMIS has to provide access to a much broader set of documents than any other Dell manufacturing facility, while still being fast and easy to use.

The team started by documenting the CFM process in two parts: desktop and notebook. The top-level CFM procedure has seven major steps as follows:

1. Reconfigure
2. Quick Test
3. Burn
4. First-line Inspection
5. Testing/Wipe Down
6. Box and Label
7. Provide Options

Figure 3.8 is a screen shot of a portion of the CFM Desktop procedure in box-and-bullet format.

Each of these steps has very specific instructions that vary by product. Before BMIS, these steps were placed into detailed documents, reviewed, and filed. Production workers were trained using these documents, but the very nature of the documents made them unwieldy as reference documents in the production areas. Over time, the methods called out in the written procedures were replaced by personal shortcuts, assumptions, and guesses and passed on by word of mouth. It became harder and harder to maintain any consistency in work processes as new products were introduced. BMIS would provide a vehicle to capture this core information in an easily accessible Web document that would allow any operator to find the information necessary to perform any of the seven procedure steps without having to rely on memory or verbal instructions.

The production operations team worked closely with the BMIS team to document the seven steps of the CFM procedure into box-and-bullet format. Each of the seven steps led to another box-and-bullet document that provided greater detail on the next level of procedures, which in turn provided links to work instructions and work aids. Work instructions generally were box-and-bullet documents that provided a deeper level of detail for the operation being performed.

Desktops - Procedure

Receive unit from parts kitting	
RECONFIGURE UNIT	• Verify System • Reconfigure • Verify and Assemble
PERFORM QUICK TEST	• Create SDR Diskette • Prepare Unit for Test • Run Quick Test • Prepare To Route
PERFORM BURN	• Check Unit Type • Prepare and Test Unit • Assess Test Results • Prepare To Route
PERFORM 1ST LINE INSPECTION	• Power On and Inspect • Assess Inspection Results • Prepare to Route
PERFORM HI POT TESTING/WIPEDOWN	• Prepare Unit for Test • Assess Test Result • Clean Unit • Prepare to Route

FIGURE 3.8. Part of the CFM Desktop procedure.

Work aids take many forms. The aid shown in Figure 3.9 gives clear instructions on how a tray should be placed on the conveyor for movement to the next station. Another example of a work aid is a list of memory part numbers that can be substituted for each other. Other work aids show the exact placement of a memory module on a motherboard and the proper torque settings for powered screwdrivers.

Where necessary, box-and-bullet documents and work aids were created for products and models that had unique requirements, particularly where new technology had been introduced into Dell's product lines.

Following CFM, the team branched out into other areas of the operation: receiving; materials handling; inventory management; material and production planning; process, manufacturing, and production engineering; quality engineering and management; and finished goods inventory and shipping. In each area the BMIS team worked in partnership with line management

Pass Tray - Work Aid

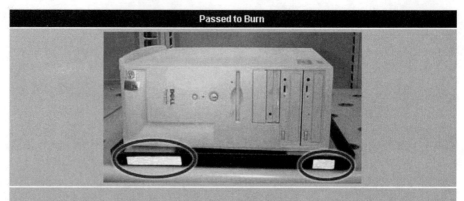

FIGURE 3.9. The Pass Tray work aid

and employees to develop the procedures, processes, work instructions, and work aids unique to each function. Each new area provided an opportunity to validate the BMIS model and to enhance it where needed to satisfy the needs of the business. The ARB team collaborated to find creative solutions to address unique information requirements and maintain the core BMIS structure.

While the production operations processes and procedures were being documented, a parallel effort was taking place in the marketing and sales functions. Because the requirements of ISO 9002 focused on the operational side of a manufacturing organization, marketing and sales processes were never included in the quality management system. However, the underlying philosophy of the ARB BMS is to incorporate a continuous process improvement methodology across the enterprise. We view all processes in ARB as equally important and made the conscious decision to apply the same process discipline and focus in marketing and sales as we were applying in production operations.

A separate team began by documenting the telesales processes. The complexity of ARB's business reinforces the need for telesales representatives to field myriad calls from customers seeking to purchase laptops, consumer desktop systems, departmental and enterprise servers, and storage systems. Each telesales representative needed the tools and instructions to allow her or him to successfully resolve customer inquiries about any product to close the sale.

The telesales teams are divided into home sales and business sales. The requirements of these customer groups can be different and some level of specialization is beneficial to the sales team. However, as with operations, the sales procedure has four common steps whether the customer is a home user or a business customer.

1. **Open:** Determine customer needs, requirements, and desired features and benefits.
2. **Unit:** Review available inventory to find units matching the customer's needs.
3. **Attachments:** Discuss optional accessories, shipping methods, and any special promotions.
4. **Wrap-up:** Verify the customer information and method of payment.

The Incoming Calls procedure was captured in a box-and-bullet document and separate documents were prepared for the Open, Unit, Attachments and Wrap-up work instructions.

A key part of the wrap-up process is making certain the customer is made aware of specific sales tax information that applies to his or her state and municipality. Federal law also requires that any telesales customer be provided with specific information regarding delivery and Dell's obligation to inform the customer if delivery delays occur. Failure to inform any customer of either of these points can be considered violations of the law. Work aids were created for the sales tax and mail order scripts so that the exact wording for this essential information was readily accessible. Work aids were also prepared with instructions for credit and debit card transactions.

BMIS procedures were also created for many other functions that are key to ARB's success but would never be included in a management system focusing solely on the requirements of ISO 9000. Examples include the following:

*   Product Promotions
*   Pricing
*   Order Management
*   Sales Operations

By December 2000, more than 85 percent of ARB's processes and procedures were on BMIS, and plans were in place to complete the rollout of Phase 2 by the end of the first quarter of 2001.

The ISO surveillance audit of ARB was conducted the week of December 11, 2000. There were still areas ARB needed to address, and a few nonconformances were issued, but there were no surprises. Although we had made tremendous progress since May 2000, we had much work ahead to fully deploy BMIS Phase 2. We were gratified, however, by the registrar's glowing assessment of the ARB BMS.

"The web-based document system recently produced by ARB is considered to be approaching best in class in the industry. The potential to click and access relevant linked information was most impressive. The linkages to relevant metric information relating to the defined processes and relevant training data (etc.) is a very useful feature . . . The fact . . . that it includes Sales, Finance, Engineering (etc.) is considered a major plus."

As we continued the implementation of BMIS across the rest of ARB, we also began looking at processes and procedures that had been completed prior to the audit. We found that BMIS users had suggestions to extend and improve the usability of the system. We started adding additional levels of detail where needed. For example, we added pictures of component placements and removal along with pictures of the internal layout of newly announced systems. We also created work aids for information, such as settings for torque screw drivers that had been kept in individual locations, and made them available on the intranet. We also created a page that listed all the changes made to BMIS during the last 30 days; the reason for the change; and a link to the process, procedure, work instruction, or work aid that had changed.

In December 2000 ARB had also introduced an e-commerce web site. The site is accessible by selecting any of the Consumer or Business Online Shopping links at *http://www.dell.com* and then clicking on "Refurbished Systems" at the top of the page. This Web site allows a customer to browse a real-time database of refurbished equipment available for sale, select a system, add a monitor and other peripheral devices to the order, move these items to an electronic shopping cart, and place the order by providing shipping and billing information and a credit card. Customers can do all of these 24 hours a day, seven days a week, without having to speak to a telesales representative. The customer still has the option of speaking to someone in telesales at any time before or during the process. The telesales representative can take over and complete a customer's order at any time during the transaction should a customer make that request. As part of the implementation of this e-commerce capability, new processes and procedures were written to train telesales representatives on how to handle calls from customers who were in the process of creating an order and needed assistance on the e-commerce site. This procedure was added to the BMIS site where it joined the telesales and other marketing and sales processes and procedures.

So far we have discussed the history and implementation of the ARB BMS. Like any other management system, though, assessment and continuous improvement must be an integral part of the process. As mentioned earlier, continuous improvement is embedded in the design of the system. We've already made many improvements based on user feedback and business imperatives and we also have expanded the scope of assessments of BMIS processes beyond checking for compliance.

In March 2001 we developed a training program to prepare auditors to assess all aspects of an operation and its processes (see Figure 3.10). The audit scope includes examining the extent to which the processes and procedures on BMIS are followed in the day-to-day business and whether they are current. Further, the scope of process audits in ARB has been expanded to include assessments of the efficiency and effectiveness of processes as they are measured by metrics established by the departments and against overall business metrics. The reviews also examine audit control points to assess effectiveness of processes and procedures in managing assets and maintaining appropriate internal controls.

Internal Assessment System - Procedure

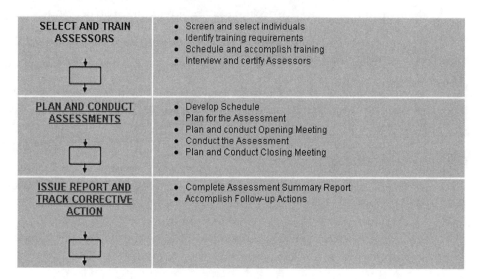

FIGURE 3.10. The BMS internal assessment procedure.

Summary

An effective management system must yield measurable improvements in business operations. Control of processes and procedures are essential in any company. The company, however, may well be focusing on the wrong processes unless the effects of these controls can be validated through results. It may be very efficient in maintaining control but ineffective in improving the operation.

The comparison of key results between November 1999 and December 2000 clearly demonstrates that the intranet-based ARB Business Management System is both efficient and effective. By year-end 2000, all key business measurement indicators reflected significant year-over-year improvements. Our ISO registrar stated that the web-based management system was approaching best-in-class in the industry.

BMIS also provided the foundation for ARB to engage in Dell's Business Process Improvement (BPI) initiative. BPI is a methodology used to understand, interrogate, and improve processes thereby adding value to every customer interaction with Dell. It requires looking at all aspects of the business (from order to post-sales service) from the customer's perspective asking, "How can we improve our business processes?" The BPI Methodology is designed to:

- Focus on projects that drive the customer experience and key business metrics
- Produce financially validated cost savings and process improvements
- Use quality tools to provide a structured approach to improving processes and productivity

The ARB Business Management System is not the sole reason for the strong improvement in business results. But the results could not have been achieved and sustained in such a short time without the focus on process definition, communication, and compliance provided by the Business Management Interactive System.

4

THE 2000 REVISION

The first revision to ISO 9000:1987 came in 1994. It was a combination of minor enhancements and clarification of ambiguities. The 2000 revision is a total rewrite of the 1994 standard. Twenty elements have been replaced

Significant Changes

- 20 Elements contained in 5 Clauses, but now includes...
  - Customer focus
  - Internal communication
  - Customer communication
  - Customer satisfaction
  - Continual improvement

by five clauses. Although all 20 of the elements are contained in the five clauses, there are substantial changes and new requirements. They include the following:

- Elimination of ISO 9002 and ISO 9003
- The ability to exclude sections of ISO 9001 that do not apply to your organization
- Redefinition of ISO 9000 to "Fundamentals and Vocabulary," which eliminated ISO 8402
- Redefinition of ISO 9004 to "Guidelines for Performance Improvements"
- Commonality of the formats of ISO 9000, ISO 9001, and ISO 9004
- Change from "Quality Assurance System" to "Quality Management System" (QMS)
- Encouragement of using "the process approach"
- Calling your company the "organization" instead of the "supplier"
- Changing the name "subcontractor" to "supplier"
- "Product" defined to mean hardware, software, services, and processed materials

- Change from 18 documented procedures required to 6
- Change from 17 required records to 21
- Identification of processes, their sequence, and interaction
- Establishing the need for criteria and methods for effective operations and control of processes
- Evidence of management commitment to the QMS
- Establishment of measurable quality objectives
- Opening channels of internal communications
- Addressing customer satisfaction
- Identifying competency needs
- Evaluating training effectiveness
- Making employees aware of how their work effects the QMS
- Managing the human and physical work environment
- Focus on meeting customers' needs and expectations
- Communicating awareness of customer requirements
- Communicating with the customer at all levels
- Measuring customer satisfaction
- Expanding monitoring and measuring activities to run the QMS
- Controlling processes as well as products
- Expanding statistical techniques to data analysis and taking action on the data
- Building a continual improvement model

Some of the changes are dramatic, some subtle. Table 4.1 provides a cross-reference to the 20 elements of the 1994 revision. Chapter 6 defines in detail the requirements contained in each clause. Chapter 8 provides a roadmap to plan the transition from the 1994 revision to the 2000 standard.

TABLE 4.1 *Changes From ISO 9001:1994 to ISO 9001:2000*

Clause (2000)	Title	ISO 9001: 1994 Element(s)	Changes From ISO 9001:1994
4	Quality Management System (title only)		No longer a "Quality Assurance System"
4.1	General Requirements	4.2.1	Added requirements to continually improve system effectiveness; determine process sequence and interaction; monitor, measure, and analyze processes; continually improve processes; and document and control outsourced processes
4.2	Documentation Requirements (title only)		
4.2.1	General	4.2.2	More clearly defines the types of documentation; first mention of "competence of personnel"
4.2.2	Quality Manual	4.2.1	New requirements: to document exclusions in the manual, to include or make reference to procedures, and to document the sequence and interaction of processes
4.2.3	Control of Documents	4.5.1, 4.5.2, 4.5.3	Records now included as documents; clarified the need to ensure documents remain legible and identifiable
4.2.4	Control of Records	4.16	Clarified requirement to ensure that records remain legible, identifiable, and retrievable
5	Management Responsibility (title only)		
5.1	Management Commitment	4.1.1	Added requirements to communicate the importance of meeting customer, statutory, and regulatory requirements; continually improve QMS effectiveness

(continued)

TABLE 4.1 *Changes From ISO 9001:1994 to ISO 9001:2000 (continued)*

Clause (2000)	Title	ISO 9001: 1994 Element(s)	Changes From ISO 9001:1994
5.2	Customer Focus	4.3.2	New requirement to determine and meet customer requirements and aim to enhance customer satisfaction
5.3	Quality Policy	4.1.1	Added requirement for a commitment to comply with the policy, to continually improve QMS effectiveness, and to establish and review quality objectives
5.4	Planning (title only)		
5.4.1	Quality Objectives	4.1.1, 4.2.1	New requirement to clearly establish measurable and consistent quality objectives
5.4.2	Quality Management System Planning	4.2.3	Added a requirement to ensure the integrity of the QMS when changes are planned and implemented
5.5	Responsibility, Authority, and Communication (title only)		
5.5.1	Responsibility and Authority	4.1.2.1	Essentially unchanged
5.5.2	Management Representative	4.1.2.3	Added the duty to promote awareness of customer requirements
5.5.3	Internal Communication	New requirement	Added the requirement for top management to communicate the effectiveness of the QMS
5.6	Management Review (title only)		
5.6.1	General	4.1.3	Essentially unchanged
5.6.2	Review Input	New requirement	Added a specific list of inputs for management reviews

(*continued*)

TABLE 4.1 *Changes From ISO 9001:1994 to ISO 9001:2000 (continued)*

Clause (2000)	Title	ISO 9001: 1994 Element(s)	Changes From ISO 9001:1994
5.6.3	Review Output	New requirement	Added a specific list of outputs from management reviews, including the only reference to improving products
6	Resource Management (title only)		
6.1	Provision of Resources	4.1.2.2	Added requirements to implement and continually improve the QMS and enhance customer satisfaction by meeting their requirements
6.2	Human Resources (title only)		
6.2.1	General	4.1.2.2	Added references to competence and skills required when selecting personnel working on processes
6.2.2	Competence, Awareness, and Training	4.18	Again discusses competence, plus determining the effectiveness of training; requires awareness training of relevance of activities and contribution to meeting quality objectives; requires records of education, skills, and experience to be maintained
6.3	Infrastructure	4.9	For the first time, requires organizations to consider facilities, equipment, and supporting services in achieving conformance
6.4	Work Environment	4.9	Expands process control to consider the work environment in achieving conformance as clarity to "controlled conditions"
7	Product Realization (title only)		

TABLE 4.1 *Changes From ISO 9001:1994 to ISO 9001:2000 (continued)*

Clause (2000)	Title	ISO 9001: 1994 Element(s)	Changes From ISO 9001:1994
7.1	Planning of Product Realization	4.2.3, 4.9, 4.10.1, 4.15, 4.19	Specific planning steps must now be taken to plan the processes within the QMS; quality objectives must be part of the planning; processes must be validated for effectiveness
7.2	Customer-Related Processes (title only)		
7.2.1	Determination of Requirements Related to the Product	New requirement	New requirements are added to determine customer stated requirements and those necessary for known intended use, determine applicable statutory and regulatory requirements, and include any other needed requirements
7.2.2	Review of Requirements Related to the Product	4.3.2, 4.3.3, 4.3.4	Minor enhancements in the area of contract review
7.2.3	Customer Communication	New requirement	A specific requirement is added to open channels of communication with customers regarding product information, inquiries, feedback, and customer complaints
7.3	Design and Development (title only)		
7.3.1	Design and Development Planning	4.4.2, 4.4.3	Essentially unchanged
7.3.2	Design and Development Inputs	4.4.4	Added the need to consider functional performance requirements, information from previous designs, and other essential requirements
7.3.3	Design and Development Outputs	4.4.5	Added an output to provide information to purchasing, production, and service

(continued)

TABLE 4.1 *Changes From ISO 9001:1994 to ISO 9001:2000 (continued)*

Clause (2000)	Title	ISO 9001: 1994 Element(s)	Changes From ISO 9001:1994
7.3.4	Design and Development Review	4.4.6	Added review requirements to evaluate the ability of designs to meet requirements, identify problems and propose actions, ensure reviews are systematic, and record necessary actions
7.3.5	Design and development Verification	4.4.7	Essentially unchanged
7.3.6	Design and Development Validation	4.4.8	Added a requirement to perform validation prior to implementation or delivery, when practicable
7.3.7	Control of Design and Development Changes	4.4.9	Added requirements to review, verify, and validate changes as appropriate; and evaluate the effect of changes on delivered products
7.4	Purchasing (title only)		
7.4.1	Purchasing Process	4.6.2	Essentially unchanged
7.4.2	Purchasing Information	4.6.3	Purchasing information requirements expanded to include requirements for procedures, processes, and equipment; personnel qualification requirements; and QMS requirements
7.4.3	Verification of Purchased Product	4.6.4, 4.10.2	Essentially unchanged
7.5	Production and Service Provision (title only)		
7.5.1	Control of Production and Service Provision	4.9, 4.15.6, 4.19	Added control requirements for having the information that describes product characteristics and the implementation of release, delivery, and postdelivery activities

TABLE 4.1 *Changes From ISO 9001:1994 to ISO 9001:2000 (continued)*

Clause (2000)	Title	ISO 9001: 1994 Element(s)	Changes From ISO 9001:1994
7.5.2	Validation of Processes for Production and Service Provision	4.9	Adds requirements to validate processes and to revalidate them as necessary; validation proves that the processes meet their intended outcome
7.5.3	Identification and Traceability	4.8, 4.10.5, 4.12	Essentially unchanged
7.5.4	Customer Property	4.7	Essentially unchanged
7.5.5	Preservation of Product	4.15.2, 4.15.3, 4.15.4, 4.15.5	Combined all aspects of handling, storage, packaging, preservation, and delivery into one subclause that could more accurately be called "inventory control"
7.6	Control of Monitoring and Measuring Devices	4.11.1, 4.11.2	Added clarifications to the requirements for calibration, gives an option to "verify" as opposed to "calibrate," and addresses the validation of test software prior to use
8	Measurement, Analysis, and Improvement (title only)		
8.1	General	4.10.1, 4.20.1, 4.20.2	Combined the functions of inspection and data gathering to ensure that conformity verification processes collect the data necessary to not only ensure conformity, but to continually improve the QMS
8.2	Monitoring and Measurement (title only)		
8.2.1	Customer Satisfaction	New requirement	Adds a new requirement to monitor customer satisfaction as a performance measure

(continued)

TABLE 4.1   *Changes From ISO 9001:1994 to ISO 9001:2000 (continued)*

Clause (2000)	Title	ISO 9001: 1994 Element(s)	Changes From ISO 9001:1994
8.2.2	Internal Audit	4.17	Clarifies selection of internal auditors who have no conflict of interest in the area being audited and emphasizes the need to resolve audit issues expediently
8.2.3	Monitoring and Measurement of Processes	4.17, 4.20.1, 4.20.2	Combines internal audit tools and statistics with a new requirement to specifically monitor processes for effectiveness and to use the data collected to affect corrective actions
8.2.4	Monitoring and Measurement of Product	4.10.2, 4.10.3, 4.10.4, 4.10.5, 4.20.1, 4.20.2	Combines inspection requirements and statistics with more emphasis on monitoring and measuring product conformance
8.3	Control of Nonconforming Product	4.13.1, 4.13.2	Essentially unchanged, except for a new requirement to take accountability for nonconformities found after a product is delivered or in use
8.4	Analysis of Data	4.14, 4.20.1, 4.20.2	Now a comprehensive set of requirements to gather data from all appropriate sources and to use that data to evaluate effectiveness of the QMS and for continual improvement
8.5	Improvement (title only)		
8.5.1	Continual Improvement	4.1.3	Essentially a new requirement to use all of the information gathered to continually improve the QMS
8.5.2	Corrective Action	4.14.1, 4.14.2	More clearly defined as elimination of nonconformities and taking actions to prevent recurrence

(continued)

TABLE 4.1   *Changes From ISO 9001:1994 to ISO 9001:2000 (continued)*

Clause (2000)	Title	ISO 9001: 1994 Element(s)	Changes From ISO 9001:1994
8.5.3	Preventive Action	4.14.1, 4.14.3	More clearly defined as eliminating potential nonconformities before they occur

Figure 4.1 depicts the journey of quality from its early days of inspection and detection to its ultimate achievement: world-class quality[1]. The relative positions of ISO 9000 on the continuum indicate where they are in relation to earlier initiatives. BMS refers to the integration of quality and processes into a Business Management System, as opposed to having adversarial operations and quality organizations.

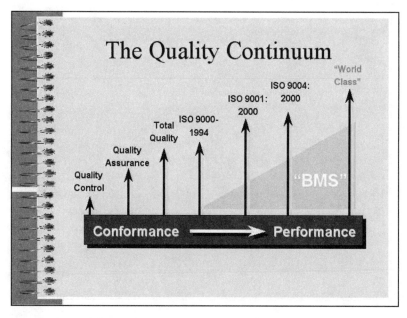

FIGURE 4.1.   The quality continuum.

1. *World-class-quality can be defined as reaching excellence levels contained in tools such as the Malcolm Baldrige National Quality Award and other State and industry models.*

5

THE RELATIONSHIP AMONG ISO 9000:2000, ISO 9001:2000, AND ISO 9004:2000

In Chapter 2, we reviewed the history of ISO 9000. In Chapter 4, we discussed the 2000 revision of ISO 9001. In Chapter 6, we explore the actual wording of ISO 9001. In Chapter 16, we list other standards in the ISO 9000 and related families. In this chapter, we explore the relationship of the three documents that make up the "coherent" series of the 2000 revision.

ISO 9000:2000 is titled "Quality Management Systems—Fundamentals and Vocabulary." It is not a requirements document, but it is provided as an adjunct to ISO 9001:2000 to add clarity in understanding the underlying principles behind ISO 9001 and to define the vocabulary used in the standard. In its introduction, it includes the interrelationship between the coherent set of standards and a list of "Quality Management Principles." According to Paragraph 0.2, "Eight quality management principles have been identified that can be used by top management in order to lead the organization to improved performance." It also states, "These eight quality management principles form the basis for the quality management system standards within the ISO 9000 family." These principles are as follows:

- Customer focus: Organizations depend on their customers and therefore should understand current and future customer needs, meet customer requirements, and strive to exceed customer expectations.

- Leadership: Leaders establish unity of purpose and the direction of the organization. They should create and maintain an internal environment in which people can become fully involved in achieving the organization's objectives.
- Involvement of people: People at all levels are the essence of an organization and their full involvement enables their abilities to be used for the organization's benefit.
- Process approach: A desired result is achieved more efficiently when activities and related resources are managed as a process.
- System approach to management: Identifying, understanding, and managing interrelated processes as a system contributes to the organization's effectiveness and efficiency in achieving its objectives.
- Continual improvement: Continual improvement of the organization's overall performance should be a permanent objective of the organization.
- Factual approach to decision making: Effective decisions are based on the analysis of data and information.
- Mutually beneficial supplier relationships: An organization and its suppliers are interdependent and a mutually beneficial relationship enhances the ability of both to create value.

Of the eight quality management principles, only customer focus and continual improvement are specifically mentioned in ISO 9001:2000 as requirements. The rest are referred to only in ISO 9004:2000, "Guidelines for Performance Improvements," and most are mentioned only once. Curiously, involvement of people is mentioned 68 times in ISO 9004! How then do the other six principles apply to ISO 9001? Because ISO 9000 states that these principles were used in developing the family of standards, it would make business sense to embrace the eight principles as critical to the success of any viable QMS. It is recommended that these principles be utilized when writing the Quality Policy Manual and when designing the QMS, not as imposed requirements, but as valuable guidance principles. For instance, Paragraph 7.4 of ISO 9001 gives minimum requirements for establishing relationships with suppliers. Paragraph 0.2 of ISO 9000 suggests that not only should minimum controls be established, but also that mutually beneficial relationships with suppliers will lead to the objectives of continual improvement and customer satisfaction, the key themes of the coherent standards. If ISO 9001 implementation in your company is to pay its own way (as opposed to being an overhead burden), these guidelines are invaluable implementation tools.

Section 1 of ISO 9000:2000 sets forth the following elements:

- The scope of the standard
- Rationale for QMSs
- Requirements for QMSs as distinguished from requirements for products
- Steps in the "QMS approach"
- A discussion of "the process approach"
- Definitions of the quality policy and quality objectives
- The role of top management in the QMS
- The value of documentation
- The types of documentation used in a QMS
- Evaluating processes within the QMS
- Auditing the QMS
- Reviewing the QMS
- Self-assessment techniques
- The aim of continual improvement
- The role of statistical techniques
- The focus of the QMS
- Relationship between a QMS and quality excellence models

These topics are essentially a primer on QMSs. For those new to the discipline, the primer provides sound logic and background for QMS implementation. For seasoned quality professionals, it establishes some evolutionary guidelines that help move us from traditional adversarial roles between quality and the rest of the company to a proactive approach to achieving overall business success.

Section 3 of ISO 9000:2000 is a glossary of the terminology used in all three standards. Annex A provides concept diagrams of how the terminology interrelates.

To really confuse matters, Paragraph 2 of ISO 9001:2000 refers to ISO 9000:2000 as a "normative reference." Therefore, any time ISO 9001 refers to fundamentals defined in ISO 9000, they become part of the requirements in ISO 9001. In other words, among other items, there is a clear need to incorporate the definitions and their interrelationships into the design of the QMS. Although we have already determined that only two of the eight quality management principles of Paragraph 0.2 of ISO 9000 are referenced in ISO 9001 (and therefore become provisions of ISO 9001), we must show due diligence in correlating the fundamentals in Sections 1 and 2 of ISO 9000 for any "normative references" in ISO 9001. It is incumbent on your organization, either internally or with the help of outside expertise, to determine and document the impact of the fundamentals in ISO 9000 and how they are used to define your QMS and its requirements.

ISO 9001:2000 is the "requirements" document of the three standards. Clauses 4 through 8 contain the required elements of the QMS. The discussions in Chapter 6 and the Audit Checklist in Appendix D provide a detailed look at all of the clauses and their meanings. Organizations that choose to exclude any subclauses of ISO 9001 because they are not directly applicable to their business may do so only from those in Clause 7. When any exclusion is claimed, the rationale for exclusion must be documented in the Quality System Manual.

ISO 9004 is entitled "Guidelines for Performance Improvements." It is devoted to providing information to those who would use ISO 9001 not only as a conformance document, but also as the foundation of an excellence model of business management. Each clause of ISO 9001 is built on to give guidance in returning the greatest benefit from the intent of the clauses. It also introduces topics, such as financial measures and self-assessment, that are not found in ISO 9001, but are logical extensions of the QMS requirements for organizations that seek to become models of excellence or "best in class." In Chapter 6, we include the guidelines from ISO 9004 after each relevant clause of ISO 9001. This was done not to infer that these are added requirements, but to suggest that there is a wealth of data in these guidelines to help with designing the most viable QMS that your organization desires. Annex A of ISO 9004 even provides an assessment tool for organizations to use to evaluate their own performance and continual improvement. It assigns "maturity levels" (much like the CMM Software Model1) to help organizations rate themselves. Only time will tell if this model will be embraced, especially with the existence of established Malcolm Baldrige2 assessment tools and other industry-association self-evaluation tools.

Don't become bogged down in ISO 9004, but do read it and extract the tools that will help you successfully implement ISO 9001.

---

1. *This is a series of models developed by Carnegie Mellon's Software Engineering Institute. See* http://www.sei.cmu.edu/cmm/ *for more information.*

2. *The Malcolm Baldrige National Quality Award is presented annually by the President of the United States to organizations that have demonstrated the highest level of excellence in their business management. It is based on a numerical scoring system that is widely used in evaluating business performance.*

6

THE FIVE CLAUSES
OF ISO 9001:2000

In this chapter, we explore in depth the 2000 revision to ISO 9001. Each clause and subclause is stated verbatim.

Following each key requirement, implementation guidelines, tips, and techniques are provided. These are based on more than a decade of experience by the authors and from experiential and anecdotal data researched and found to be sound approaches to implementation.

When appropriate, potential pitfalls and problem areas are included. These are also based on experience and information gathered about how to avoid non-value-added activities while developing, modifying, or implementing your QMS.

Finally, ISO 9004 Performance Improvement Guidelines are included after each clause and paragraph where appropriate. Although these are not requirements, they provide valuable information, tools, and reference data for designing or improving your QMS. For instance, there are frequent references to "interested parties" in ISO 9004 but no such references in ISO 9001. In fact, you must take into account "interested parties" such as regulatory agencies, local governing bodies, and even critical suppliers when implementing ISO 9001. Therefore, using ISO 9004 as a guide is a reasonable and prudent step toward achieving ISO 9001 compliance. At the same time, ISO 9004 stresses excellence models and sophisticated concepts (e.g., supplier partnerships) that may not be immediately applicable to newly developing QMSs. Take care not to overdesign or overdocument your processes based on ISO 9004 guidelines and recommendations. ISO 9001 is the only "requirements" document. Although the writers of the standards have attempted to make ISO 9001 and 9004 "coherent" documents, it will become obvious that the guidelines don't always fit precisely under each clause. You may have to look at context, scope of the guideline and relativity, and the location of the guideline within this chapter.

4 QUALITY MANAGEMENT SYSTEM

4.1 GENERAL REQUIREMENTS

The organization shall establish, document, implement and maintain a quality management system and continually improve its effectiveness in accordance with the requirements of this International Standard.

Implementation Guidelines, Tips, and Techniques

The QMS encompasses all activities, from determining customer needs to evaluating customer satisfaction. This normally includes all aspects of the value delivery system. There can be a case made for excluding the financial operations and human resources operations, because those activities are heavily regulated and often well documented. However, because the standard does deal with human needs and requirements and tying process metrics to business performance, it is wise to establish the interface with these organizations when designing the QMS.

Convention suggests that the documentation of the QMS include a Quality Policy Manual supported by operational procedures and work instructions to the level necessary for your business, industry, and culture. The documents may be electronic or written. The procedures and work instructions can be written or in the form of controlled process aides (photos, flowcharts, checklists, diagrams, etc.).

The standard requires organizations to "maintain" the QMS, which means that the system must be self-perpetuating. It also requires that the QMS continually improve its effectiveness. These objectives are often best accomplished with a standing cross-functional "continual improvement committee" that is chartered to keep the system compliant, alive, and robust.

Potential Pitfalls

There is no requirement to redesign or redocument an existing QMS just to conform to the format or language of the standard. If your system is currently robust and meets the requirements, a crosswalk or reference matrix might be all that is necessary for conformance auditing. Conducting a detailed gap analysis is warranted, however.

4.1 GENERAL REQUIREMENTS (CONTINUED)

The organization shall:

a. identify the processes needed for the quality management system and their application throughout the organization,

b. determine the sequence and interaction of these processes,

c. determine criteria and methods needed to ensure that both the operation and control of these processes are effective

Implementation Guidelines, Tips, and Techniques

Although ISO 9000, 9001, and 9004 suggest (as opposed to require) a "process approach" to organizational infrastructure, these three requirements make it clear that organizations that have not identified all required processes, their sequence of operation, interaction, control, support, monitoring, measurement, and analysis will likely not achieve compliance with the standard. These processes must include management activities and any outsourcing activities. This gives great impetus for using the "process approach" defined in ISO 9001, Paragraph 0.2, as a model for implementation. Flowcharting and process mapping are very effective tools for documenting, validating, and improving processes.

Potential Pitfalls

Every organization employs "processes" to achieve their desired outcome. Awareness of the function and outcome of each process and the interrelationship of processes is often unconscious and undocumented in smaller companies. Larger companies may have evolved convoluted and disassociated processes as a result of unplanned growth or crisis management. In either case, failure to identify each process in the value delivery system, to map the interrelationship of those processes, and to measure their effectiveness will inevitably lead to a dysfunctional and nonauditable QMS that is costly and wasteful.

4.1 GENERAL REQUIREMENTS (CONTINUED)

d. ensure the availability of resources and information necessary to support the operation and monitoring of these processes

Implementation Guidelines, Tips, and Techniques

Resources are defined as human resources, tools (computers, etc.), and the environment to support the operation. Information can be drawings, documents, standards, work instructions, customer requirements, or any applicable statutory or regulatory requirements.

Potential Pitfalls

Determination of "availability" should be defined for your culture. Ambiguity will lead to confusion within the workforce and difficulty in auditing for conformance. For instance, availability may mean that consumable supplies are always on hand and ready for use in one organization. In another company, it might mean that consumables are ordered as they are needed. Don't leave determination of the definition of availability to your internal or external auditors.

4.1 GENERAL REQUIREMENTS (CONTINUED)

e. monitor, measure and analyze these processes, and

f. implement actions necessary to achieve planned results and continual improvement of these processes.

Implementation Guidelines, Tips, and Techniques

All of the business processes must be continually monitored, measured, and analyzed to ensure that they are performing as intended. The data collected must be used to continually improve the processes.

Potential Pitfalls

Organizations that produce durable products or measurable commodities often have objective and straightforward approaches to measuring and monitoring processes. Often sensors, gauges, and computers can collect quantitative data and provide immediate indications of process effectiveness or ineffectiveness. Companies that produce less tangible products or services also have compelling business reasons to determine process effectiveness, although data collection may require creative methods that produce less exact data points. In any case, the processes must be monitored, appropriate data collected, and actions taken to ensure that the desired results are being met and that the data is being used as a tool of continual improvement.

4.1 GENERAL REQUIREMENTS (CONTINUED)

These processes shall be managed by the organization in accordance with the requirements of this International Standard.

Implementation Guidelines, Tips, and Techniques

Compliance of the QMS is required to the "International Standard," which is ISO 9001:2000 and the U.S. version, Q9001:2000.

4.1 GENERAL REQUIREMENTS (CONTINUED)

Where an organization chooses to outsource any process that affects product conformity with requirements, the organization shall ensure control over such processes. Control of such outsourced processes shall be identified within the quality management system.

Implementation Guidelines, Tips, and Techniques

Many companies are outsourcing rather than building in-house expertise. Others outsource particular processes or services. Using subcontractors or suppliers to perform value-added processes does not relieve an organization of ensuring that conformity to requirements is met at a level comparable to that established for in-house processes. The QMS documentation must address how subcontracted processes are controlled. The extent of the controls must be commensurate with the importance of the process or service.

Potential Pitfalls

If you are subcontracting critical services, specific requirements and expectations must be stated in drawings, procedures, process procedures, or purchasing documents. This requirement does not, however, imply any specific methodology for control of outsourced processes. It is not necessary to perform on-site inspections if there is no sound business reason to do so. Good business practices might include having subcontractors perform all verification and monitoring activities or having a representative of your company as an on-site auditor.

4.1 GENERAL REQUIREMENTS (CONTINUED)

NOTE Processes needed for the quality management system referred to above should include processes for management activities, provision of resources, product realization and measurement.

Implementation Guidelines, Tips, and Techniques

This note highlights the fact that the QMS includes more in its scope than the value delivery system. It includes management and provision of resources as defined processes within the QMS.

Potential Pitfalls

As stated earlier, any ambiguity in process definition inevitably leads to unwanted variability in process outcome. Although management activities are often reactive to the dictate of changing situations, the fundamental methodology for managing the QMS must be specified. This should include the steps in the chain of command necessary to deal with planned activities and key decision points that occur in product realization and measurement, including allocation of resources.

ISO 9004 Performance Improvement Guidelines

Managing Systems and Processes

Leading and operating an organization successfully requires managing it in a systematic and visible manner. Success should result from implementing and maintaining a management system that is designed to continually improve the effectiveness and efficiency of the organization's performance by considering the needs of interested parties. Managing an organization includes quality management, among other management disciplines. Top management should establish a customer-oriented organization:

    a. by defining systems and processes that can be clearly understood, managed and improved in effectiveness as well as efficiency, and;

    b. by ensuring effective and efficient operation and control of processes and the measures and data used to determine satisfactory performance of the organization.

Examples of activities to establish a customer-oriented organization include:

- defining and promoting processes that lead to improved organizational performance,
- acquiring and using process data and information on a continuing basis,
- directing progress towards continual improvement, and
- using suitable methods to evaluate process improvement, such as self-assessments and management review.

Examples of self-assessment and continual improvement processes are given in Annexes A and B of ISO 9004:2000.

4.2 DOCUMENTATION REQUIREMENTS

4.2.1 GENERAL

The quality management system documentation shall include

a. documented statements of a quality policy and quality objectives,

b. a quality manual,

c. documented procedures required by this International Standard,

d. documents needed by the organization to ensure the effective planning, operation and control of its processes, and

e. records required by this International Standard.

Implementation Guidelines, Tips, and Techniques

The definition of required documentation includes that which is specified in (a) through (e). It specifically mentions the procedures and records required within the clauses of the standard, but it also includes documents "needed" to ensure effective planning, operation, and process control.

Potential Pitfalls

Care must be exercised in determining what process documentation is needed and to what extent the QMS is codified. There is a tendency to over-document the QMS, resulting in unnecessary self-constraints. A test of reason should always include this question: What minimal level of documentation must I have to provide training and guidance to known-competent process operators? In determining record retention needs, consider liability issues, statutory and regulatory requirements, and the need to provide ongoing support to customers after products or services are delivered.

4.2.1 GENERAL (CONTINUED)

NOTE 1 Where the term "documented procedure" appears within this International Standard, this means that the procedure is established, documented, implemented and maintained.

Potential Pitfalls

Document control procedures must contain provisions for maintenance of the documents. This follows the "continual improvement" theme of the standard. This note also reinforces the imperative that all documented procedures must be implemented. Evidence of implementation is demonstrated most often by audit results.

4.2.1 GENERAL (CONTINUED)

NOTE 2 The extent of the quality management system documentation can differ from one organization to another due to

    a. the size of organization and type of activities,

    b. the complexity of processes and their interactions, and

    c. the competence of personnel.

Implementation Guidelines, Tips, and Techniques

This note acknowledges that QMS documentation does not have to follow any particular form; it should be tailored to the needs of the organization. It should not necessarily be designed to follow the clauses of the standard, although a quality manual that follows the sequence of the standard facilitates compliance auditing. It also acknowledges that, if you establish competency criteria for your personnel, the level of documentation need only be as complex as events dictate.

Potential Pitfalls

Again, there is a tendency to overdocument and try to fit the culture of an organization into some standard documentation formats. The documentation should be only as complex as your company can effectively use and maintain. Verification of competency, however, should not be underdocumented. Concise definitions of skills and knowledge required to perform specific job functions are vital to the streamlining of process procedures. Identifying the required knowledge level of each process operator minimizes the number of detailed work instructions necessary to assure product or process conformance.

4.2.1 GENERAL (CONTINUED)

NOTE 3 The documentation can be in any form or type of medium.

Implementation Guidelines, Tips, and Techniques

It is becoming common to replace paper manuals with Web-based documentation and electronic manuals that are controlled and accessible. There are many cost-effective systems available to allow dynamic updates and controlled access, while providing a robust platform for process control, inspection, and training. Flowcharts, photographs, and laminated work aides are also effective media.

Potential Pitfalls

This note does not advocate "informal" documentation that is inappropriate to the product or service. The medium gives freedom to be creative, not to minimize the need for effective documentation.

4.2.2 QUALITY MANUAL

The organization shall establish and maintain a quality manual that includes

    a. the scope of the quality management system, including details of and justification for any exclusions,

b. the documented procedures established for the quality management system, or reference to them, and

c. a description of the interaction between the processes of the quality management system.

Implementation Guidelines, Tips, and Techniques

The quality manual must be a very robust document and the centerpiece of the QMS. At the same time, there is great flexibility in how the QMS documentation is structured. The only required elements of the quality manual are the stated scope of what the manual covers and justification for any exclusions claimed. For instance, the scope might be "the processing of insurance claims for the medical industry." Exclusions could include "The XYZ company is a reseller of manufactured products and does not perform design. Therefore, Clause 7.3 of ISO 9001:2000 is excluded." The remainder of the quality manual can include policy statements and make reference to operational procedures or it can be a single document with all procedures and work instructions included. There is also a requirement to describe the interaction of all processes. This may be done most effectively with process flowcharts included with a functional organizational chart. See the sample quality manual in Appendix B. For organizations utilizing Web-based documentation, the quality manual may be part of a document hierarchy that is connected by hyperlinks of increasing detail or by navigation to reference documents.

Potential Pitfalls

Quality manuals have tended to be a compilation of policy statements and references. In (c), there is a specified need to document the interaction of processes and their procedures within the quality manual. Clearly, the quality manual must have a role as a dynamic tool that is used to document process flow rather than a reference that collects dust on a shelf.

4.2.3 CONTROL OF DOCUMENTS

Documents required by the quality management system shall be controlled. Records are a special type of document and shall be controlled according to the requirements given in 4.2.4. A documented procedure shall be established to define the controls needed

   a. to approve documents for adequacy prior to issue,

   b. to review and update as necessary and re-approve documents,

   c. to ensure that changes and the current revision status of documents are identified,

   d. to ensure that relevant versions of applicable documents are available at points of use,

   e. to ensure that documents remain legible and readily identifiable,

   f. to ensure that documents of external origin are identified and their distribution controlled, and

   g. to prevent the unintended use of obsolete documents, and to apply suitable identification to them if they are retained for any purpose.

Implementation Guidelines, Tips, and Techniques

The requirements for document control are straightforward and concise. This is also a clause that requires a documented procedure. The definition of a document, however, has never been universally clear. Documents required by the QMS include any forms, computer screens or reports, checklists, routing documents, customer documents, supplier documents, specifications, references, software, and other paper or media that is integral to the effective control of the processes within the value delivery system. If there is a need for a point of control, such as document revisions or forms widely used, then an appropriate level of control must be in place. Procedures must be reviewed and approved by those accountable for the processes they control. If the procedures are on paper, signatures and dates (or some other form of revision control) must be present. If documents are on computer systems, there must be appropriate password or access controls to ensure their integrity. There must also be a library system for these forms or documents to ensure the use of the correct revision. This includes identifying changes to documents and ensuring that the revisions and change information arrive at the appropriate work centers in a timely manner. Documents used frequently or in hostile environments must be audited for identification and legibility and replaced when they are no longer usable for their intended purpose. The document control system must be robust enough to serve the needs of those who use the documents and data. It must not be so controlling, however, that "work-arounds" and informal documentation are needed to keep processes moving.

Potential Pitfalls

Be sure to include software and software media in the document control system. This applies to any software that is used in the value delivery system (e.g., process control software, diagnostic software, etc.). You need not include software, such as word processing programs, used for clerical duties. Also be sure to include outside standards that you might use for reference and customer-furnished drawings, specifications, and standards.

4.2.4 CONTROL OF RECORDS

Records shall be established and maintained to provide evidence of conformity to requirements and of the effective operation of the quality management system. Records shall remain legible, readily identifiable and retrievable. A documented procedure shall be established to define the controls needed for the identification, storage, protection, retrieval, retention time and disposition of records.

Implementation Guidelines, Tips, and Techniques

Control of records has broad implications. Any document or computer data that is used to give evidence of conformity (ergo, nonconformity) must be handled in accordance with this clause. Measures must exist to:

- Ensure records are identifiable
- Allow appropriate access to the records
- Ensure these records remain legible during their intended lifetime

Because many records are now computer files, procedures must be defined to ensure the integrity of electronic data. These control methods should be implemented only to the extent dictated by your industry, your business needs, your customer, and regulatory and statutory requirements. They must, however, include records of the effective operation of the QMS, which may involve virtually all business records kept by your organization. A fact-finding process is recommended to identify all records that are kept, the business reasons for keeping them, and the period for which they should be kept. As part of this process, a "test of reason" should be invoked to ensure sufficient data exists to ensure customer needs and avoidance of liability issues.

Documented procedures must exist for identification, storage, protection, retrieval, retention time, and disposition of records. Storage, retention, and retrieval should be to the extent dictated by the importance of the records and your need to access them.

Potential Pitfalls

This clause often causes organizations to create administrative nightmares for themselves. There is no ISO requirement to build massive data control and retrieval systems unless there is a business imperative to do so. If you have never had occasion to refer back to certain records and data, do a test of reason to discover why you keep it. If you build a record retention system that includes disposition procedures, you must have a methodology to ensure that the procedures are followed and records are disposed of as prescribed. A more robust method is to devise disposition procedures that state "Discard no earlier than *xx/yy/zzzz*." This allows you to keep records beyond their retention periods without violating your own procedures. Also, procedures must specify the method for disposing of records (shredding, archiving, etc.).

ISO 9004 Performance Improvement Guidelines

Documentation

Management should define the documentation, including the relevant records, needed to establish, implement and maintain the quality management system and to support an effective and efficient operation of the organization's processes.

The nature and extent of the documentation should satisfy the contractual, statutory and regulatory requirements, and the needs and expectations of customers and other interested parties and should be appropriate to the organization. Documentation may be in any form or medium suitable for the needs of the organization.

In order to provide documentation to satisfy the needs and expectations of interested parties management should consider:

- contractual requirements from the customer and other interested parties,
- acceptance of international, national, regional and industry sector standards,
- relevant statutory and regulatory requirements,
- decisions by the organization,
- sources of external information relevant for the development of the organization's competencies, and
- information about the needs and expectations of interested parties.

The generation, use and control of documentation should be evaluated with respect to the effectiveness and efficiency of the organization against criteria such as:

- functionality (such as speed of processing),
- user friendliness,
- resources needed,
- policies and objectives,
- current and future requirements related to managing knowledge,
- benchmarking of documentation systems, and
- interfaces used by organization's customers, suppliers and other interested parties.

Access to documentation should be ensured for people in the organization and to other interested parties, based on the organization's communication policy.

5 MANAGEMENT RESPONSIBILITY

5.1 MANAGEMENT COMMITMENT

Top management shall provide evidence of its commitment to the development and implementation of the quality management system and continually improving its effectiveness by

a. communicating to the organization the importance of meeting customer as well as statutory and regulatory requirements,

b. establishing the quality policy,

c. ensuring that quality objectives are established,

d. conducting management reviews, and

e. ensuring the availability of resources.

Implementation Guidelines, Tips, and Techniques

Top management, however that is defined in your organization, must be the architect and the driver of all quality management and planning activities. There must be auditable evidence of their commitment to the QMS and its continual improvement, to conducting management reviews, and to providing needed resources. The quality department cannot solely own the QMS. It must be enterprisewide and passionately driven from the top. Evidence of commitment must be manifested in actions more robust than reacting to customer complaints or quality problems. This evidence must include regular communication and reinforcement of quality policies and objectives from top management and availability of resources to execute the quality objectives. For instance, a quality policy that includes the idea that the organization will meet all customer stated and implied needs must be communicated to all who are part of the value delivery system. Specifically, top management must define measurable actions and accountabilities to achieve this goal. They must establish metrics to ensure that the goals and objectives are being carried out and they must take corrective action when measures indicate that the stated actions and accountabilities are not being met. Another example would be a quality objective that states that software will perform to the organization's specifications at all times. Without resources to conduct validation testing, customer feedback surveys, and quantification of results to a predetermined standard, this objective is hollow, ineffective, and meaningless.

Potential Pitfalls

If your quality initiatives are "grass roots" or exist only for liability abatement, you will not be compliant with ISO 9001:2000 and you will not realize a meaningful return on your investment in quality-related activities. Top management must develop a quality policy and quality objectives that are truly a shared vision of their expectations, not marketing hype for potential customers. These expectations include their vision for the image the company projects, their expectations from each employee, and the imperative of meeting customer and regulatory requirements. Management reviews must be a forum for companywide evaluation of QMS effectiveness, not an agenda item at the annual sales meeting. Placards espousing the quality policy posted in the break room and motivational posters are not evidence of management commitment. Continual improvement is not evidenced by resolving nonconformities or lack of customer complaints.

ISO 9004 Performance Improvement Guidelines

Leadership, commitment and the active involvement of the top management are essential for developing and maintaining an effective and efficient quality management system to achieve benefits for interested parties. To achieve these benefits, it is necessary to establish, sustain and increase customer satisfaction. Top management should consider actions such as

- establishing a vision, policies and strategic objectives consistent with the purpose of the organization,
- leading the organization by example, in order to develop trust within its people,
- communicating organizational direction and values regarding quality and the quality management system,

- participating in improvement projects, searching for new methods, solutions and products,
- obtaining feedback directly on the effectiveness and efficiency of the quality management system,
- identifying the product realization processes that provide added value to the organization,
- identifying the support processes that influence the effectiveness and efficiency of the realization processes,
- creating an environment that encourages the involvement and development of people, and
- provision of the structure and resources that are necessary to support the organization's strategic plans

Top management should also define methods for measurement of the organization's performance in order to determine whether planned objectives have been achieved. Methods include

- financial measurement,
- measurement of process performance throughout the organization,
- external measurement, such as benchmarking and third party evaluation,
- assessment of the satisfaction of customers, people in the organization and other interested parties,
- assessment of the perceptions of customers and other interested parties of performance of products provided, and
- measurement of other success factors identified by management.

Information derived from such measurements and assessments should also be considered as input to management review in order to ensure that continual improvement of the quality management system is the driver for performance improvement of the organization.

Issues to Be Considered

When developing, implementing and managing the organization's quality management system, management should consider the quality management principles outlined in 4.3.

On the basis of these principles, top management should demonstrate leadership in, and commitment to, the following activities:

- understanding current and future customer needs and expectations, in addition to requirements;
- promoting policies and objectives to increase awareness, motivation and involvement of people in the organization;
- establishing continual improvement as an objective for processes of the organization;
- planning for the future of the organization and managing change;
- setting and communicating a framework for achieving the satisfaction of interested parties.

In addition to small-step or ongoing continual improvement, top management should also consider breakthrough changes to processes as a way to improve the organization's performance. During such changes, management should take steps to ensure that the resources and communication needed to maintain the functions of the quality management system are provided.

Top management should identify the organization's product realization processes, as these are directly related to the success of the organization. Top management should also identify those support processes that affect either the effectiveness and efficiency of the realization processes or the needs and expectations of interested parties.

Management should ensure that processes operate as an effective and efficient network. Management should analyze and optimize the interaction of processes, including both realization processes and support processes. Consideration should be given to

- ensuring that the sequence and interaction of processes are designed to achieve the desired results effectively and efficiently,
- ensuring process inputs, activities and outputs are clearly defined and controlled,
- monitoring inputs and outputs to verify that individual processes are linked and operate effectively and efficiently,
- identifying and managing risks, and exploiting performance improvement opportunities,
- conducting data analysis to facilitate continual improvement of processes,

- identifying process owners and giving them full responsibility and authority,
- managing each process to achieve the process objectives, and
- the needs and expectations of interested parties.

5.2 CUSTOMER FOCUS

Top management shall ensure that customer requirements are determined and are met with the aim of enhancing customer satisfaction.

Potential Pitfalls

Some service providers and leading-edge technology companies may see little value in this requirement, believing that "if you build it, they will come." Others may believe that the fact that customers buy their products or services is evidence of their customer focus. This clause, however, places the responsibility for determining and meeting customer requirements and enhancement of customer satisfaction clearly on the top management that sets all business priorities. Companies that have no proactive procedures in this area will find gaining compliance nearly impossible. Those who excel in customer focus will reap enormous marketing and financial benefits.

ISO 9004 Performance Improvement Guidelines

Needs and Expectations of Interested Parties

General

Every organization has interested parties, each party having needs and expectations. Interested parties of organizations include

- customers and end-users,
- people in the organization,
- owners/investors (such as shareholders, individuals or groups, including the public sector, that have a specific interest in the organization),

- suppliers and partners, and
- society in terms of the community and the public affected by the organization or its products.

Needs and Expectations

The success of the organization depends on understanding and satisfying the current and future needs and expectations of present and potential customers and end-users, as well as understanding and considering those of other interested parties.

In order to understand and meet the needs and expectations of interested parties, an organization should

- identify its interested parties and maintain a balanced response to their needs and expectations,
- translate identified needs and expectations into requirements,
- communicate the requirements throughout the organization, and
- focus on process improvement to ensure value for the identified interested parties.

To satisfy customer and end-user needs and expectations, the management of an organization should

- understand the needs and expectations of its customers, including those of potential customers,
- determine key product characteristics for its customers and end-users,
- identify and assess competition in its market, and
- identify market opportunities, weaknesses and future competitive advantage.

Examples of customer and end-user needs and expectations, as related to the organization's products, include

- conformity,
- dependability,
- availability,

- delivery,
- post-realization activities,
- price and life-cycle costs,
- product safety,
- product liability, and
- environmental impact.

The organization should identify its people's needs and expectations for recognition, work satisfaction, and personal development. Such attention helps to ensure that the involvement and motivation of people are as strong as possible.

The organization should define financial and other results that satisfy the identified needs and expectations of owners and investors.

Management should consider the potential benefits of establishing partnerships with suppliers to the organization, in order to create value for both parties. A partnership should be based on a joint strategy, sharing knowledge as well as gains and losses. When establishing partnerships, an organization should

- identify key suppliers, and other organizations, as potential partners,
- jointly establish a clear understanding of customers' needs and expectations,
- jointly establish a clear understanding of the partners' needs and expectations, and
- set goals to secure opportunities for continuing partnerships.

In considering its relationships with society, the organization should

- demonstrate responsibility for health and safety,
- consider environmental impact, including conservation of energy and natural resources,
- identify applicable statutory and regulatory requirements, and
- identify the current and potential impacts on society in general, and the local community in particular, of its products, processes and activities.

Statutory and Regulatory Requirements

Management should ensure that the organization has knowledge of the statutory and regulatory requirements that apply to its products, processes and activities and should include such requirements as part of the quality management system. Consideration should also be given to

- the promotion of ethical, effective and efficient compliance with current and prospective requirements,
- the benefits to interested parties from exceeding compliance, and
- the role of the organization in the protection of community interests.

5.3 QUALITY POLICY

Top management shall ensure that the quality policy

a. is appropriate to the purpose of the organization,

b. includes a commitment to comply with requirements and continually improve the effectiveness of the quality management system,

c. provides a framework for establishing and reviewing quality objectives,

d. is communicated and understood within the organization, and

e. is reviewed for continuing suitability.

Implementation Guidelines, Tips, and Techniques

The term quality policy is often used interchangeably with mission statement, vision statement, or value statement. It can have different meanings, depending on your culture, industry, and value system. Regardless of its name, it is a statement of the value and beliefs that those who lead the organization wish to impart to their employees, customers, and suppliers. It is the statement of quality values by which the organization wants to be known. Because there is no universal definition of quality, this statement defines what quality means to the organization. For example, a contract manufacturing operation might adopt this quality policy: "We are an extension of the customer's processes." Within those few words, the leaders of the company convey that they exist to supplement the resources of their customers, using the customer's quality and value requirements. For all of the employees, this means that their jobs are focused on becoming an extension of their customers, not designing new products or writing their own workmanship standards. A credit-card processing center might write this into its quality policy: "The XYZ service group will ensure a seamless transition between the consumer and the banking industry." This informs everyone that their sole reason for existence is to ensure that the funds from credit card sales move to the appropriate banking institution without error or delay.

The quality policy is often accompanied by a list of specific values that more clearly define the policy; for example, "We will meet the customer's stated and implied needs," or "We will continually advance the technology of our industry." The values might even include a dedication to return value to the community or provide a return on investment for shareholders. To be meaningful, each must be a true representation of the key values of the business leaders, each must be implemented (as opposed to being a slogan), and each must be measurable to demonstrate effectiveness. They cannot be marketing hype or unmeasurable catchphrases.

Items (b) through (e) go on to require a demonstrated commitment to comply with the policy, a mechanism to use it for continually improving the quality system, and a plan from which to evolve quality objectives. They also require that the policy be communicated to everyone who can affect the value delivery system and that the policies be continually reviewed for suitability.

Potential Pitfalls

Quality policies written by advertising agencies to adorn brochures, Web sites, and annual reports will be ineffective tools in communicating a teachable set of values to everyone who can have an effect on processes, products, and customers. Having employees memorize quality policy statements for internal and external audits is a waste of time and energy when the meaning of the policy is not integral to every activity of every job function.

ISO 9004 Performance Improvement Guidelines

Quality Policy

Top management should use the quality policy as a means of leading the organization toward improvement of its performance.

An organization's quality policy should be an equal and consistent part of the organization's overall policies and strategy.

In establishing the quality policy, top management should consider

- the level and type of future improvement needed for the organization to be successful,
- the expected or desired degree of customer satisfaction,
- the development of people in the organization,
- the needs and expectations of other interested parties,
- the resources needed to go beyond ISO 9001 requirements, and
- the potential contributions of suppliers and partners.

The quality policy can be used for improvement provided that

- it is consistent with top management's vision and strategy for the organization's future,
- it permits quality objectives to be understood and pursued throughout the organization,
- it demonstrates top management's commitment to quality and the provision of adequate resources for achievement of objectives,
- it aids in promoting a commitment to quality throughout the organization, with clear leadership by top management,
- it includes continual improvement as related to satisfaction of the needs and expectations of customers and other interested parties, and
- it is effectively formulated and efficiently communicated.

As with other business policies, the quality policy should be periodically reviewed.

5.4 PLANNING

5.4.1 QUALITY OBJECTIVES

Top management shall ensure that quality objectives, including those needed to meet requirements for product, are established at relevant functions and levels within the organization. The quality objectives shall be measurable and consistent with the quality policy.

Implementation Guidelines, Tips, and Techniques

Once we have defined what quality means to an organization (through the quality policy and value statements) we must then establish meaningful objectives for realization of them. These strategic objectives must be integral to the value delivery system and shared by everyone. To be effective, there must be consequences for not meeting them and recognition or reward for improving them. As with the quality policy, objectives for quality must be real and measurable. For instance, a quality objective might be "Customer returns will be no greater than 0.1% of the quantity of product shipped each quarter." This objective must be communicated to everyone who can affect it and it must be continually measured. Action has to be taken if returns approach or reach the control limit. It must also be regularly assessed against business objectives and revised as necessary to meet strategic and customer needs.

Potential Pitfalls

A statement such as "We will minimize customer returns" is not a viable quality objective. It has no measurable parameters and no way of determining its effectiveness. It also gives process operators no guidelines by which to operate or be evaluated.

ISO 9004 Performance Improvement Guidelines

Planning

Quality Objectives

The organization's strategic planning and the quality policy provide a framework for the setting of quality objectives.

Top management should establish these objectives, leading to improvement of the organization's performance. The objectives should be capable of being measured in order to facilitate an effective and efficient review by management. When establishing these objectives, management should also consider

- current and future needs of the organization and the markets served,
- relevant findings from management reviews,
- current product and process performance,
- levels of satisfaction of interested parties,
- self-assessment results,
- benchmarking, competitor analysis, opportunities for improvement, and
- resources needed to meet the objectives.

The quality objectives should be communicated in such a way that people in the organization can contribute to their achievement. Responsibility for deployment of quality objectives should be defined. Objectives should be systematically reviewed and revised as necessary.

5.4.2 QUALITY MANAGEMENT SYSTEM PLANNING

Top management shall ensure that

a. the planning of the quality management system is carried out in order to meet the requirements given in 4.1, as well as the quality objectives, and

b. the integrity of the quality management system is maintained when changes to the quality management system are planned and implemented.

Implementation Guidelines, Tips, and Techniques

This requirement builds on the need for a process approach to operations and a system approach to management. It identifies the need for master planning of all activities affecting quality, a continual monitoring of the plan's effectiveness, and a method to evolve and perpetuate the values in the quality policy. Effective and integrated planning of resources and requirements to obtain the desired results must be demonstrated. There must also be a mechanism to ensure control while changes are planned and implemented.

Potential Pitfalls

Planning cannot be a one-time event that happens when the QMS is designed. It must be an ongoing process dictated by changing business and customer needs. In organizations with multiple disciplines or products and services, planning must be coordinated across all disciplines and remain dynamic as dictated by the criticality of the products or services.

ISO 9004 Performance Improvement Guidelines

Quality Planning

Management should take responsibility for the quality planning of the organization. This planning should focus on defining the processes needed to meet effectively and efficiently the organization's quality objectives and requirements consistent with the strategy of the organization.
Inputs for effective and efficient planning include

- strategies of the organization,
- defined organizational objectives,
- defined needs and expectations of the customers and other interested parties,
- evaluation of statutory and regulatory requirements,
- evaluation of performance data of the products,
- evaluation of performance data of processes,

- lessons learned from previous experience,
- indicated opportunities for improvement, and
- related risk assessment and mitigation data.

Outputs of quality planning for the organization should define the product realization and support processes needed in terms such as

- skills and knowledge needed by the organization,
- responsibility and authority for implementation of process improvement plans,
- resources needed, such as financial and infrastructure,
- metrics for evaluating the achievement of the organization's performance improvement,
- needs for improvement including methods and tools, and
- needs for documentation, including records.

Management should systematically review the outputs to ensure the effectiveness and efficiency of the processes of the organization.

5.5 RESPONSIBILITY, AUTHORITY, AND COMMUNICATION

5.5.1 RESPONSIBILITY AND AUTHORITY

Top management shall ensure that responsibilities and authorities are defined and communicated within the organization.

Implementation Guidelines, Tips, and Techniques

The specific responsibilities and authority level of those who execute the quality policy and quality plans must be defined through some consistent means. The most common method is through concise job descriptions tied to an organizational chart of responsibilities. Specifics must be communicated to all those who require this information to perform their duties and all who interface with them or are affected. Purchasing agents must know what is expected of them, what levels of authority they possess, and how they should interact with the functions around them. Those who submit purchase orders to them and those who receive the goods or services they acquire must also be trained in the interdependencies of the various functions and processes.

Potential Pitfalls

An organization chart in the quality manual will not suffice for this requirement. Responsibility and authority must be clearly defined and communicated to all process owners and operators. The levels of command and authority must be clearly defined so that key decision points are dealt with at the appropriate level of competence and authority. At first blush, this may seem overly regimented, but absence of clear authority usually results in anarchy, not creativity.

ISO 9004 Performance Improvement Guidelines

Responsibility, Authority, and Communication

Responsibility and Authority

Top management should define and then communicate the responsibility and authority in order to implement and maintain an effective and efficient quality management system.

People throughout the organization should be given responsibilities and authority to enable them to contribute to the achievement of the quality objectives and to establish their involvement, motivation and commitment.

5.5.2 MANAGEMENT REPRESENTATIVE

Top management shall appoint a member of management who, irrespective of other responsibilities, shall have responsibility and authority that includes

　　a. ensuring that processes needed for the quality management system are established, implemented and maintained,

　　b. reporting to top management on the performance of the quality management system and any need for improvement, and

c. ensuring the promotion of awareness of customer requirements throughout the organization.

NOTE The responsibility of a management representative can include liaison
with external parties on matters relating to the quality management system.

Implementation Guidelines, Tips, and Techniques

The job requirements for the management representative might include attributes such as:

- Training in systems and process development and implementation.
- Ability to lead the implementation of stated goals, plans, and
  objectives.
- Tenacity to ensure ongoing effectiveness and success.
- Ability to openly and genuinely dialogue with others at every level
  of the organization.
- Desire and skills to represent the stated and implied needs of the
  customer to all who affect product or service quality.

Nowhere in the attributes is there a need for formal training in classic
quality methods. In fact, my key requirement is a passion to ensure the success of the company through successful implementation of the quality policy. If this person has multiple job duties, the ability to act as the management representative must be uninhibited and uncompromised.

Authority of the management representative must include open access
to top management and the ability to communicate and effect appropriate
strategic and tactical actions in a timely manner. The representative need
not be a member of "top" management, unless the organizational structure
has strict lines of command and rank. The function might be more accurately defined as the facilitator and interfunctional coordinator or liaison.

Potential Pitfalls

The traditional quality manager is often not the best candidate for this role,
unless that person is a proactive agent of continual improvement, as op-

posed to one who is a classic student of detective and remedial quality control. This need not be a full-time job, unless the size of the organization requires that level of resource.

ISO 9004 Performance Improvement Guidelines

Management Representative

A management representative should be appointed and given authority by top management to manage, monitor, evaluate and coordinate the quality management system. This appointment is to enhance effective and efficient operation and improvement of the quality management system. The representative should report to top management and communicate with customers and other interested parties on matters pertaining to the quality management system.

5.5.3 INTERNAL COMMUNICATION

Top management shall ensure that appropriate communication channels are established within the organization and that communication takes place regarding the effectiveness of the quality management system.

Implementation Guidelines, Tips, and Techniques

A common myth of traditional management training is that sharing information diminishes power and exposes management to microscopic scrutiny. Nothing could be further from the truth. Continually sharing performance results and measures of achievement of quality objectives turns process operators into process owners. Establishment of open, honest, and appropriate metrics is a powerful tool in creating risk for noncompliance and reward for exceeding expectations. Sharing information on a regular and ongoing basis is a key to eliminating variability and inconsistency from processes.

Potential Pitfalls

A five-minute pep talk at the annual company meeting will not suffice for internal communication. Depending on organizational culture, this requirement can be a combination of verbal and visual presentations at all levels along with control charts, newsletters, or intranet news sites. Organizations that do not publicize hard numbers can show sufficient information in anecdotal stories, pie charts, and trend charts to communicate effectively.

ISO 9004 Performance Improvement Guidelines

Internal Communication

The management of the organization should define and implement an effective and efficient process for communicating the quality policy, requirements, objectives and accomplishments. Providing such information can aid in the organization's performance improvement and directly involves its people in the achievement of quality objectives. Management should actively encourage feedback and communication from people in the organization as a means of involving them.

Activities for communicating include, for example

- management-led communication in work areas,
- team briefings and other meetings, such as for recognition of achievement,
- notice-boards, in-house journals/magazines,
- audio-visual and electronic media, such as e-mail and Web sites, and
- employee surveys and suggestion schemes.

5.6 MANAGEMENT REVIEW

5.6.1 GENERAL

Top management shall review the organization's quality management system, at planned intervals, to ensure its continuing suitability, adequacy and effectiveness. This review shall include assessing opportunities for improvement and the need for changes to the quality management system, including the quality policy and quality objectives.

Records from management reviews shall be maintained.

Implementation Guidelines, Tips, and Techniques

This paragraph requires top management to regularly and systematically review the effectiveness of their quality planning. This is best accomplished through physical or virtual meetings of those in the organization charged with implementing the quality policy and quality plans. In the next two sections, 5.6.2 provides specific recommendations for the agenda of the meetings and 5.6.3 lists outcomes that must result from the review. When, where, who, and how often should be determined by the complexity of the organization and the importance of ensuring continual process effectiveness. The agenda items are clear (5.6.2) and the need to consider change and improvement at every meeting is critical to the long-term success of the organization.

Potential Pitfalls

Again, a five-minute interlude at the annual sales meeting will not suffice for management review. The specific inputs and outputs must be covered effectively and reviewed often enough to ensure that processes do not drift out of control or that customer requirements are not compromised.

ISO 9004 Performance Improvement Guidelines

Management Review

General

Top management should develop the management review activity beyond verification of the effectiveness and efficiency of the quality management system into a process that extends to the whole organization, and which also evaluates the efficiency of the system. Management reviews should be platforms for the exchange of new ideas, with open discussion and evaluation of the inputs being stimulated by the leadership of top management.

To add value to the organization from management review, top management should control the performance of realization and support processes by systematic review based on the quality management principles. The frequency of review should be determined by the needs of the organization. Inputs to the review process should result in outputs that extend beyond the effectiveness and efficiency of the quality management system. Outputs from reviews should provide data for use in planning for performance improvement of the organization.

5.6.2 REVIEW INPUT

The input to management review shall include information on

a. results of audits,

b. customer feedback,

c. process performance and product conformity,

d. status of preventive and corrective actions,

e. follow-up actions from previous management reviews,

f. changes that could affect the quality management system, and

g. recommendations for improvement.

ISO 9004 Performance Improvement Guidelines

Review Input

Inputs to evaluate efficiency as well as effectiveness of the quality management system should consider the customer and other interested parties and should include

- status and results of quality objectives and improvement activities,
- status of management review action items,

- results of audits and self-assessment of the organization,
- feedback on the satisfaction of interested parties, perhaps even to the point of their participation,
- market-related factors such as technology, research and development, and competitor performance,
- results from benchmarking activities,
- performance of suppliers,
- new opportunities for improvement,
- control of process and product nonconformities,
- marketplace evaluation and strategies,
- status of strategic partnership activities,
- financial effects of quality-related activities, and
- other factors which may impact the organization, such as financial, social or environmental conditions, and relevant statutory and regulatory changes.

5.6.3 REVIEW OUTPUT

The output from the management review shall include any decisions and actions related to

a. improvement of the effectiveness of the quality management system and its processes,

b. improvement of product related to customer requirements, and

c. resource needs.

ISO 9004 Performance Improvement Guidelines

Review Output

By extending management review beyond verification of the quality management system, the outputs of management review can be used by top management as inputs to improvement processes. Top management can use this review process as a powerful tool in the identification of opportunities for performance improvement of the organization. The schedule of reviews should facilitate the timely provision of data in the context of strategic planning for the organization. Selected output should be communicated to demonstrate to the people in the organization how the management review process leads to new objectives that will benefit the organization. Additional outputs to enhance efficiency include, for example

- performance objectives for products and processes,
- performance improvement objectives for the organization,
- appraisal of the suitability of the organization's structure and resources,
- strategies and initiatives for marketing, products, and satisfaction of customers and other interested parties,
- loss prevention and mitigation plans for identified risks, and
- information for strategic planning for future needs of the organization.

Records should be sufficient to provide for traceability and to facilitate evaluation of the management review process itself, in order to ensure its continued effectiveness and added value to the organization.

5 MANAGEMENT RESPONSIBILITY (CONTINUED)

ISO 9004 Performance Improvement Guidelines

There is no corresponding requirement to use the following principles in ISO 9001. These are performance improvement guidelines only found in ISO 9004.

Use of Quality Management Principles

To lead and operate an organization successfully, it is necessary to manage it in a systematic and visible manner. The guidance to management offered in this International Standard is based on eight quality management principles. These principles have been developed for use by top management in order to lead the organization toward improved performance. These quality management principles are integrated in the contents of this International Standard and are listed below

- **Customer focus.** Organizations depend on their customers and therefore should understand current and future customer needs, should meet customer requirements and strive to exceed customer expectations.
- **Leadership.** Leaders establish unity of purpose and direction of the organization. They should create and maintain the internal environment in which people can become fully involved in achieving the organization's objectives.
- **Involvement of people.** People at all levels are the essence of an organization and their full involvement enables their abilities to be used for the organization's benefit.
- **Process approach.** A desired result is achieved more efficiently when activities and related resources are managed as a process.
- **System approach to management.** Identifying, understanding and managing interrelated processes as a system contributes to the organization's effectiveness and efficiency in achieving its objectives.
- **Continual improvement.** Continual improvement of the organization's overall performance should be a permanent objective of the organization.
- **Factual approach to decision making.** Effective decisions are based on the analysis of data and information.
- **Mutually beneficial supplier relationships.** An organization and its suppliers are interdependent and a mutually beneficial relationship enhances the ability of both to create value.

Successful use of the eight management principles by an organization will result in benefits to interested parties, such as improved monetary returns, the creation of value and increased stability.

6 RESOURCE MANAGEMENT

6.1 PROVISION OF RESOURCES

The organization shall determine and provide the resources needed

    a. to implement and maintain the quality management system and continually improve its effectiveness, and

    b. to enhance customer satisfaction by meeting customer requirements.

Implementation Guidelines, Tips, and Techniques

This clause provides the imperative for organizations to support their quality plans with resources appropriate to achieve their stated objectives and the requirements of their customers. A quality objective of being at the leading edge of technology development can't be realized without an appropriate research and development budget and the time and facilities to carry out the work.

Potential Pitfalls

Defining appropriate levels of resources is a difficult task for many companies. Those that do not typically plan for future resources will likely face internal strife in committing to make a link between physical resources and quality objectives. As with all other implementation guidelines, use the test of business sense to judge what actions to take and how quickly to implement them.

ISO 9004 Performance Improvement Guidelines

Introduction

Top management should ensure that the resources essential to the implementation of strategy and the achievement of the organization's objectives are identified and made available. This should include resources for operation and improvement of the quality management system, and the satisfaction of customers and other interested parties. Resources may be people, infrastructure, work environment, information, suppliers and partners, natural resources and financial resources.

Issues to Be Considered

Consideration should be given to resources to improve the performance of the organization, such as

- effective, efficient and timely provision of resources in relation to opportunities and constraints,
- tangible resources such as improved realization and support facilities,
- intangible resources such as intellectual property,
- resources and mechanisms to encourage innovative continual improvement,
- organization structures, including project and matrix management needs,
- information management and technology,
- enhancement of competence via focused training, education and learning,
- development of leadership skills and profiles for the future managers of the organization,
- use of natural resources and the impact of resources on the environment, and
- planning for future resource needs.

6.2 HUMAN RESOURCES

6.2.1 GENERAL

Personnel performing work affecting product quality shall be competent on the basis of appropriate education, training, skills and experience.

Implementation Guidelines, Tips, and Techniques

Competency requirements for each function within the quality management system must be defined. Communicating the skill sets and training required for each function is key to minimizing documentation. Comprehensive job descriptions that capture the required competency, education, skills, training, and experience should be written for each functional area.

Potential Pitfalls

Training programs are no longer optional for most organizations. Failure to satisfy needs is not only a nonconformity, but also a symptom of a business with a limited future.

ISO 9004 Performance Improvement Guidelines

People

Involvement of People

Management should improve both the effectiveness and efficiency of the organization, including the quality management system, through the involvement and support of people. As an aid to achieving its performance improvement objectives, the organization should encourage the involvement and development of its people

- ◆ by providing ongoing training and career planning,
- ◆ by defining their responsibilities and authorities,

- by establishing individual and team objectives, managing process performance and evaluating results,
- by facilitating involvement in objective setting and decision making,
- by recognizing and rewarding,
- by facilitating the open, two-way communication of information,
- by continually reviewing the needs of its people,
- by creating conditions to encourage innovation,
- by ensuring effective teamwork,
- by communicating suggestions and opinions,
- by using measurements of its people's satisfaction, and
- by investigating the reasons why people join and leave the organization.

6.2.2 COMPETENCE, AWARENESS, AND TRAINING

The organization shall

a. determine the necessary competence for personnel performing work affecting product quality,

b. provide training or take other actions to satisfy these needs,

c. evaluate the effectiveness of the actions taken,

d. ensure that its personnel are aware of the relevance and importance of their activities and how they contribute to the achievement of the quality objectives, and

e. maintain appropriate records of education, training, skills and experience.

Implementation Guidelines, Tips, and Techniques

Defining competency requirements for each job function in an organization is an extremely important adjunct to defining processes and their interrelationships. Competency requirements (in the form of job descriptions and requirements) specify the needed skills to perform each process. Together, job descriptions and process procedures form an effective and auditable organizational infrastructure. Once the requirements are established, they must be complemented with an effective training program to enable competency levels to be achieved by new or advancing employees. Part of the training and awareness includes QMS training to ensure each employee understands his or her role and how it relates to the other functions in his or her area of activity and the established quality objectives. Validation of competency is established through effective records of all training and awareness activities and evidence of skills and experience.

Potential Pitfalls

On-the-job-training is seldom sufficient on its own to achieve overall competency needs. Also, when critical job skills are needed (degrees, certifications, or licenses) it is a good idea to have a process to validate that the claimed degrees, certifications, or licenses are real and valid.

ISO 9004 Performance Improvement Guidelines

Competence, Awareness, and Training

Competence

Management should ensure that the necessary competence is available for the effective and efficient operation of the organization. Management should consider analysis of both the present and expected competence needs as compared to the competence already existing in the organization.

Consideration of the need for competence includes sources such as

- future demands related to strategic and operational plans and objectives,
- anticipated management and workforce succession needs,
- changes to the organization's processes, tools and equipment,
- evaluation of the competence of individual people to perform defined activities, and

- statutory and regulatory requirements, and standards, affecting the organization and its interested parties.

Awareness and Training

Planning for education and training needs should take account of change caused by the nature of the organization's processes, the stages of development of people and the culture of the organization. The objective is to provide people with knowledge and skills that, together with experience, improve their competence.

Education and training should emphasize the importance of meeting requirements and the needs and expectations of the customer and other interested parties. It should also include awareness of the consequences to the organization and its people of failing to meet the requirements. To support the achievement of the organization's objectives and the development of its people, planning for education and training should consider

- experience of people,
- tacit and explicit knowledge,
- leadership and management skills,
- planning and improvement tools,
- teambuilding,
- problem solving,
- communication skills,
- culture and social behavior,
- knowledge of markets and the needs and expectations of customers and other interested parties, and
- creativity and innovation.

To facilitate the involvement of people, education and training also include

- the vision for the future of the organization,
- the organization's policies and objectives,
- organizational change and development,
- the initiation and implementation of improvement processes,

- benefits from creativity and innovation,
- the organization's impact on society
- introductory programs for new people, and
- periodic refresher programs for people already trained.

Training plans should include

- objectives,
- programs and methods,
- resources needed,
- identification of necessary internal support,
- evaluation in terms of enhanced competence of people, and
- measurement of the effectiveness and the impact on the organization.

The education and training provided should be evaluated in terms of expectations and impact on the effectiveness and efficiency of the organization as a means of improving future training plans.

6.3 INFRASTRUCTURE

The organization shall determine, provide and maintain the infrastructure needed to achieve conformity to product requirements. Infrastructure includes, as applicable

a. buildings, workspace and associated utilities,

b. process equipment (both hardware and software), and

c. supporting services (such as transport or communication).

Implementation Guidelines, Tips, and Techniques

Achievement of quality objectives can only be attained when the work environment is adequate to support the level of complexity and required integrity of the work performed. Determination of minimal levels of resources is up to those who design the work processes. Internal audits should include assessment of infrastructure adequacy based on established resource requirements in the form of operational procedures, maintenance procedures, safety and health guidelines, or statutory and regulatory requirements.

Potential Pitfalls

Organizations with a "make do" attitude will have a very difficult time complying with this requirement. At the same time, this requirement is not a valid justification for spending money on desirable enhancements unless lack of the resources compromises the QMS, safety, or the customer. Auditing for the necessary infrastructure is often a very enlightening and objective look at the facilities and services currently in place. This audit must lead to plans and objectives to maintain and grow the infrastructure to meet the needs of the other business and quality objectives.

ISO 9004 Performance Improvement Guidelines

Infrastructure

Management should define the infrastructure necessary for the realization of products while considering the needs and expectations of interested parties. The infrastructure includes resources such as plant, workspace, tools and equipment, support services, information and communication technology, and transport facilities. The process to define the infrastructure necessary for achieving effective and efficient product realization should include the following:

- provision of an infrastructure, defined in terms such as objectives, function, performance, availability, cost, safety, security and renewal;
- development and implementation of maintenance methods to ensure that the infrastructure continues to meet the organization's

needs; these methods should consider the type and frequency of maintenance and verification of operation of each infrastructure element, based on its criticality and usage;

- ◆ evaluation of the infrastructure against the needs and expectations of interested parties; and

- ◆ consideration of environmental issues associated with infrastructure, such as conservation, pollution, waste and recycling.

Natural phenomena that cannot be controlled can impact the infrastructure. The plan for the infrastructure should consider the identification and mitigation of associated risks and should include strategies to protect the interests of interested parties.

6.4 WORK ENVIRONMENT

The organization shall determine and manage the work environment needed to achieve conformity to product requirements.

Implementation Guidelines, Tips, and Techniques

Establishment of minimal resource requirements may be adequate to achieve basic quality objectives, but consideration must also be given to optimizing the work environment as a vital component of optimizing processes and products. Compliance with this requirement should be the result of comprehensive and proactive planning and assessment processes (see 6.3).

Potential Pitfalls

Although this requirement is only a single sentence, it cannot be overlooked as trivial. Environment has broad implications, from proper lighting and ventilation to ergonomic, hygiene, and safety considerations.

ISO 9004 Performance Improvement Guidelines

Work Environment

Management should ensure that the work environment has a positive influence on motivation, satisfaction and performance of people in order to enhance the performance of the organization. Creation of a suitable work environment, as a combination of human and physical factors, should include consideration of

- creative work methods and opportunities for greater involvement to realize the potential of people in the organization,
- safety rules and guidance, including the use of protective equipment,
- ergonomics,
- workplace location,
- social interaction,
- facilities for people in the organization,
- heat, humidity, light, airflow, and
- hygiene, cleanliness, noise, vibration and pollution.

6 RESOURCE MANAGEMENT (CONTINUED)

ISO 9004 Performance Improvement Guidelines

There is no corresponding requirement to use the following principles in ISO 9001. These are performance improvement guidelines found only in ISO 9004.

Information

Management should treat data as a fundamental resource for conversion to information and the continual development of an organization's knowledge, which is essential for making factual decisions and can stimulate innovation. In order to manage information, the organization should

- identify its information needs,
- identify and access internal and external sources of information,
- convert information to knowledge of use to the organization,
- use the data, information and knowledge to set and meet its strategies and objectives,
- ensure appropriate security and confidentiality, and
- evaluate the benefits derived from use of the information in order to improve managing information and knowledge.

Suppliers and Partnerships

Management should establish relationships with suppliers and partners to promote and facilitate communication with the aim of mutually improving the effectiveness and efficiency of processes that create value. There are various opportunities for organizations to increase value through working with their suppliers and partners, such as

- optimizing the number of suppliers and partners,
- establishing two-way communication at appropriate levels in both organizations to facilitate the rapid solution of problems, and to avoid costly delays or disputes,
- cooperating with suppliers in validation of the capability of their processes,
- monitoring the ability of suppliers to deliver conforming products with the aim of eliminating redundant verifications,
- encouraging suppliers to implement programs for continual improvement of performance and to participate in other joint improvement initiatives,
- involving suppliers in the organization's design and development activities to share knowledge and effectively and efficiently improve the realization and delivery processes for conforming products,
- involving partners in identification of purchasing needs and joint strategy development, and
- evaluating, recognizing and rewarding efforts and achievements by suppliers and partners.

Natural Resources

Consideration should be given to the availability of natural resources that can influence the performance of the organization. While such resources are often out of the direct control of the organization, they can have significant positive or negative effects on its results. The organization should have plans, or contingency plans, to ensure the availability or replacement of these resources in order to prevent or minimize negative effects on the performance of the organization.

Financial Resources

Resource management should include activities for determining the needs for, and sources of, financial resources. The control of financial resources should include activities for comparing actual usage against plans, and taking necessary action.

Management should plan, make available and control the financial resources necessary to implement and maintain an effective and efficient quality management system and to achieve the organization's objectives. Management should also consider the development of innovative financial methods to support and encourage improvement of the organization's performance. Improving the effectiveness and efficiency of the quality management system can influence positively the financial results of the organization, for example

- internally, by reducing process and product failures, or waste in material and time, or
- externally, by reducing product failures, costs of compensation under guarantees and warranties, and costs of lost customers and markets.

Reporting of such matters can also provide a means of determining ineffective or inefficient activities, and initiating suitable improvement actions. The financial reporting of activities related to the performance of the quality management system and product conformity should be used in management reviews.

7 PRODUCT REALIZATION

7.1 PLANNING OF PRODUCT REALIZATION

The organization shall plan and develop the processes needed for product realization. Planning of product realization shall be consistent with the requirements of the other processes of the quality management system. In planning product realization, the organization shall determine the following, as appropriate:

    a. quality objectives and requirements for the product;

    b. the need to establish processes, documents, and provide resources specific to the product;

    c. required verification, validation, monitoring, inspection and test activities specific to the product and the criteria for product acceptance; and

    d. records needed to provide evidence that the realization processes and resulting product meet requirements.

Implementation Guidelines, Tips, and Techniques

The output of this planning must be in a form suitable for the organization's method of operations. This requirement reinforces the imperative of implementing the process approach discussed in 0.2 of ISO 9001. Planning to meet the stated quality objectives is the first step in realizing those plans. The steps outlined in (a) through (d) form the framework for a closed-loop system of coordinated processes, bringing together the activities of planning, documentation, resource provision, implementation, verification, and record keeping. In a production environment, this planning could be called manufacturing engineering. In service companies this might be operational planning. Whatever the environment, it must be a comprehensive plan of all process steps, their verification, and their interaction.

Potential Pitfalls

Although there is great flexibility in this planning process, evidence should be readily auditable. That is, it should not be necessary to travel from work center to work center to gather planning data. This would indicate a lack of planning.

7.1 PLANNING OF PRODUCT REALIZATION (CONTINUED)

NOTE 1 A document specifying the processes of the quality management system (including the product realization processes) and the resources to be applied to a specific product, project or contract, can be referred to as a quality plan.

Implementation Guidelines, Tips, and Techniques

This note better defines a quality plan, giving your organization the freedom to perform planning in any manner that is logical and consistent with the product or service and the stated quality objectives. Companies that have a single stable product or service can incorporate the quality planning within their documentation structure. Others with multiple disciplines, product lines, services, and locations or companies that regularly change their processes should consider separate quality plans for each activity.

Potential Pitfalls

It does call the quality plan a "document," meaning that it must exist in some form and be clearly referenced in process documentation.

7.1 PLANNING OF PRODUCT REALIZATION (CONTINUED)

NOTE 2 The organization may also apply the requirements given in 7.3 to the development of product realization processes.

Implementation Guidelines, Tips, and Techniques

This note refers to the "Design and Development" clause and suggests that using the methodology in 7.3 might be a viable approach to product planning activities.

ISO 9004 Performance Improvement Guidelines

Introduction

Top management should ensure the effective and efficient operation of realization and support processes and the associated process network so that the organization has the capability of satisfying its interested parties. While realization processes result in products that add value to the organization, support processes are also necessary to the organization and add value indirectly.

Any process is a sequence of related activities or an activity that has both input and output. Management should define the required outputs of processes, and should identify the necessary inputs and activities required for their effective and efficient achievement.

The interrelation of processes can be complex, resulting in process networks. To ensure the effective and efficient operation of the organization, management should recognize that the output of one process may become the input to one or more other processes.

Issues to Be Considered

Understanding that a process can be represented as a sequence of activities aids management in defining the process inputs. Once the inputs have been defined, the necessary activities, actions and resources required for the process can be determined, in order to achieve the desired outputs.

Results from verification and validation of processes and outputs should also be considered as inputs to a process, to achieve continual improvement of performance and the promotion of excellence throughout the organization. Continual improvement of the organization's processes will improve the effectiveness and efficiency of the quality management system and the organization's performance. Annex B of ISO 9004 describes a "process for continual improvement" that can be used to assist in the identification of actions needed for continual improvement of the effectiveness and efficiency of processes.

Processes should be documented to the extent necessary to support effective and efficient operation. Documentation related to processes should support

- identifying and communicating the significant features of the processes,
- training in the operation of processes,
- sharing knowledge and experience in teams and work groups,
- measurement and audit of processes, and
- analysis, review and improvement of processes.

The role of people within the processes should be evaluated in order

- to ensure the health and safety of people,
- to ensure that the necessary skills exist,
- to support coordination of processes,
- to provide for input from people in process analysis, and
- to promote innovation from people.

The drive for continual improvement of the organization's performance should focus on the improvement of the effectiveness and efficiency of processes as the means by which beneficial results are achieved. Increased benefits, improved customer satisfaction, improved use of resources and reductions of waste are examples of measurable results achieved by greater effectiveness and efficiency of processes.

Managing Processes

General

Management should identify processes needed to realize products to satisfy the requirements of customers and other interested parties. To ensure product realization, consideration should be given to associated support processes as well as desired outputs, process steps, activities, flows, control measures, training needs, equipment, methods, information, materials and other resources.

An operating plan should be defined to manage the processes, including

- input and output requirements (for example, specifications and resources),
- activities within the processes,
- verification and validation of processes and products,
- analysis of the process including dependability,
- identification, assessment and mitigation of risk,
- corrective and preventive actions,
- opportunities and actions for process improvement, and
- control of changes to processes and products.

Examples of support processes include

- managing information,
- training of people,
- finance-related activities,
- infrastructure and service maintenance,
- application of industrial safety/protective equipment, and
- marketing.

Process Inputs, Outputs, and Review

The process approach ensures that process inputs are defined and recorded in order to provide a basis for formulation of requirements to be used for verification and validation of outputs. Inputs can be internal or external to the organization. Resolution of ambiguous or conflicting input requirements can involve consultation with the affected internal and external parties. Input derived from activities not yet fully evaluated should be subject to evaluation through subsequent review, verification and validation. The organization should identify significant or critical features of products and processes in order to develop an effective and efficient plan for controlling and monitoring the activities within its processes.

Examples of input issues to consider include

- competence of people,
- documentation,
- equipment capability and monitoring, and
- health, safety and work environment.

Process outputs that have been verified against process input requirements, including acceptance criteria, should consider the needs and expectations of customers and other interested parties. For verification purposes, the outputs should be recorded and evaluated against input requirements and acceptance criteria. This evaluation should identify necessary corrective actions, preventive actions or potential improvements in the effectiveness and efficiency of the process. Verification of the product can be carried out in the process in order to identify variation. The management of the organization should undertake periodic review of process performance to ensure the process is consistent with the operating plan. Examples of topics for this review include

- reliability and repeatability of the process,
- identification and prevention of potential nonconformities,
- adequacy of design and development inputs and outputs,
- consistency of inputs and outputs with planned objectives,
- potential for improvements, and
- unresolved issues.

Product and Process Validation and Changes

Management should ensure that the validation of products demonstrates that they meet the needs and expectations of customers and other interested parties. Validation activities include modeling, simulation and trials, as well as reviews involving customers or other interested parties. Issues to consider should include

- quality policy and objectives,
- capability or qualification of equipment,

- operating conditions for the product,
- use or application of the product,
- disposal of the product,
- product life cycle,
- environmental impact of the product, and
- impact of the use of natural resources including materials and energy.

Process validation should be carried out at appropriate intervals to ensure timely reaction to changes impacting the process. Particular attention should be given to validation of processes

- for high-value and safety-critical products,
- where deficiency in product will only be apparent in use,
- which cannot be repeated, and
- where verification of product is not possible.

The organization should implement a process for effective and efficient control of changes to ensure that product or process changes benefit the organization and satisfy the needs and expectations of interested parties. Changes should be identified, recorded, evaluated, reviewed, and controlled in order to understand the effect on other processes and the needs and expectations of customers and other interested parties.

Any changes in the process affecting product characteristics should be recorded and communicated in order to maintain the conformity of the product and provide information for corrective action or performance improvement of the organization. Authority for initiating change should be defined in order to maintain control.

Outputs in the form of products should be validated after any related change, to ensure that the change has had the desired effect.

Use of simulation techniques can also be considered in order to plan for prevention of failures or faults in processes.

Risk assessment should be undertaken to assess the potential for, and the effect of, possible failures or faults in processes. The results should be used to define and implement preventive actions to mitigate identified risks. Examples of tools for risk assessment include

- fault modes and effects analysis,
- fault tree analysis,

- relationship diagrams,
- simulation techniques, and
- reliability prediction.

7.2 CUSTOMER-RELATED PROCESSES

7.2.1 DETERMINATION OF REQUIREMENTS RELATED TO THE PRODUCT

The organization shall determine

a. requirements specified by the customer, including the requirements for delivery and post-delivery activities,

b. requirements not stated by the customer but necessary for specified or intended use, where known,

c. statutory and regulatory requirements related to the product, and

d. any additional requirements determined by the organization.

Implementation Guidelines, Tips, and Techniques

This paragraph is the beginning of the "contract review" process, during which your organization must determine the customer's stated and implied needs and include any statutory and regulatory requirements that are imposed by the customer or required by regulatory bodies. Clear definition of all requirements is required prior to bidding or accepting an order. Where organizations supply a proprietary product or service that is ordered by a part number, due diligence must still be performed to ensure that the customer's expectations will be met or that your advertised performance claims are accurate and in regulatory compliance. For instance, if you manufacture electronic appliances and advertise performance parameters, you must ensure that the proposed products will meet your performance claims and that they meet national and international safety codes, as required (UL, CE, CSA, etc.).

7.2.2 REVIEW OF REQUIREMENTS RELATED TO THE PRODUCT

The organization shall review the requirements related to the product. This review shall be conducted prior to the organization's commitment to supply a product to the customer (e.g., submission of tenders, acceptance of contracts or orders, acceptance of changes to contracts or orders) and shall ensure that

a. product requirements are defined,

b. contract or order requirements differing from those previously expressed are resolved, and

c. the organization has the ability to meet the defined requirements.

Records of the results of the review and actions arising from the review shall be maintained.

Where the customer provides no documented statement of requirement, the customer requirements shall be confirmed by the organization before acceptance.

Where product requirements are changed, the organization shall ensure that relevant documents are amended and that relevant personnel are made aware of the changed requirements.

Implementation Guidelines, Tips, and Techniques

Prior to accepting an order for goods or services, your organization must ensure that it has a clear definition of what is being requested and that you have the capability and capacity to deliver within required schedules and specifications. Changes to orders must be documented, controlled, and communicated to the appropriate areas within the organization. Reasonable steps must be taken to ensure that all requirements, terms, and conditions are agreed to prior to accepting an order and there must be an audit trail to determine that competent personnel followed each of these steps.

Potential Pitfalls

The process of accepting a customer order may be a convoluted contractual process or a simple electronic order entry step. Lack of customer specifications and drawings does not relieve your company from the need to determine that there is a clear and binding contract that is free from issues that may later cause customer dissatisfaction or liability issues because these items were not clearly communicated.

7.2.2 REVIEW OF REQUIREMENTS RELATED TO THE PRODUCT (CONTINUED)

NOTE In some situations, such as Internet sales, a formal review is impractical for each order. Instead the review can cover relevant product information such as catalogues, or advertising material.

Implementation Guidelines, Tips, and Techniques

This note recognizes that much of today's business is conducted by electronic means and that there is often not a "paper trail" of the contract review process. Electronic security and password-protected access are acceptable substitutes for written signatures. The systems must, however, show an audit trail to verify that only authorized personnel have access to the computer files that affect customers and their orders.

Potential Pitfalls

Again, there must be some trail, such as a catalog listing, that defines for customers what they are ordering and what they should expect to receive.

7.2.3 CUSTOMER COMMUNICATION

The organization shall determine and implement effective arrangements for communicating with customers in relation to

a. product information,

b. enquiries, contracts or order handling, including amendments, and

c. customer feedback, including customer complaints.

Implementation Guidelines, Tips, and Techniques

Your organization must accept accountability for communicating with the customer. This is traditionally handled in sales and contracts departments, often informally and incompletely. This requirement provides for maintenance of an auditable channel of communication between supplier and customer to ensure that all issues of product information, ordering, order changes, handling, and any customer feedback are handled in a timely and effective manner. Effective methods to accomplish this include computerized contact management systems, order entry systems that allow for comments and notes, and simple customer contact forms that record verbal interactions and provide a record of matters that can affect product or service performance or delivery.

The term interested parties is mentioned often in ISO 9004. In the context of customer communications, for a company that installs fire alarms, other interested parties that would require open channels of communication might be fire departments and insurance carriers.

Potential Pitfalls

Having salespeople taking customers to lunch on a regular basis is not auditable customer communication. Many organizations utilize a customer contact form for any communication that might affect an order or requirement. This form can provide a written record of verbal or telephoned agreements, giving a clear case for revising cost or changing agreed-on needs. Copies of this form should be transmitted to the customer and the customer should be required to acknowledge any such communication (in written or electronic form).

ISO 9004 Performance Improvement Guidelines

Processes Related to Interested Parties

Management should ensure that the organization has defined mutually acceptable processes for communicating effectively and efficiently with its customers and other interested parties. The organization should implement and maintain such processes to ensure adequate understanding of the needs and expectations of its interested parties, and for translation into requirements for the organization. These processes should include identification and review of relevant information and should actively involve customers and other interested parties. Examples of relevant process information include

- requirements of the customer or other interested parties,
- market research, including sector and end-user data,
- contract requirements,
- competitor analysis,
- benchmarking, and
- processes due to statutory or regulatory requirements.

The organization should have a full understanding of the process requirements of the customer, or other interested party, before initiating its action to comply. This understanding and its impact should be mutually acceptable to the participants.

7.3 DESIGN AND DEVELOPMENT

7.3.1 DESIGN AND DEVELOPMENT PLANNING

The organization shall plan and control the design and development of product.

During the design and development planning the organization shall determine

a. the design and development stages,

b. the review, verification and validation that are appropriate to each design and development stage, and

c. the responsibilities and authorities for design and development.

The organization shall manage the interfaces between different groups involved in design and development to ensure effective communication and clear assignment of responsibility.

Planning output shall be updated, as appropriate, as the design and development progresses.

Implementation Guidelines, Tips, and Techniques

Design and development is a critical facet of ISO 9001. First, your organization must decide if it should be excluded from the scope of certification. For instance, if you design and manufacture computers, you probably cannot exclude 7.3 because your company is responsible for all phases of product design, development, and realization. On the other hand, if your company buys subassemblies from computer manufacturers and plugs components together to build a working computer, there is an argument for 7.3 being excluded from your scope because you are not performing fundamental design, only integrating commonly available and compatible products on behalf of your customer. As another example, in an insurance-claims-processing office, claims agents have a certain amount of creativity in their work, but the parameters of the services provided are prescribed by a parent company and controlled by regulatory agencies. There is no "design" work being done; therefore 7.3 could logically be excluded.

There are many ways to word the scope of registration and many gray areas of inclusion or exclusion. Inclusion or exclusion of 7.3 must be agreed on with your registrar prior to implementation of ISO 9001:2000.

Potential Pitfalls

Implementation of the requirements of 7.3 cannot be covered adequately in this book because of its complexity. Any advice given has direct implications in product and service liability issues. Adaptation to your company and culture is best accomplished through the use of professional subject matter experts who can lead you through the process from concept to validation.

ISO 9004 Performance Improvement Guidelines

General Guidance

Top management should ensure that the organization has defined, implemented and maintained the necessary design and development processes to respond effectively and efficiently to the needs and expectations of its customers and other interested parties.

When designing and developing products or processes, management should ensure that the organization is not only capable of considering their basic performance and function, but all factors that contribute to meeting the product and process performance expected by customers and other interested parties. For example, the organization should consider life cycle, safety and health, testability, usability, user-friendliness, dependability, durability, ergonomics, the environment, product disposal and identified risks. Management also has the responsibility to ensure that steps are taken to identify and mitigate potential risk to the users of the products and processes of the organization. Risk assessment should be undertaken to assess the potential for, and the effect of, possible failures or faults in products or processes. The results of the assessment should be used to define and implement preventive actions to mitigate the identified risks. Examples of tools for risk assessment of design and development include

- design fault modes and effects analysis,
- fault tree analysis,
- reliability prediction,
- relationship diagrams,
- ranking techniques, and
- simulation techniques.

7.3.2 DESIGN AND DEVELOPMENT INPUTS

Inputs relating to product requirements shall be determined and records maintained. These shall include

a. functional and performance requirements,

b. applicable statutory and regulatory requirements,

c. where applicable, information derived from previous similar designs, and

d. other requirements essential for design and development.

These inputs shall be reviewed for adequacy. Requirements shall be complete, unambiguous and not in conflict with each other.

7.3.3 DESIGN AND DEVELOPMENT OUTPUTS

The outputs of design and development shall be provided in a form that enables verification against the design and development input and shall be approved prior to release.

Design and development outputs shall

a. meet the input requirements for design and development,

b. provide appropriate information for purchasing, production and for service provision,

c. contain or reference product acceptance criteria, and

d. specify the characteristics of the product that are essential for its safe and proper use.

ISO 9004 Performance Improvement Guidelines

Design and Development Input and Output

The organization should identify process inputs that affect the design and development of products and facilitate effective and efficient process performance in order to satisfy the needs and expectations of customers, and those of other interested parties. These external needs and expectations, coupled with those internal to the organization, should be suitable for translation into input requirements for the design and development processes.

Examples are as follows:

- external inputs such as
    - customer or marketplace needs and expectations,
    - needs and expectations of other interested parties,
    - supplier's contributions,
    - user input to achieve robust design and development,
    - changes in relevant statutory and regulatory requirements,
    - international or national standards, and
    - industry codes of practice;

- internal inputs such as
  - policies and objectives,
  - needs and expectations of people in the organization, including those receiving the output of the process,
  - technological developments,
  - competence requirements for people performing design and development,
  - feedback information from past experience,
  - records and data on existing processes and products, and
  - outputs from other processes;

- inputs that identify those characteristics of processes or products that are crucial to safe and proper functioning and maintenance, such as
  - operation, installation and application,
  - storage, handling and delivery,
  - physical parameters and the environment, and
  - requirements for disposal of the products.

Product-related inputs based on an appreciation of the needs and expectations of end users, as well as those of the direct customer, can be important. Such inputs should be formulated in a way that permits the product to be verified and validated effectively and efficiently.

The output should include information to enable verification and validation to planned requirements. Examples of the output of design and development include

- data demonstrating the comparison of process inputs to process outputs,
- product specifications, including acceptance criteria,
- process specifications,
- material specifications,
- testing specifications,
- training requirements,
- user and consumer information,
- purchase requirements, and
- reports of qualification tests.

Design and development outputs should be reviewed against inputs to provide objective evidence that outputs have effectively and efficiently met the requirements for the process and product.

7.3.4 DESIGN AND DEVELOPMENT REVIEW

At suitable stages, systematic reviews of design and development shall be performed in accordance with planned arrangements

a. to evaluate the ability of the results of design and development to meet requirements, and

b. to identify any problems and propose necessary actions.

Participants in such reviews shall include representatives of functions concerned with the design and development stage(s) being reviewed. Records of the results of the reviews and any necessary actions shall be maintained.

7.3.5 DESIGN AND DEVELOPMENT VERIFICATION

Verification shall be performed in accordance with planned arrangements to ensure that the design and development outputs have met the design and development input requirements. Records of the results of the verification and any necessary actions shall be maintained.

7.3.6 DESIGN AND DEVELOPMENT VALIDATION

Design and development validation shall be performed in accordance with planned arrangements to ensure that the resulting product is capable of meeting the requirements for the specified application or intended use, when known. Wherever practicable, validation shall be completed prior to the delivery or implementation of the product. Records of the results of validation and any necessary actions shall be maintained.

7.3.7 CONTROL OF DESIGN AND DEVELOPMENT CHANGES

Design and development changes shall be identified and records maintained. The changes shall be reviewed, verified and validated, as appropriate, and approved before implementation. The review of design and development changes shall include evaluation of the effect of the changes on constituent parts and product already delivered.

Records of the results of the review of changes and any necessary actions shall be maintained.

ISO 9004 Performance Improvement Guidelines

Design and Development Review

Top management should ensure that appropriate people are assigned to manage and conduct systematic reviews to determine that design and development objectives are achieved. These reviews may be conducted at selected points in the design and development process as well as at completion. Examples of topics for such reviews include

- adequacy of input to perform the design and development tasks,
- progress of the planned design and development process,
- meeting verification and validation goals,
- evaluation of potential hazards or fault modes in product use,
- life-cycle data on performance of the product,
- control of changes and their effect during the design and development process,
- identification and correction of problems,
- opportunities for design and development process improvement, and
- potential impact of the product on the environment.

At suitable stages, the organization should also undertake reviews of design and development outputs, as well as the processes, in order to satisfy the needs and expectations of customers and people within the organization who receive the process output. Consideration should also be given to the needs and expectations of other interested parties.

Examples of verification activities for output of the design and development process include

- comparisons of input requirements with the output of the process,
- comparative methods, such as alternative design and development calculations,

- evaluation against similar products,
- testing, simulations or trials to check compliance with specific input requirements, and
- evaluation against lessons learned from past process experience, such as nonconformities and deficiencies.

Validation of the output of the design and development processes is important for the successful reception and use by customers, suppliers, people in the organization and other interested parties.

Participation by the affected parties permits the actual users to evaluate the output by such means as

- validation of engineering designs prior to construction, installation or application,
- validation of software outputs prior to installation or use, and
- validation of services prior to widespread introduction.

Partial validation of the design and development outputs may be necessary to provide confidence in their future application.

Sufficient data should be generated through verification and validation activities to enable design and development methods and decisions to be reviewed. The review of methods should include

- process and product improvement,
- usability of output,
- adequacy of process and review records,
- failure investigation activities, and
- future design and development process needs.

7.4 PURCHASING

7.4.1 PURCHASING PROCESS

The organization shall ensure that purchased product conforms to specified purchase requirements. The type and extent of control applied to the supplier and the purchased product shall be dependent upon the effect of the purchased product on subsequent product realization or the final product.

The organization shall evaluate and select suppliers based on their ability to supply product in accordance with the organization's requirements. Criteria for selection, evaluation and re-evaluation shall be established. Records of the results of evaluations and any necessary actions arising from the evaluation shall be maintained.

Implementation Guidelines, Tips, and Techniques

Organizations must demonstrate that they have taken appropriate steps to determine necessary controls over their purchasing activities, and that they qualify the companies from which they acquire products and services that directly affect the final product and that which is delivered to the customer. This can run from a formal purchasing process and a supplier approval and reapproval process based on objective criteria and formal surveys to evaluating capability by sample orders and tracking delivery performance. It is good business sense to ensure that you are getting what you are ordering in a timely manner and to rate suppliers on their performance. If supplied products or components are critical to your operation, it makes even more sense to follow guidelines suggested in ISO 9004 to form partnerships with your suppliers and have continual dialogue about your needs, expectations, and results. If you purchase off-the-shelf generic parts, it might not make much difference which distributor you purchase from. If you purchase only operational supplies to support a service organization, this clause may be excluded.

7.4.2 PURCHASING INFORMATION

Purchasing information shall describe the product to be purchased, including where appropriate

a. requirements for approval of product, procedures, processes and equipment,

b. requirements for qualification of personnel, and

c. quality management system requirements.

The organization shall ensure the adequacy of specified purchase requirements prior to their communication to the supplier.

Implementation Guidelines, Tips, and Techniques

When purchasing a supplier part number, that number may be the only information required to ensure that you get what you need. If you are having external services performed to your drawings or to industry specifications, it is reasonable that more precise information be included in your purchasing documents. In this clause, "appropriate" is definitely a function of the importance of the product or service you are buying. The test of reason is to determine if there is any possibility of a key requirement being unclearly communicated in your purchasing documents. As with design, liability issues should be considered when placing terms and conditions on a supplier to avoid receiving items that may not be suitable because either the supplier or customer made assumptions.

Potential Pitfalls

Many of the issues discussed in 7.2 (between you and your customer) are germane to the relationship between you and your suppliers. This is particularly true in the areas of open communication, reaching complete agreements, and being clearly communicative when changes are made.

7.4.3 VERIFICATION OF PURCHASED PRODUCT

The organization shall establish and implement the inspection or other activities necessary for ensuring that purchased product meets specified purchase requirements.

Where the organization or its customer intends to perform verification at the supplier's premises, the organization shall state the intended verification arrangements and method of product release in the purchasing information.

Implementation Guidelines, Tips, and Techniques

When the acquisition process results in delivery of a commodity or service, some attention must be given to ensuring that you received what you requested and specified. In some cultures, this includes physical inspection, testing, or validation. In others, controls are established with suppliers to ensure that requirements are met prior to shipment. In other cases, non-criticality of a commodity may require no more than visual inspection for identification and damage before it is accepted. Exercise whatever level of control makes business sense for your organization in receiving purchased products or services. When intended verification activities are not clearly implied, they must be stated in the purchasing document (e.g., preshipment inspections or tests).

Potential Pitfalls

Service organizations may look to exclude this clause as not applicable. The term verification may be as simple, however, as looking at incoming commodities to determine if they are the correct product and if they were damaged in shipping. Verification may also be as innocuous as verifying revision levels of purchased software.

ISO 9004 Performance Improvement Guidelines

Purchasing Process

Top management of the organization should ensure that effective and efficient purchasing processes are defined and implemented for the evaluation and control of purchased products, in order that purchased products satisfy the organization's needs and requirements, as well as those of interested parties.

Use of electronic linkage with suppliers should be considered in order to optimize communication of requirements.

To ensure the effective and efficient performance of the organization, management should ensure that purchasing processes consider the following activities:

- timely, effective and accurate identification of needs and purchased product specifications;
- evaluation of the cost of purchased product, taking account of product performance, price and delivery;
- the organization's need and criteria for verifying purchased products;
- unique supplier processes;

- consideration of contract administration, for both supplier and partner arrangements;
- warranty replacement for nonconforming purchased products;
- logistic requirements;
- product identification and traceability;
- preservation of product;
- documentation, including records;
- control of purchased product which deviates from requirements;
- access to suppliers' premises;
- product delivery, installation or application history;
- supplier development; and
- identification and mitigation of risks associated with the purchased product.

Requirements for suppliers' processes and product specifications should be developed with suppliers in order to benefit from available supplier knowledge. The organization could also involve suppliers in the purchasing process in relation to their products in order to improve the effectiveness and efficiency of the organization's purchasing process. This could also assist the organization in its control and availability of inventory.

The organization should define the need for records of purchased product verification, communication and response to nonconformities in order to demonstrate its own conformity to specification.

Supplier Control Process

The organization should establish effective and efficient processes to identify potential sources for purchased materials, to develop existing suppliers or partners, and to evaluate their ability to supply the required products in order to ensure the effectiveness and efficiency of overall purchasing processes. Examples of inputs to the supplier control process include

- evaluation of relevant experience,
- performance of suppliers against competitors,
- review of purchased product quality, price, delivery performance and response to problems,

- audits of supplier management systems and evaluation of their potential capability to provide the required products effectively and efficiently and within schedule,
- checking supplier references and available data on customer satisfaction,
- financial assessment to assure the viability of the supplier throughout the intended period of supply and cooperation,
- supplier response to inquiries, quotations and tendering,
- supplier service, installation and support capability and history of performance to requirements,
- supplier awareness of and compliance with relevant statutory and regulatory requirements,
- the supplier's logistic capability including locations and resources, and
- the supplier's standing and role in the community, as well as perception in society.

Management should consider actions needed to maintain the organization's performance and to satisfy interested parties in the event of supplier failure.

7.5 PRODUCTION AND SERVICE PROVISION

7.5.1 CONTROL OF PRODUCTION AND SERVICE PROVISION

The organization shall plan and carry out production and service provision under controlled conditions. Controlled conditions shall include, as applicable

a. the availability of information that describes the characteristics of the product,

b. the availability of work instructions, as necessary,

c. the use of suitable equipment,

d. the availability and use of monitoring and measuring devices,

e. the implementation of monitoring and measurement, and

f. the implementation of release, delivery and post-delivery activities.

Implementation Guidelines, Tips, and Techniques

Regardless of your products or services, there must be some effective production planning and control activity that merges requirements, drawings, specifications, and resources and logically plans and executes implementation of your processes. This function must also be responsible for merging and staging the customer orders in their correct priority and for making midcourse corrections to account for unexpected interruptions or process variations. This combination of capacity planning and resource maximization is a key to profitability and minimization of production expenses. In manufacturing environments, a computer-supported planning and control function is common. In service organizations, a scheduler or operations director may be responsible for resource coordination with customer needs.

Potential Pitfalls

This planning and control cannot be random or ill defined. Organizations that require flexibility in their planning and production should have clear methodology and decision points that direct the required resources to the proper places at the appropriate times. For instance, a software development organization must plan the steps of development and have a road map that coordinates all development and testing activities.

7.5.2 VALIDATION OF PROCESSES FOR PRODUCTION AND SERVICE PROVISION

The organization shall validate any processes for production and service provision where the resulting output cannot be verified by subsequent monitoring or measurement. This includes any processes where deficiencies become apparent only after the product is in use or the service has been delivered. Validation shall demonstrate the ability of these processes to achieve planned results. The organization shall establish arrangements for these processes including, as applicable

a. defined criteria for review and approval of the processes,

b. approval of equipment and qualification of personnel,

c. use of specific methods and procedures,

d. requirements for records, and

e. revalidation.

Implementation Guidelines, Tips, and Techniques

The process approach referred to in ISO 9000, ISO 9001, and ISO 9004 is a key to ensuring that the needs and desires of the customer are continually implemented. Definition of each process, the interrelationship of the processes, and the individual and collective validation steps must be defined, monitored, and executed in a consistent and predictable manner. In special cases in which the outcome of the process cannot be readily measured or tested, special controls must be exhibited to ensure that all prerequisites are in place before the process is carried out and that controls are in place and monitored during execution. For example, with plastic injection molding, once the part is molded, verification of conformance usually can only be accomplished through destructive testing. To ensure an effective process, the raw materials must be validated as correct; molds cleaned and inspected prior to use; and temperature, pressure, and time monitored throughout the process so predictable outcomes are achieved. In a service industry, you cannot make adjustments to what a customer service representative discusses with every customer while it is happening. Scripting the scenarios and giving the representative the tools and training is the only effective method for ensuring process conformity and customer satisfaction. In this scenario, process validation might be accomplished through monitoring phone conversations, making adjustments to scripts, retraining representatives, and revalidating the process.

Potential Pitfalls

It will be difficult to find clear scenarios for excluding this requirement because most organizations perform some defined processes in a logical order to achieve the outcome desired by the customer.

ISO 9004 Performance Improvement Guidelines

Operation and Realization

Top management should go beyond control of the realization processes in order to achieve both compliance with requirements and provide benefits to interested parties. This may be achieved through improving the effectiveness and efficiency of the realization processes and associated support processes, such as

- reducing waste,
- training of people,
- communicating and recording information,
- developing supplier capability,
- improving infrastructure,
- preventing problems,
- processing methods and process yield, and
- methods of monitoring.

7.5.3 IDENTIFICATION AND TRACEABILITY

Where appropriate, the organization shall identify the product by suitable means throughout product realization.

The organization shall identify the product status with respect to monitoring and measurement requirements.

Where traceability is a requirement, the organization shall control and record the unique identification of the product.

NOTE In some industry sectors, configuration management is a means by which identification and traceability are maintained.

Implementation Guidelines, Tips, and Techniques

This requirement may be as simple as a control number on a document or software or as complex as tracking batches of raw products for formulating a chemical compound. Whenever there is a stated or business need to trace the individual components of a product or service or there is a need to identify lots and batches as compounds or assemblies become more and more combined during production, appropriate steps must be taken to ensure the integrity and identification of lots, batches, or assemblies. This is often accomplished by bar coding or some other positive identification method.

Potential Pitfalls

Avoid overcomplicating this requirement. If you have no clear need to track batches or serial numbers for warranty or liability purposes, this clause may be excluded.

ISO 9004 Performance Improvement Guidelines

Identification and Traceability

The organization can establish a process for identification and traceability that goes beyond the requirements in order to collect data that can be used for improvement.

The need for identification and traceability may arise from

- status of products, including component parts,
- status and capability of processes,
- benchmarking performance data, such as marketing,
- contract requirements, such as product recall capability,
- relevant statutory and regulatory requirements,
- intended use or application,
- hazardous materials, and
- mitigation of identified risks.

7.5.4 CUSTOMER PROPERTY

The organization shall exercise care with customer property while it is under the organization's control or being used by the organization. The organization shall identify, verify, protect and safeguard customer property provided for use or incorporation into the product. If any customer property is lost, damaged or otherwise found to be unsuitable for use, this shall be reported to the customer and records maintained.

NOTE Customer property can include intellectual property.

Implementation Guidelines, Tips, and Techniques

Customer property can be anything from drawings and specifications to raw materials, subassemblies, tooling, test fixtures, or software. Procedures must exist to keep from commingling customer property with other materials. The procedures must also specify methods to identify the customer property, handling procedures specified by the customer, and disposition instructions when the project is completed. These procedures and controls are particularly critical in repair operations.

Potential Pitfalls

Organizations that never deal with customer property may exclude this clause.

ISO 9004 Performance Improvement Guidelines

Customer Property

The organization should identify responsibilities in relation to property and other assets owned by customers and other interested parties and under the control of the organization, in order to protect the value of the property. Examples of such property are

- ingredients or components supplied for inclusion in a product,
- product supplied for repair, maintenance or upgrading,
- packaging materials supplied directly by the customer,
- customer materials handled by service operations such as storage,
- services supplied on behalf of the customer, such as transport of customer property to a third party, and

- customer intellectual property, including specifications, drawings and proprietary information.

7.5.5 PRESERVATION OF PRODUCT

The organization shall preserve the conformity of product during internal processing and delivery to the intended destination. This preservation shall include identification, handling, packaging, storage and protection. Preservation shall also apply to the constituent parts of a product.

Implementation Guidelines, Tips, and Techniques

An oversimplification of the purpose of this clause might be inventory control. It is included to ensure that all materials, products, and supplies are controlled in a manner consistent with the identified needs for handling, packaging, packing, or storage. Any organization with reasonable inventory control procedures and hazardous material control will be compliant with this requirement.

Potential Pitfalls

Organizations that do not deal with inventory, raw materials, or finished products may exclude this clause. Before claiming exclusion, be certain that there are no components that must be controlled. For example, a software company may have to control computer media and documents as inventory items.

ISO 9004 Performance Improvement Guidelines

Preservation of Product

Management should define and implement processes for handling, packaging, storage, preservation and delivery of product that prevent damage, deterioration or misuse during internal processing and final delivery of the product. Management should involve suppliers and partners in defining and implementing effective and efficient processes to protect purchased material.

Management should consider the need for any special requirements arising from the nature of the product. Special requirements can be associated with software, electronic media, hazardous materials, products requiring special people for service, installation or application, and products or materials that are unique or irreplaceable.

Management should identify resources needed to maintain the product throughout its life cycle to prevent damage, deterioration or misuse. The organization should communicate information to the interested parties involved about the resources and methods needed to preserve the intended use of the product throughout its life cycle.

7.6 CONTROL OF MONITORING AND MEASURING DEVICES

The organization shall determine the monitoring and measurement to be undertaken and the monitoring and measuring devices needed to provide evidence of conformity of product to determined requirements.

The organization shall establish processes to ensure that monitoring and measurement can be carried out and are carried out in a manner that is consistent with the monitoring and measurement requirements.

Where necessary to ensure valid results, measuring equipment shall

a. be calibrated or verified at specified intervals or prior to use, against measurement standards traceable to international or national measurement standards; where no such standards exist, the basis used for calibration or verification shall be recorded;

b. be adjusted or re-adjusted as necessary;

c. be identified to enable calibration status to be determined;

d. be safeguarded from adjustments that would invalidate the measurement result; and

e. be protected from damage and deterioration during handling, maintenance and storage.

In addition, the organization shall assess and record the validity of the previous measuring results when the equipment is found not to conform to requirements. The organization shall take appropriate action on the equipment and any product affected. Records of the results of calibration and verification shall be maintained (see 4.2.4).

When used in the monitoring and measurement of specified requirements, the ability of computer software to satisfy the intended application shall be confirmed. This shall be undertaken prior to initial use and reconfirmed as necessary.

NOTE See ISO 10012-1 and ISO 10012-2 for guidance.

Implementation Guidelines, Tips, and Techniques

Organizations that utilize monitoring, measuring equipment, or software must employ appropriate controls to ensure that the planned results of their use are achieved. Such equipment might include instrumentation, gauges, verification tooling, or software diagnostic programs. In general, whenever there is a need to verify a quantitative or qualitative result, the means to make that measurement or analysis must be of known accuracy. The procedures for use of those tests and measurements must also be controlled.

Potential Pitfalls

Organizations that do not perform quantitative or qualitative measures may exclude this clause. Great care must be exercised before claiming exclusion because these devices may be as innocuous as a scale in a shipping department, if that scale is used to bill a customer for freight charges.

ISO 9004 Performance Improvement Guidelines

Control of Measuring and Monitoring Devices

Management should define and implement effective and efficient measuring and monitoring processes, including methods and devices for verification and validation of products and processes to ensure the satisfaction of customers and other interested parties. These processes include surveys, simulations, and other measurement and monitoring activities.

In order to provide confidence in data, the measuring and monitoring processes should include confirmation that the devices are fit for use and are maintained to suitable accuracy and accepted standards, as well as a means of identifying the status of the devices.

The organization should consider means to eliminate potential errors from processes, such as "fool-proofing," for verification of process outputs in order to minimize the need for control of measuring and monitoring devices, and to add value for interested parties.

8 MEASUREMENT, ANALYSIS, AND IMPROVEMENT

8.1 GENERAL

The organization shall plan and implement the monitoring, measurement, analysis and improvement processes needed

    a. to demonstrate conformity of the product,

    b. to ensure conformity of the quality management system, and

    c. to continually improve the effectiveness of the quality management system.

This shall include determination of applicable methods, including statistical techniques, and the extent of their use.

Implementation Guidelines, Tips, and Techniques

This clause launches the requirement to utilize "management by fact" when operating a business; that is, process-based businesses must objectively evaluate each process step and use the data gathered to ensure conformity and plan corrective actions and continual improvement. It requires that the company satisfy itself that all processes have led to the desired outcome, whether a service or a product. The most effective methods for your culture should be employed and metrics assigned to each logical step to ensure compliance and help with planning for future improvements.

Potential Pitfalls

This clause does not prescribe any specific measurements or tests, nor does it require complex statistical data gathering and analysis if there is no need or benefit to your organization. It is not a subject for exclusion however, because every business needs to employ some methodology for evaluating processes and quantifying results against plans, objectives, and customer needs.

ISO 9004 Performance Improvement Guidelines

Introduction

Measurement data are important for making fact-based decisions. Top management should ensure effective and efficient measurement, collection and validation of data to ensure the organization's performance and the satisfaction of interested parties. This should include review of the validity and purpose of measurements and the intended use of data to ensure added value to the organization.

Examples of measurement of performance of the organization's processes include

+ measurement and evaluation of its products,
+ capability of processes,
+ achievement of project objectives, and
+ satisfaction of customers and other interested parties.

The organization should continually monitor its performance improvement actions and record their implementation, as this can provide data for future improvements.

The results of the analysis of data from improvement activities should be one of the inputs to management review in order to provide information for improving the performance of the organization.

Issues to Be Considered

Measurement, analysis and improvement include the following considerations:

- measurement data should be converted to information and knowledge to be of benefit to the organization;
- measurement, analysis and improvement of products and processes should be used to establish appropriate priorities for the organization;
- measurement methods employed by the organization should be reviewed periodically, and data should be verified on a continual basis for accuracy and completeness;
- benchmarking of individual processes should be used as a tool for improving the effectiveness and efficiency of processes;
- measurements of customer satisfaction should be considered as vital for evaluation of the organization's performance;
- use of measurements, and the generating and communicating of the information obtained, are essential to the organization and should be the basis for performance improvement and the involvement of interested parties; such information should be current, and its purpose should be clearly defined;
- appropriate tools for the communication of information resulting from the analyses of the measurements should be implemented;
- the effectiveness and efficiency of communicating with interested parties should be measured to determine whether the information is timely and clearly understood;
- where process and product performance criteria are met, it may still be beneficial to monitor and analyze performance data in order to understand better the nature of the characteristic under study;
- the use of appropriate statistical or other techniques can help in the understanding of both process and measurement variation, and can thereby improve process and product performance by controlling variation;
- self-assessment should be considered on a periodic basis to assess the maturity of the quality management system and the level of the organization's performance, as well as to define opportunities for performance improvement (see Annex A of ISO 9004).

8.2 MONITORING AND MEASUREMENT

8.2.1 CUSTOMER SATISFACTION

As one of the measurements of the performance of the quality management system the organization shall monitor information relating to customer perception as to whether the organization has met customer requirements. The methods for obtaining and using this information shall be determined.

Implementation Guidelines, Tips, and Techniques

This is, perhaps, the most controversial clause of ISO 9001:2000. Objectively measuring customer satisfaction should be part of every organization's procedures, but it is often overlooked, ignored, or subjectively evaluated. Many companies look at profit and lack of customer complaints as indicators of customer satisfaction, yet profit can only report nonspecific historical results and lack of complaints will not indicate lack of repeat business or unstated customer dissatisfaction. This clause does not imply that every organization must employ an independent testing service to monitor customer satisfaction. It does require, however, that some proactive steps be taken and objective data gathered to ensure that customer needs and expectations are being met. This process must be ongoing and the data must be used to take corrective action and be part of future planning for customer needs.

ISO 9004 Performance Improvement Guidelines

Monitoring and Measurement

Measurement and Monitoring of System Performance

Top management should ensure that effective and efficient methods are used to identify areas for improvement of the quality management system performance. Examples of methods include

- satisfaction surveys for customers and other interested parties,
- internal audits,

- financial measurements, and
- self-assessment.

Measurement and Monitoring of Customer Satisfaction

Measurement and monitoring of customer satisfaction is based on review of customer-related information. The collection of such information may be active or passive. Management should recognize that there are many sources of customer-related information, and should establish effective and efficient processes to collect, analyze and use this information for improving the performance of the organization. The organization should identify sources of customer and end-user information, available in written and verbal forms, from internal and external sources. Examples of customer-related information include

- customer and user surveys,
- feedback on aspects of product,
- customer requirements and contract information,
- market needs,
- service delivery data, and
- information relating to competition.

Management should use measurement of customer satisfaction as a vital tool. The organization's process for requesting, measuring and monitoring feedback of customer satisfaction should provide information on a continual basis. This process should consider conformity to requirements, meeting needs and expectations of customers, as well as the price and delivery of product.

The organization should establish and use sources of customer satisfaction information and should cooperate with its customers in order to anticipate future needs. The organization should plan and establish processes to listen effectively and efficiently to the "voice of the customer." Planning for these processes should define and implement data-collection methods, including information sources, frequency of collection, and data-analysis review. Examples of sources of information on customer satisfaction include

- customer complaints,
- communicating directly with customers,

- questionnaires and surveys,
- subcontracted collection and analysis of data,
- focus groups,
- reports from consumer organizations,
- reports in various media, and
- sector and industry studies.

8.2.2 INTERNAL AUDIT

The organization shall conduct internal audits at planned intervals to determine whether the quality management system

a. conforms to the planned arrangements, to the requirements of this International Standard and to the quality management system requirements established by the organization, and

b. is effectively implemented and maintained.

An audit program shall be planned, taking into consideration the status and importance of the processes and areas to be audited, as well as the results of previous audits. The audit criteria, scope, frequency and methods shall be defined. Selection of auditors and conduct of audits shall ensure objectivity and impartiality of the audit process. Auditors shall not audit their own work.

The responsibilities and requirements for planning and conducting audits, and for reporting results and maintaining records shall be defined in a documented procedure.

The management responsible for the area being audited shall ensure that actions are taken without undue delay to eliminate detected nonconformities and their causes. Follow-up activities shall include the verification of the actions taken and the reporting of verification results.

NOTE See ISO 10011-1, ISO 10011-2 and ISO 10011-3 for guidance.

Implementation Guidelines, Tips, and Techniques

Internal auditing is a key element of the ISO 9001 QMS. It continually validates that the QMS is effective and that quality plans and objectives are being met. It is also a tool for planning continual improvement based on objective evidence from audits. Perhaps the word assessment would be a better description of this function, because audit has negative and punitive connotations from financial auditing.

Internal audits are systematic verifications of process effectiveness. They have nothing to do with personnel performance and should not be used against those who are performing the work. In most cases, negative audit findings are the result of poor procedures, ineffective processes, or lack of training. Secondary benefits of using cross-functional audit teams are an increased awareness about how processes interact and increased awareness about the needs of internal customers. Companies that have not been exposed to this methodology should seek professional training to ensure that the benefits are realized.

Potential Pitfalls

Whenever possible, avoid full-time auditors who are part of an inspection or assurance organization. Having "quality cops" is counterproductive to the nonadversarial methodology of effective internal auditing. In smaller organizations, consultants may be used as members of the internal audit team. Some companies form support groups in their community and share auditing duties with other companies that are not in competing businesses.

ISO 9004 Performance Improvement Guidelines

Internal Audit

Top management should ensure the establishment of an effective and efficient internal audit process to assess the strengths and weaknesses of the quality management system. The internal audit process acts as a management tool for independent assessment of any designated process or activity. The internal audit process provides an independent tool for use in obtaining objective evidence that the existing requirements have been met, since the internal audit evaluates the effectiveness and efficiency of the organization.

It is important that management ensure improvement actions are taken in response to internal audit results. Planning for internal audits should be flexible in order to permit changes in emphasis based on findings and objective evidence obtained during the audit. Relevant input from the area to be audited, as well as from other interested parties, should be considered in the development of internal audit plans.

Examples of subjects for consideration by internal auditing include

- effective and efficient implementation of processes,
- opportunities for continual improvement,
- capability of processes,
- effective and efficient use of statistical techniques,
- use of information technology,
- analysis of quality cost data,
- effective and efficient use of resources,
- process and product performance results and expectations,
- adequacy and accuracy of performance measurement,
- improvement activities, and
- relationships with interested parties.

Internal audit reporting sometimes includes evidence of excellent performance in order to provide opportunities for recognition by management and motivation of people.

Financial Measures

Management should consider the conversion of data from processes to financial information in order to provide comparable measures across processes and to facilitate improvement of the effectiveness and efficiency of the organization. Examples of financial measures include

- prevention and appraisal costs analysis,
- nonconformity cost analysis,
- internal and external failure cost analysis, and
- life-cycle cost analysis.

Self-Assessment

Top management should consider establishing and implementing self-assessment. This is a careful evaluation, usually performed by the organization's own management, that results in an opinion or judgment of the effectiveness and efficiency of the organization and the maturity of the quality management system. It can be used by the organization to benchmark its performance against that of external organizations and world-class performance. Self-assessment also aids in evaluating the performance improvement of the organization, whereas the internal audit process of an organization is an independent audit used to obtain objective evidence that existing policies, procedures or requirements have been met, as it evaluates the effectiveness and efficiency of the quality management system. The range and depth of self-assessment should be planned in relation to the organization's objectives and priorities. The self-assessment approach described in Annex A of ISO 9004 focuses on determining the degree of the effectiveness and efficiency of the implementation of the organization's quality management system. Some of the advantages of using the self-assessment approach given in Annex A are that

+ it is simple to understand,
+ it is easy to use,
+ it has minimal impact on the use of management resources, and
+ it provides input for enhancing the performance of the organization's quality management system.

Annex A of ISO 9004 is only one example of self-assessment. Self-assessment should not be considered as an alternative to internal or external quality auditing. Use of the approach described in Annex A can provide management with an overall view of the performance of the organization and the degree of maturity of the quality management system. It can also provide input for identifying areas in the organization requiring performance improvement and in helping to determine priorities.

8.2.3 MONITORING AND MEASUREMENT OF PROCESSES

The organization shall apply suitable methods for monitoring and, where applicable, measurement of the quality management system processes. These methods shall demonstrate the ability of the processes to achieve planned results. When planned results are not achieved, correction and corrective action shall be taken, as appropriate, to ensure conformity of the product.

Implementation Guidelines, Tips, and Techniques

Although implied elsewhere in the standard, this clause specifies the need to have monitoring steps included in each process that produce measurable outcomes. These verification and measuring activities must be part of a closed-loop system of process metrics and corrective action being used to validate, fix, and improve processes.

ISO 9004 Performance Improvement Guidelines

Measurement and Monitoring of Processes

The organization should identify measurement methods and should perform measurements to evaluate process performance. The organization should incorporate these measurements into processes and use the measurements in process management.

Measurements should be used for managing daily operations, for evaluation of the processes that may be suitable for small-step or ongoing continual improvements, as well as for breakthrough projects, according to the vision and strategic objectives of the organization.

Measurements of process performance should cover the needs and expectations of interested parties in a balanced manner. Examples include

- capability,
- reaction time,
- cycle time or throughput,
- measurable aspects of dependability,
- yield,
- the effectiveness and efficiency of the organization's people,
- utilization of technologies,
- waste reduction, and
- cost allocation and reduction.

8.2.4 MONITORING AND MEASUREMENT OF PRODUCT

The organization shall monitor and measure the characteristics of the product to verify that product requirements have been met. This shall be carried out at appropriate stages of the product realization process in accordance with the planned arrangements.

Evidence of conformity with the acceptance criteria shall be maintained. Records shall indicate the person(s) authorizing release of product.

Product release and service delivery shall not proceed until the planned arrangements have been satisfactorily completed, unless otherwise approved by a relevant authority and, where applicable, by the customer.

Implementation Guidelines, Tips, and Techniques

Once processes are deemed under control, their outcomes must be monitored for conformance. This can be manifested as inspections and tests of products or determination by other means that services were rendered in accordance with customer requirements and expectations. Whatever methods are used, there must be positive indicators that all required steps have been successfully accomplished, all prerequisites have been met, and that the product or service is authorized for release or delivery.

Potential Pitfalls

This clause does not necessarily require formal inspection and test steps. Many organizations build validation steps into processes, negating the need for tollgate inspection steps. Some even use tools such as Six Sigma evaluation to completely eliminate the need for inspections and tests based on statistical data-gathering techniques. Others may include specific "go/no-go" steps to ensure defective product does not have any more value-added steps performed before validation of previous processes is complete. Most organizations utilize a final check to ensure all requirements are met before the product or service is dispatched to the customer. Still others require customer authorization prior to shipment. Select the methods most appropriate to your product, service, culture, and customer requirements.

ISO 9004 Performance Improvement Guidelines

Measurement and Monitoring of Product

The organization should establish and specify the measurement requirements (including acceptance criteria) for its products. The measurement of product should be planned and performed in order to verify that the requirements of interested parties have been achieved and used to improve the realization processes.

When selecting measurement methods for ensuring that products conform to requirements and when considering customer needs and expectations, the organization should consider the following:

- the types of product characteristics, which then determine the types of measurement, suitable measurement means, the accuracy required and skills needed;
- equipment, software and tools required;
- the location of suitable measurement points in the realization process sequence;
- characteristics to be measured at each point, and the documentation and acceptance criteria to be used;
- customer-established points for witness or verification of selected characteristics of a product;
- inspections or testing required to be witnessed or performed by statutory and regulatory authorities;
- where, when and how the organization intends, or is required by the customer or statutory and regulatory authorities, to engage qualified third parties to perform
  - type testing,
  - in-process inspections or testing,
  - product verification,
  - product validation, and
  - product qualification;
- qualification of people, materials, products, processes, and the quality management system;
- final inspection to confirm that verification and validation activities have been completed and accepted; and
- recording the results of product measurements.

The organization should review the methods used for measuring products and the planned records of verification, to consider opportunities for performance improvement. Typical examples of product measurement records that could be considered for performance improvement include

- inspection and test reports,
- material release notices,
- product acceptance forms, and
- certificates of conformity as required.

Measurement and Monitoring the Satisfaction of Interested Parties

The organization should identify the measurement information required to meet the needs of interested parties (other than customers), in relation to the processes of the organization in order to balance the allocation of resources. Such information should include measurements relating to the people in the organization, owners and investors, suppliers and partners, as well as society. Measurement examples are as follows:

- For people in the organization, the organization should
  - survey the opinions of its people regarding how well the organization satisfies their needs and expectations, and
  - assess individual and collective performances and their contribution to organizational results.
- For owners and investors, the organization should
  - assess its capacity to attain defined objectives,
  - assess its financial performance,
  - evaluate the impact of external factors on its results, and
  - identify the value contributed by the actions taken.
- For suppliers and partners, the organization should
  - survey the opinions of suppliers and partners on their satisfaction with the purchasing processes of the organization,
  - monitor and supply feedback on the performance of suppliers and partners and their compliance with the organization's purchasing policy, and

- assess the quality of product purchased, contributions from suppliers and partners, and mutual benefits derived from the relationship.
- For society, the organization should
  - define and track suitable data relative to its objectives, in order to achieve satisfactory interaction with society, and
  - periodically assess the effectiveness and efficiency of its actions and the perceptions of its performance by relevant parts of society.

8.3 CONTROL OF NONCONFORMING PRODUCT

The organization shall ensure that product which does not conform to product requirements is identified and controlled to prevent its unintended use or delivery. The controls and related responsibilities and authorities for dealing with nonconforming product shall be defined in a documented procedure.

The organization shall deal with nonconforming product by one or more of the following ways:

a. by taking action to eliminate the detected nonconformity;

b. by authorizing its use, release or acceptance under concession by a relevant authority and, where applicable, by the customer; and

c. by taking action to preclude its original intended use or application.

Records of the nature of nonconformities and any subsequent actions taken, including concessions obtained, shall be maintained.

When nonconforming product is corrected it shall be subject to reverification to demonstrate conformity to the requirements.

When nonconforming product is detected after delivery or use has started, the organization shall take action appropriate to the effects, or potential effects, of the nonconformity.

Implementation Guidelines, Tips, and Techniques

Nonconforming material procedures should be only as complex as the criticality of your products or services. If you purchase and build only catalog part-numbered items and your only options are to return them to the vendor or scrap them, your procedures should be relatively simple. If you are required to notify your customer when a nonconformity occurs, your system will be more cumbersome. In either event, there must be a clear audit trail of what happened, what is to be done, what was done, and how the cycle was completed. A mature system also generates corrective action and continual improvement data from this process. If you provide services, nonconformities must be documented and resolved in a manner similar to products. When your procedures do allow rework or repair resulting in the product being less than brand new, you need procedures to include reinspection and assurances that the prescribed rework or repair was performed satisfactorily.

Potential Pitfalls

The need for formal material review boards and secure bonded storage is not implied by this standard. Often, line organizations, purchasing agents, and inspectors dispose of nonconformities. Criticality of dispositions, competence of personnel, customer requirements, and liability considerations should be utilized to build a nonconforming material (or service) disposition procedure.

ISO 9004 Performance Improvement Guidelines

Control of Nonconformity

Top management should empower people in the organization with the authority and responsibility to report nonconformities at any stage of a process in order to ensure timely detection and disposition of nonconformities. Authority for response to nonconformities should be defined to maintain achievement of process and product requirements. The organization should effectively and efficiently control nonconforming product identification, segregation and disposition in order to prevent misuse.

Where practical, nonconformities should be recorded, together with their disposition, to assist learning and to provide data for analysis and improvement activities. The organization may also decide that nonconformities to both product realization and support processes should be recorded and controlled.

The organization can also consider recording information on those nonconformities that are corrected in the normal course of work. Such data can provide valuable information for improving the effectiveness and efficiency of processes.

Nonconformity Review and Disposition

The management of the organization should ensure the establishment of an effective and efficient process to provide for review and disposition of identified nonconformities. Review of nonconformities should be conducted by authorized people to determine if any trends or patterns of occurrence require attention. Negative trends should be considered for improvement, and as input to management review where reduction goals and resource needs are considered.

People carrying out the review should have the competence to evaluate the total effects of the nonconformity and should have the authority and resources to disposition the nonconformity and to define appropriate corrective action. Acceptance of nonconformity disposition may be a contractual requirement of the customer, or a requirement of other interested parties.

8.4 ANALYSIS OF DATA

The organization shall determine, collect and analyze appropriate data to demonstrate the suitability and effectiveness of the quality management system and to evaluate where continual improvement of the effectiveness of the quality management system can be made. This shall include data generated as a result of monitoring and measurement and from other relevant sources. The analysis of data shall provide information relating to

a. customer satisfaction,

b. conformity to product requirements,

c. characteristics and trends of processes and products including opportunities for preventive action, and

d. suppliers.

Implementation Guidelines, Tips, and Techniques

This clause galvanizes the need, stated elsewhere in the standard, to collect and analyze data as a method of determining process effectiveness, determining customer satisfaction, and building a model for continual improvement. Product liability and customer loyalty issues should be enough impetus to establish effective data collection and analysis procedures.

Potential Pitfalls

A common hazard is to become data rich and information poor; that is, many organizations gather data but neglect to intellectualize its meaning and then use the information from the data to take actions in process correction and improvement. The results of data analysis must be the foundation for evaluating quality plans and objectives and for validating business results, leading to corrective action and revised strategic planning.

ISO 9004 Performance Improvement Guidelines

Analysis of Data

Decisions should be based on analysis of data obtained from measurements and information collected as described in this International Standard. In this context, the organization should analyze data from its various sources to assess performance against plans, objectives and other defined goals, and to identify areas for improvement including possible benefits for interested parties.

Decisions based on facts require effective and efficient actions such as

- valid analysis methods,
- appropriate statistical techniques, and
- making decisions and taking actions based on results of logical analyses, as balanced with experience and intuition.

Analysis of data can help to determine the root cause of existing or potential problems, and therefore guide decisions about the corrective and preventive actions needed for improvement.

For an effective evaluation by management of the total performance of the organization, data and information from all parts of the organization should be integrated and analyzed. The organization's overall performance should be presented in a format that is suitable for different levels of the organization. The results of this analysis can be used by the organization to determine

- trends,
- customer satisfaction,
- satisfaction of other interested parties,
- effectiveness and efficiency of its processes,
- supplier contribution,
- success of its performance improvement objectives,
- economics of quality, financial and market-related performance,
- benchmarking of its performance, and
- competitiveness.

8.5 IMPROVEMENT

8.5.1 CONTINUAL IMPROVEMENT

The organization shall continually improve the effectiveness of the quality management system through the use of the quality policy, quality objectives, audit results, analysis of data, corrective and preventive actions and management review.

Implementation Guidelines, Tips, and Techniques

The word continual was chosen carefully to indicate that organizations must be on an ongoing journey of improvement as part of their planned business activities. This does not imply that products or services must be constantly changing, nor does it necessitate a day-by-day improvement process. It means that a regular and methodical methodology must be established to use data and information collected to improve processes as the opportunity for improvement presents itself. Often, data analysis points to low-hanging fruit that can be immediately harvested for rapid process enhancement. Other data may indicate a need for a long-term strategy to upgrade equipment or facilities.

ISO 9004 Performance Improvement Guidelines

Improvement

Management should continually seek to improve the effectiveness and efficiency of the processes of the organization, rather than wait for a problem to reveal opportunities for improvement. Improvements can range from small-step ongoing continual improvement to strategic breakthrough improvement projects. The organization should have a process in place to identify and manage improvement activities. These improvements may result in change to the product or processes and even to the quality management system or to the organization.

8.5.2 CORRECTIVE ACTION

The organization shall take action to eliminate the cause of nonconformities in order to prevent recurrence. Corrective actions shall be appropriate to the effects of the nonconformities encountered.

A documented procedure shall be established to define requirements for

a. reviewing nonconformities (including customer complaints),

b. determining the causes of nonconformities,

c. evaluating the need for action to ensure that nonconformities do not recur,

d. determining and implementing action needed,

e. records of the results of action taken, and

f. reviewing corrective action taken.

Implementation Guidelines, Tips, and Techniques

Corrective action is the documentation and resolution of deviations from any stated requirements in your QMS. Corrective action is not necessarily a part of nonconforming material control, unless repeated nonconformities lead to a corrective action request (CAR). CARs are usually the result of deviations found during internal audits. In mature quality systems, CARs may be generated from observations in nonaudit situations.

The CAR has several finite components. The first is an objective description of the finding and reference to the procedure or ISO 9001 element that is at variance. Without specific reference to a written procedure, there can be no legitimate CAR (they are process related, never subjective, and never used to accuse individuals). Second, the CAR must be issued to a responsible individual for investigation and response. There is always a specific time period allowed for response and a follow-up mechanism to ensure that it does not remain an issue beyond a reasonable time period. Finally, there is always an analysis and follow-up process to ensure that the root cause was identified and rectified so that recurrence of the same finding is very unlikely. Great attention is paid to the corrective action system because it is an indicator of how seriously companies depend on their quality management and their continual improvement systems. Most companies have some informal corrective action systems that do not prevent the same problem from occurring repeatedly. This expediency in solving tactical problems is not sound long-term business practice and will show in an audit as a lack of commitment to the company's quality policy.

ISO 9004 Performance Improvement Guidelines

Corrective Action

Top management should ensure that corrective action is used as a tool for improvement. Corrective action planning should include evaluation of the significance of problems, and should be in terms of the potential impact on such aspects as operating costs, costs of nonconformity, product performance, dependability and the safety and satisfaction of customers and other interested parties. People from appropriate disciplines should participate in the corrective action process. Also, the effectiveness and efficiency of processes should be emphasized when actions are taken and the actions should be monitored to ensure that desired goals are met. Corrective actions should be considered for inclusion in management review.

In pursuing corrective action, the organization should identify sources of information, and collect information to define the necessary corrective actions. The defined corrective action should be focused on eliminating causes of nonconformities in order to avoid recurrence. Examples of sources of information for corrective action consideration include

- customer complaints,
- nonconformity reports,
- internal audit reports,
- outputs from management review,
- outputs from data analysis,
- outputs from satisfaction measurements,
- relevant quality management system records,
- the organization's people,
- process measurements, and
- results of self-assessment.

There are many ways to determine the causes of nonconformity, including analysis by an individual or the assignment of a corrective-action project team. The organization should balance the investment in the corrective action against the impact of the problem being considered.

In evaluating the need for actions to ensure that nonconformities do not recur, the organization should consider providing appropriate training for people assigned to corrective-action projects.

The organization should incorporate root-cause analysis, as appropriate, into the corrective action process. Root-cause analysis results should be verified by testing prior to defining and initiating corrective action.

8.5.3 PREVENTIVE ACTION

The organization shall determine action to eliminate the causes of potential nonconformities in order to prevent their occurrence. Preventive actions shall be appropriate to the effects of the potential problems.

A documented procedure shall be established to define requirements for

a. determining potential nonconformities and their causes,

b. evaluating the need for action to prevent occurrence of nonconformities,

c. determining and implementing action needed,

d. records of results of action taken, and

e. reviewing preventive action taken.

Implementation Guidelines, Tips, and Techniques

An effective preventive action program establishes a systematic process of continually avoiding problems before they occur. This element does not advocate the use of a Ouija board to predict the future; it suggests that specific activities leave valuable evidence of processes that are on the verge of being outside control limits. Companies that employ sound business practices seize these opportunities to prevent problems as found money.

Potential Pitfalls

The corrective and preventive action processes can be handled in the same manner, but provisions for preventive action must be clearly stated.

ISO 9004 Performance Improvement Guidelines

Loss Prevention

Management should plan to mitigate the effects of loss to the organization in order to maintain the performance of processes and products. Loss prevention in the form of planning should be applied to realization and support processes, activities and products to ensure the satisfaction of interested parties.

To be effective and efficient, planning for loss prevention should be systematic. This should be based on data from appropriate methods, including evaluation of historical data for trends, and criticality relative to the performance of the organization and its products, in order to generate data in quantitative terms. Data can be generated from

- use of risk analysis tools such as fault mode and effects analysis,
- review of customer needs and expectations,
- market analysis,
- management review output,
- outputs from data analysis,
- satisfaction measurements,
- process measurements,
- systems that consolidate sources of information from interested parties,
- relevant quality management system records,
- lessons learned from past experience,
- results of self-assessment, and
- processes that provide early warning of approaching out-of-control operating conditions.

Such data will provide information to develop an effective and efficient plan for loss prevention and prioritization appropriate to each process and product, in order to satisfy the needs and expectations of interested parties.

Results of the evaluation of the effectiveness and efficiency of loss prevention plans should be an output from management review, and should be used as an input for the modification of plans and as input to the improvement processes.

Continual Improvement of the Organization

To aid in ensuring the future of the organization and the satisfaction of interested parties, management should create a culture that involves people actively seeking opportunities for improvement of performance in processes, activities and products.

To involve people, top management should create an environment where authority is delegated so that people are empowered and accept responsibility to identify opportunities where the organization can improve its performance. This can be achieved by activities such as

- setting of objectives for people, projects and the organization,
- benchmarking competitor performance and best practice,
- recognition and reward for achievement of improvement, and
- suggestion schemes including timely reaction by management.

To provide a structure for improvement activities, top management should define and implement a process for continual improvement that can be applied to realization and support processes and activities. To ensure the effectiveness and efficiency of the improvement process, consideration should be given to realization and support processes in terms of

- effectiveness (such as outputs meeting requirements),
- efficiency (such as resources per unit in terms of time and money),
- external effects (such as statutory and regulatory change),
- potential weakness (such as lack of capability and consistency),
- the opportunity to employ better methods,
- control of planned and unplanned change, and
- measurement of planned benefits.

Such a process for continual improvement should be used as a tool for improving the organization's internal effectiveness and efficiency, as well as to improve the satisfaction of customers and other interested parties.

Management should support improvements in the form of small-step ongoing activities integral to existing processes as well as breakthrough opportunities, in order to gain maximum benefit for the organization and interested parties.

Examples of inputs to support the improvement process include information derived from

- validation data,
- process yield data
- test data,
- data from self-assessment,
- stated requirements and feedback from interested parties,
- experience of people in the organization,
- financial data,
- product performance data, and
- service delivery data.

Management should ensure that product or process changes are approved, prioritized, planned, provisioned and controlled to satisfy interested party requirements and avoid exceeding the capability of the organization.

A process presenting continual process improvement for implementation by an organization is described in Annex B of ISO 9004.

7

ISO 9001 Implementation and Transition Strategy

This chapter outlines the steps that companies of all sizes can use to make ISO 9001 the cornerstone of their strategic planning for the future. It covers the most economical methods for implementation of ISO 9001 and how companies can utilize their internal resources to minimize cost and maximize the benefits. The chapter also details how companies can capture what has made them successful and use it to model their future by replacing management by feel with management by fact.

It also deals specifically with organizations that are currently certified to the 1994 versions of ISO 9001, 9002, or 9003 and are looking to plan a successful transition to ISO 9001:2000. It is also for companies that are in the implementation process of the 1994 Standard and need guidance in planning their approach to certification. Using the information presented here, along with that in Chapters 4 through 6 and Appendix D, you should have enough information to successfully plan the transition process.

SMALL COMPANIES

The good news is that small companies derive the most dramatic benefit from a well-implemented ISO 9001 QMS. The bad news is that most small companies haven't budgeted strategic quality initiatives into their already tight cash flow. In the context of this book, a small company is defined as one that has been in business for x number of years and has y number of employees (where x and y are relatively unimportant), but has evolved pragmatically and persists by the will of those in charge. That is, these companies have never taken the time to take an objective and strategic look at where they are and where they are going, at least not to the point of documenting what has made them successful. These small businesses run on word of mouth, instinct, the problem du jour, knee jerks, and he who yells the loudest. Their employees are dedicated and find solutions to the daily challenges, despite minimal direction and limited resources.

My definition may sound negative, but most small businesses that are paying their bills and making payroll every month are actually a testimonial to ingenuity and entrepreneurship. When the success model is not well defined, small business owners and employees must rely on keen instinct to keep the ship pointed into the wind and away from the rocks.

Those small businesses that want to make the move from management by crisis to management by fact can find a viable first step by using ISO 9001 as a model for the implementation process. My suggested methodology is very much in concert with the tenets of ISO 9001: Define your infrastructure, charter your mission, and communicate it to everyone. Chapter 8 contains an outline for executing a strategic plan. The following work needs to be done before you launch into the strategic plan.

Designing a Strategic Plan

Gather up the key players in your company. Include not only those who own a piece of the business or those on the management staff, but those who have a passionate emotional interest in the success of the company. Reserve a suite at a golf resort or a cabin in the woods and plan two quiet days away from the daily hassle of the office. If you have the resources, retain a professional facilitator to help you through this process. He or she can help make this process a glowing success on your first outing. Take with you plenty of flip-chart paper, masking tape, and broad-tip markers.

Begin by brainstorming in four areas:

- All products and services you provide, or plan to provide in the next two years
- Your physical resources

- Your personnel resources
- Your financial resources

Attack the four bullets one at a time. Don't worry about listing the contents in any order: The contents will be ranked later. Ask for one idea from each individual. Keep going around the room until you have run out of items to list (these are the basic rules of brainstorming). Tape all of the lists to the walls so they can be seen. For the four topics, find consensus and rank each item in descending order of importance or value. Cross out any that are duplications or have no real importance or value to the company. You should now have a crude but objective look at what your company resources are.

Starting with your products and services, spend a generous amount of time defining your core business. Define what quality means in your organization (see the discussion in Chapter 1). What exactly is it that you do? Refer to your three resource lists to determine exactly what your charter entails. If you have more than one core business, rank them by the amount of resources you currently dedicate to each one. From that list, decide if that is really what business(es) you want to be in. This may sound arcane, but are you doing what you are good at? Do you enjoy doing it, or have you stuck yourselves in a niche that pays the bills but takes every ounce of energy you have to keep doing the same thing every day? This discovery process usually leads to some interesting and intense conversations. You must all be introspective, communicative, and brutally honest with each other if this is to be of any real value.

Once you have decided exactly what you do today, spend another generous amount of time brainstorming to determine what you think you will be doing in the next year. This can't be a pie-in-the-sky budgetary guess, but, rather, it must be specific products and services that you need or want to provide with not much more talent and resources than you already have on board or to which you have immediate access.

As a result of this process, you should identify two or three key objectives. More is too many to tackle, and fewer are usually not ambitious enough. When you have reached agreement on the products or services (or have decided to sell the business and become golf pros), spend the rest of the first day fitting your resources into how you are going to accomplish this one-year goal. If you come up short on resources, plan how you will acquire the resources. Next, decide (not merely based on financial results) how you will know how well you have achieved your objectives a year from now. When you are done, get in a round of golf or some fishing, and sleep on what you have done the first day.

The second day should be devoted to performing a reality check, documenting your results, and deciding how you are going to share the plan with everyone in the company. Go back through the logic of the first day and convince yourselves that you did not get involved in "groupthink" or allow one individual to suboptimize the outcome. Write a one-sentence mission statement (ISO 9001 calls it the quality policy) that states the core values of your business. This will become the marching orders for everyone in your company. If you feel compelled, write a set of value statements that support the mission statement. I do not offer any suggestions because this needs to be spontaneous (and this is also one of the reasons a facilitator would be helpful).

Prepare an outline of how you are going to accomplish your mission (resources and priorities). You are now ready to go back to the office and tackle the strategic plan outlined in Chapter 8. If all went well, you will also have developed a smug glow of new understanding and a newfound synergistic relationship with those who participated.

Obviously, this technique is not for every small company. The point is, by whatever means available, your company must take an objective look at itself and decide where it is headed. You must also develop a plan to capture your success so it can be replicated in the future. Once that is done, you must communicate that information to everyone in the value delivery system. This is a prerequisite to beginning ISO 9001 implementation or any other strategic improvement initiative.

Launching Your New Plan

You still have to launch these initiatives, and you probably have not budgeted for a consultant or other professional resources. If you can work it into your plan, engage a facilitator who has broad experience in successfully implementing ISO 9001 in a variety of business environments. Check his or her references carefully and find out from the references how much their business has improved as a result of ISO 9001 implementation. It doesn't matter much if the consultant got them certified on the first pass. The important question is, "Did the process add value to the company and will it be able to sustain continual improvement when the consultant is gone?"

Of course, this book is intended to help you launch your ISO 9001 initiative and it contains much of the generic information you will need. You can also obtain local help through your college system or through a local section of the ASQ (*www.asq.org*). Many business schools have small-business development offices that have resources to help you with your implementation. They can often refer you to support groups of business professionals who are also making the ISO 9001 journey. These voluntary groups are often very helpful with shared experiences. The downside to support groups is that misinformation can be propagated just as effectively as valid information. Be sure to validate any data you receive from support groups. The same is true for Internet discussion groups. The Internet has spawned a massive body of discussion participants. You can't be sure of the expertise of the people answering questions in a discussion group.

Once you have decided which resources you will employ, the most effective method for launching your strategic quality initiative is with a cross-functional implementation team. This is described in detail in Chapter 9. This team, or steering committee, should have the ad-hoc assignment of leading the implementation of ISO 9001. At this point, they must have a clear charter, the authority to act, and sufficient time and resources to be successful. Without any one of these elements, the entire cultural change is doomed to failure.

MEDIUM-SIZED COMPANIES

Companies that have survived the pains of startup and growth and have achieved a defined culture and infrastructure may find ISO 9001 an unwelcome irritation. It is sometimes analogous to asking someone to change a pair of shoes that they've just worn to a comfortable fit. To the uninitiated, ISO 9001 might appear as a threat to recently codified and validated methods and processes. This chapter shows companies how to integrate ISO 9001 into their newly defined culture without causing major rifts and how to use WIIFM ("What's in it for me?") to make allies of middle managers who might perceive the standard as a threat to their autonomy.

The first step in ISO 9001 implementation in a medium-sized company is to ensure that your company has taken the preparatory steps of defining its mission. Most have not. It is more difficult to accomplish this task in more mature companies because those in charge have evolved success methodologies that they replicate daily to ensure that what made them successful keeps them successful. In other words, they have developed a largely unconscious behavior pattern that has not been codified or transmitted down the chain of command. Because this behavior pattern is the essence of the company's culture, it is taken for granted and it is what separates the leaders from the doers. Asking successful business managers to document their mission and communicate it to all may be perceived as a threat to their power base and as a deterrent to their ability to change the business on the whims of external influences. Again, a consultant is often the only person who can bring clarity to developing the quality policy and convincing the business managers that it is a wise thing to do.

Convince Management

Once the mission has been established, the remaining major hurdle is to get all the top and middle managers to buy into it. If you have a dynamic group of managers who embrace the opportunity to improve, you have an easy row to hoe. In most companies, top management wants to delegate the entire program and middle managers usually resist change because it is seen as a threat to their autonomy and to achieving departmental objectives. Change is also perceived to add workload to already taxed departments.

The only way to make allies of managers is to educate them about ISO 9001 implementation and continually show them how implementation will make their work easier. For instance, hold lunchtime training sessions. Bring food in once a week and pick key clauses of ISO 9001 to review and discuss. Stress that each element exists to ensure that the value delivery system works effectively, not as a bureaucratic overhead requirement.

Reinforce the theme that, unless it makes good business sense, you don't have to do anything differently just to satisfy ISO 9001. Ask what the managers see as their greatest deterrents to productivity and find ways to use ISO 9001 to help them fix their problems. Find local companies that have successfully implemented ISO 9001 and arrange field trips for your managers to show them the positive results of the ISO 9001 journey. Make joint commitments with the managers to achieve key quality improvement objectives if they will fully support the ISO 9001 efforts. The term *fully support* is a key to the success of this initiative. Managers who passively allow it to happen are usually bottlenecks to the process and those who are silent are usually sabotaging the effort by their lack of commitment.

As the process evolves, it will become easier and easier to win management support because the benefits of documenting processes, training workers, and using internal auditing as a building tool make their work easier and easier. The ISO 9001 champions must seize every opportunity to point out the improvements as they occur (that is why sound metrics are essential to measuring progress). Blow your horn as often as possible and make every stage of implementation a win–win scenario.

LARGER AND MORE MATURE COMPANIES

In many large companies, ISO 9001 is looked on as a step backward in the evolution of quality. It is shunned as too basic or too parochial for mature quality systems. It may be that your company has a viable QMS, in which case your quality professionals need only develop a compliance matrix and perform internal audits that will verify that their current systems will meet an ISO 9001 compliance audit. For established systems, it is also true that the tenets of ISO 9001 can shore up outdated strategic quality initiatives and help replace expensive tollgate inspection systems with nonconfrontational process controls.

Larger companies often have a quality department or some formal infrastructure responsible for quality assurance or quality control. A few of these organizations have direct responsibility for continual quality improvement, but most are gatekeepers to ensure that defective products or services do not reach the customers. It is likely that each of these organizations has volumes of procedures written as prescriptive and adversarial checks and balances with the other departments in the value delivery system. Many of these procedures were written as a compliance exercise and a reference to cite when infractions occur, rather than as a proactive QMS.

Determining the Extent of ISO 9001 Updates

For companies with existing quality systems, the first step to ISO 9001 implementation is to perform a gap analysis (see Appendix D). This formal exercise compares the key elements of ISO 9001 to the existing procedures to determine conformance of the existing system to the tenets of ISO 9001. For each element, compliance or noncompliance is determined and a compliance matrix is generated. This matrix reveals elements of the existing system that satisfy the ISO 9001 elements and any deficiencies as well.

Most of the time, internal auditing is nonexistent in traditional organizations. Also, corrective and preventive action may be informal or not well executed. For areas in which deficiencies exist, the procedures must be updated prior to conducting formal audits.

Some Companies Require Little Change

In companies with formal quality organizations, there is rarely a need for a steering committee, as the quality professionals usually lead the ISO 9001 implementation and serve as internal auditors. Avoid the trap of having quality engineers read more into the ISO 9001 elements than may be there (many of us were guilty of just that in the days of MIL-I-45208 and MIL-Q-9858). Aside from internal auditing and formal corrective and preventive action, most quality departments will need very little reengineering to be ISO 9001 compliant. Often, the reengineering streamlines existing processes and controls.

Most formal quality systems can be made compliant with very little effort. In fact, some are so far advanced from the baseline ISO 9001 system that compliance is virtually assured. For others that have been relying on outdated procedures that are only followed in crisis situations, this process can be a great catharsis. The gap analysis points out the weaknesses in your current system and the process of internal auditing quantifies how effective your system is.

Quality Management Is a Team Sport

The other area to be stressed in larger companies is that quality is often left up to the quality department; that is, most other departments have no vested interest in the quality program and do not have a clue what is going on behind the closed doors and white smocks. ISO 9001 certification is fully dependent on everyone in the value delivery system being a player in the QMS. Each process operator must be cognizant of the quality policy, be trained in the QMS, be following their own written procedures, and be walking the walk of continual improvement. This can be the most difficult and time-consuming part of ISO 9001 implementation in larger companies, but it also provides the greatest payback in productivity and profit improvement.

ORGANIZATIONS TRANSITIONING FROM EARLIER ISO STANDARDS

The ISO is charged with keeping the ISO 9001 standard current with the needs of changing business climates and the improvements found as the standard is implemented in new environments and cultures. The initial plan was to have a revision every five years. Since its introduction in 1987, it had been revised only once, in 1994, before the 2000 revision. There are technical committees and advisory groups continually meeting and assessing suggested changes to the standard. Because it is a global standard, it takes protracted periods of time to coordinate task groups and then to gain consensus about changes affecting practitioners from vastly diverse cultures. Each of these issues was dealt with in the 2000 revision to ISO 9001.

Any proactive steps to make changes before the standard was actually released in December 2000 were premature because substantive changes were made as late as September 2000. Any publications and training materials released prior to 2001 should be carefully scrutinized for technical accuracy. If you encounter any books or articles that do not contain references to Clause 4 of ISO 9001:2000, that is an indication that the information was based on the draft international standard issued early in 2000 and that the information does not include the final changes made before the standard was released. Any reference to the term *permissible exclusions* is also an indicator of outdated information. Although exclusions are permitted to ISO 9001:2000 Clause 7, they are no longer referred to as permissible exclusions. Also, as mentioned in Chapter 1, the actual implementation of ISO 9001:2000 is just beginning and there is no knowledge base yet established on the realities of transition to the new revision. (The data in this book is the result of 10 years of experience in ISO 9001 implementation and data gathered from registrars and from the first few companies to become certified to ISO 9001:2000 early in 2001).

In October 2000, ISO published Document ISO/TC176/SC 2/N474R, entitled "Transition Planning Guidance for ISO 9001:2000." It is available on the ISO Web site (*www.iso.ch*). It sets forth transition guidelines that were released before the standard was published in December 2000. There is a great deal of useful background data in this document, but it is also written in "ISO babble" and might be confusing to an organization that is looking for specific implementation information in a concise format.

Also recently released (and available at *www.iso.ch*) are the following documents:

- ISO/TC 176/SC 2/N526 (October 2000): Guidance on the terminology used in ISO 9001:2000 and ISO 9004:2000
- ISO/TC 176/SC 2/N544 (December 2000): Guidance to the Process Approach to quality management systems
- ISO/TC 176/SC 2/N525R (March 2001) Guidance on the documentation requirements of ISO 9001:2000
- ISO/TC 176/SC 2/N5242 (March 2001): Guidance on ISO 9001:2000 Clause 1.2 "Application"

All of these are useful documents, the salient points of which are addressed in this chapter.

First, if you are presently well along in the implementation of ISO 9000:1994 but not yet certified, be advised that there is a three-year window (through December 2003) in which both the 1994 and the 2000 standards will coexist. It will be a strategic decision on the part of your organization as to whether you want to complete your current certification initiative before contemplating the transition to 2000. If you do not have established procedures for customer satisfaction, regulatory compliance, and continual improvement, you should probably complete your 1994 certification while planning the transition as an element of continual improvement. Although difficult to qualify, I strongly recommend the use of a competent professional consulting firm that is well grounded in the new revision to give you transition planning guidance.

Second, I have participated in most of the major conferences held in early 2001 at which the subject of ISO 9001:2000 was discussed and presented. The presentations and the networking conversations reinforced my belief that many organizations are either overwhelmed by the new revision, misunderstand its impact, or are looking for shortcuts to become minimally compliant. Misinformation is another imperative for finding a qualified consultant to help with your transition planning.

Third, in a joint communiqué issued in September 1999 by ISO and the International Accreditation Foundation, a great deal of responsibility was placed on registrars to ensure that the new revision was implemented in accordance with the intent of the standard, especially in the area of clauses excluded as not applicable. Therefore, if you are currently certified, it is in your best interest to have a transition planning meeting with your registrar to obtain guidelines for timing and conformance demonstration requirements. In fact, you should have a written agreement in place with your registrar that includes the steps and timelines you can agree to for making the transition to ISO 9001:2000.

With all of these caveats in place, here are the recommended steps of transition planning:

- Awareness: Arrange for an awareness session about the 2000 revision to be conducted for top management and those presently responsible for ISO 9001 in your organization. See Chapter 4 for the relevant information.
- Gap analysis: Perform a gap analysis of your current processes and clauses of ISO 9001:2000. Use Appendix D for the checklist. Use Chapter 4 and Appendix C for guidance about the differences between the 1994 and 2000 standards.
- Document findings: Document the findings of the gap analysis into a format that identifies any deficiencies in your current quality system and documentation. Prioritize the list, putting the most significant and resource demanding deficiencies first on the list.
- Draft an implementation plan: From the findings, draft a transition planning document and schedule to present to top management. Include the needed resources, reasons, and benefits for any proposed changes.
- Conduct strategic planning: Use the draft implementation plan as the agenda for a strategic planning meeting with top management. Obtain consensus on the plan, timeline, and resources. Tie the plan to measurable outcomes. See Chapter 8 for guidance.
- Develop a tactical plan: Before implementing the strategic plan, define intermediate plans for making any needed transitions. Define implementation guidelines to ensure that parallel systems are combined in a planned sequence. Implement necessary training as transition steps occur.
- Training: Conduct training at all levels on the strategic and tactical plans.
- Implement the plans: Have a committee oversee the transition efforts. Monitor the strategic and tactical plans. Tie activities to the master schedule. Reschedule as necessary to maintain continuity. Measure results against planned results.
- Conduct internal audits: Revise the internal audit schedule to allow for transition audits. Retrain internal auditors to familiarize them with the 2000 revision. Devise new audit checklists for the transition and for the new revision. Conduct audits, document results,

and affect corrective action as necessary. Revise procedures as necessary based on audit results.

- Conduct management review(s): Conduct management reviews to assess the effectiveness of the transition implementation.
- Evolve the continual improvement process: Utilize the internal audit and corrective action processes to establish a viable continual improvement process. To be effective, this must be an ongoing activity that has measurable results tied to business and quality objectives.

Above all, common sense must prevail in planning the transition process. Some organizations are striving to be among the first to be certified to the 2000 revision for prestige and for a marketing advantage. Others are waiting until the last minute to make the transition. Most should evolve the transition as an integral part of their continual improvement efforts. Establishing a budget and timelines that will allow customer needs to continue to be top priority while phasing in the most useful and productive changes in order of priority is the most sensible approach. Done well, each change can be implemented and documented as a productivity and profitability improvement project, with measurable gains over expense.

Attend as many public seminars as possible on the 2000 revision. Read *Quality Digest, Quality Progress,* and *Quality Systems Update* to keep on top of the evolving implementation conventions and precedents. Find local support groups through the ASQ. Utilize all resources available to you to keep informed on the progress of the ISO 9001:2000 transition. Be careful not to follow any advice until it is validated by business logic. I'm sure there will soon be a wave of companies offering to help you determine your customer satisfaction index to comply with ISO 9001:2000. If that service has no intrinsic value to your company, don't do it just to satisfy a perceived requirement of the standard. The operative questions should always be "Does this make sense for my business?" and "Does this add value to my customer or to my stockholders?"

8

STRATEGIC AND TACTICAL PLANNING

Before any ISO 9001 implementation can begin, you need to devise and roll out a strategic plan, which should define the organization's objectives, allocate resources, and establish ways to measure success along the journey. It should also contain contingency plans for variations in business activities (when business takes a seasonal downturn, some companies put their ISO 9001 implementation on hold, when it is really an ideal time to accelerate the project by using idle resources).

This chapter discusses successful strategic planning and outlines how to devise a tactical ISO 9001 implementation plan using existing resources and without disrupting the work that must be done each day. ISO 9001 cannot be implemented at the expense of customer needs, nor can it be implemented if it always comes second to every daily crisis.

When we begin a new journey with a plan to achieve certain milestones, it is most desirable to have a road map of where we are and where we want to go. If we are out for a Sunday drive, a road map may detract from the spontaneity of the trip. In running a business, however, navigating by feel will almost certainly steer you into a ditch or cause you to arrive at an unplanned destination.

The Plan Outline

The strategic implementation plan is very much an outline. We've defined the meat of the strategic plan in the first seven chapters. We discuss how to make each piece successful in subsequent chapters. We have selected the key elements that need to be included in the plan outline and incorporated them into the following topical categories. Because we've selected the theme of using ISO 9001 as the foundation for our strategic quality initiative, we construct the strategic plan around it.

I. The Infrastructure
   1. Define the Quality Policy and Mission Statement (5.1, 5.2, 5.3)
   2. Establish a System of Internal Quality Communication (5.5)
   3. Build a Functional Organization Chart (5.5)
      a. Define the responsible leadership positions
      b. Define the organizational structure and interrelationships
   4. Steering Committee (Chapter 9)
      a. Define who will coordinate and implement the strategic plan
   5. Appoint a Management Representative to Be the Quality Coordinator (5.5)
   6. Define the Scope of the Plan (5.4)

Determine if the plan is to encompass the entire company and all of its business entities. Will it be specific to a plant, operation, product line, or service center? Define exactly what the certification will cover.

   7. Define the Boundaries (5.4)

Decide if the plan will be limited only to those functions and processes that directly affect the value delivery system, or if it will be a strategic plan that encompasses all functions (administration, human resources, and accounting are sometimes not included in an ISO 9001 QMS).

   8. Define the Budget Issues (6.1)

If your company requires a specific budget for each department or project, determine how the costs associated with developing the plan will be budgeted and expensed and how you will you track costs versus budget.

   9. Set Up a Perpetual Renewal Plan (4.1)

Establish a charter that makes the strategic plan a perpetually evolving activity, regardless of who occupies which chairs. Make the required budget part of your long-range projections.

    10. Establish a Management Review System (5.6)
    11. Develop a Tactical Plan (this chapter)

Determine how will you deal with short-term problems and issues while you are developing and implementing this plan.

  II. The QMS
    1. Document the QMS (4.2)
    2. Document the Strategic Implementation Plan and Include Quality Objectives (5.4)
    3. Set Up a Perpetual Review and Maintenance Plan
  III. Human Interface
    1. Define the Role of the Jobholders (5.5)

Determine how they will be empowered to be responsible for their own actions, how they will be rewarded, and what risks and remedies they will face.

    2. Define How Everyone Will Be Trained (6.2)

Develop a master training plan that includes QMS training, job-related training, technical skills training (computers, software, etc.), and personal growth training and education.

  IV. Customer Interface
    1. Develop a Plan for Customer Interface (7.2)
      a. Develop business partnerships. You should posture yourself to become a strategic partner with your customers instead of just another vendor or peddler. Culturally involve your customers as the focus of your business. Ask them what they need and show them what is possible.
      b. Control document and contract flow. Ensure that there is no chance for miscommunication between you and your customers. Control their documentation and reach agreement on all contractual requirements.

    c. Develop a feedback loop for corrective and preventive action. Develop a working communication system with your customers to ensure that any problems are resolved quickly and equitably and that the same problems do not recur.

V.   Business Operations

   1. Design Control (7.3)

     a. Document and control the design and development process. Use the ISO 9001 model.

   2. Documentation Control (4.2)

     a. Document the paperwork and data flow. If it affects the QMS, be sure that the flow of information is auditable.

     b. Develop a system of positive control. Ensure that only the correct versions of documents are available for use in the value delivery system.

     c. Develop a change control system. Ensure that any changes are positively communicated to those affected by the changes. Determine point of effectiveness for every change and document what is to be done with existing products and services.

     d. Develop a method to control quality records. The integrity of historical records must be maintained for them to be of any use in configuration management or liability control.

   3. Supplier Interface (7.4)

     a. Develop a plan for supplier interface

       1. Business partnership. Replace peddlers and vendors with companies that will share your vision of success and support you through the ups and downs of your business.

       2. Control document and contract flow. Ensure that your partners control your documentation and specifications and that you reach agreement on all contractual terms.

       3. Develop a feedback loop for corrective and preventive action. Develop a working communication system with your suppliers to ensure that any problems are resolved quickly and equitably and that the same problems do not recur.

   4. Inventory Control (7.5)

     a. Product identification and traceability. As applicable for your industry, be sure that all products and materials are identified and traceable.

b. Control of customer-supplied product. If your customers provide material, equipment, or supplies, be sure they are controlled and accounted for.

c. Handling, storage, packaging, preservation, and delivery. Ensure that your methods of handling, inventory, packaging, preparation, and delivery maintain the integrity of your product.

5. Process Control (7.1, 7.5)

a. Develop a plan for controlling all processes within the value delivery system. Each activity that adds value to your product or service is a process. Each process should be documented to the degree necessary to measure its effectiveness and to the extent required to train new operators.

6. Quality Conformance (7.5, 8.3)

a. Develop a plan for inspection and testing. Each product and service must be verified as compliant before delivery to a customer. Effective systems for ensuring this compliance should be in place.

b. Develop a plan for controlling inspection measuring and test equipment. Any equipment used to verify published specifications or demonstrate conformance should be controlled and calibrated to a source of known accuracy.

c. Develop a plan to identify inspection and test status. Identification of the stage of inspection and test of any product should be clear and evident to the degree that is indicated by the importance of the commodities.

d. Develop a plan for controlling nonconforming product. Develop a system to segregate nonconformities from the workflow and to dispose of them in a timely fashion.

7. Corrective and Preventative Action (8.5)

a. Develop a corrective action plan. Ensure that deviations from policies and procedures are documented and resolved in a timely manner. Follow up to ensure effectiveness of the corrective action.

b. Develop a preventive action plan. Ensure that deviations and nonconformities do not recur.

8. Internal Audits (8.2)

   a. Develop an internal auditing system. Develop an effective program of routinely verifying the effectiveness of the QMS.

9. Develop a Family of Measures (8.2)

   a. Implement a series of barometers that effectively measure the performance of all key processes in the value delivery system.

10. Develop a Continual Improvement Program (8.5)

   a. Develop a methodology to use the results of metrics and internal audits to continually improve the QMS.

THE TACTICAL PLAN

Strategic plans are an excellent business tool when well conceived and smartly executed. The downfall of a great strategic plan is often what to do in the interim. You need to have a tactical plan ancillary to the strategic plan that forms a bridge between existing systems that will be phased out and new systems that will be implemented. For instance, if you have never made an attempt to control the forms you use, your strategic plan may call for a formal document control function to be established. Answer these questions:

- What happens until that function is implemented?
- Who will collect all of the obsolete forms?
- Who will perform awareness training as each new group of forms is released?
- Who will stay in touch with the process owners to ensure that the new system is supporting their needs?

There is nothing more tragic in business than a great strategic plan that fails because its implementation transition was not planned and its effects were not monitored. Tactical planning also serves as the "midcourse correction" that must be implemented when a strategic plan is not as viable and robust as the planners visualized. Continually evaluating and refining the implementation of the strategic plan is the essence of effective tactical execution. Most companies do not plan to fail, but failing to plan for contingencies can be just as fatal. Also, new procedures are often overly optimistic about what is and is not possible. Plan for bridges from the old to the new and plan for detours in the roadway when you encounter quicksand or mountains of resistance.

9

THE IMPLEMENTERS AND INTERNAL AUDITS

As alluded to earlier, the most effective method for implementing ISO 9001 in most companies is a cross-functional steering committee. The importance of the steering committee cannot be stressed enough: It can make or break an ISO 9001 implementation. The keys to success include the following:

- Recruit members from diverse backgrounds and disciplines throughout the company. Do not use the same management committee that is tagged for every ad-hoc assignment that comes along.
- Recruit members from all levels, especially those who are most vocal and most likely to stimulate creative ideas.
- Do not try to select a purely harmonious group. A little bit of controversy helps the thought processes and avoids "groupthink," in which everyone agrees on everything.
- Invite members of management only when you need their help with a specific issue or you want to report on progress. If the group is empowered and has a clear charter, you will not need permission or forgiveness on a regular basis.
- Change the makeup of the committee when change is warranted. The process of ISO 9001 implementation may take six months to two years. In all likelihood, you will not end up with the same group

that you started with. Some members will not be comfortable with the committee and some will change job assignments. Some will grow restless and some will try to take control. Accept changing membership in stride.

- Keep the membership between five and nine people. Any more than that will not be able to get anything done. Any fewer than five may put too much work on individuals. Remember, you are trying to minimize the impact on workflow. I constantly remind committee members that their primary tasks come first, but their committee duties must be part of their workday, not an afterthought.

- Meet once per week for one hour. Do not routinely let the meeting go beyond the time limit. During particularly intense efforts, such as internal auditing training, the meetings may be scheduled for longer periods. Everyone should have, and is expected to do, homework outside the meeting.

- Have a chairperson who sets the agenda and forces the group to stick to it. The chairperson may also be the guardian of the implementation schedule and may regularly remind the committee of the progress they are making within the agreed-on schedule.

- Have a scribe who is charged with recording and publishing the meeting minutes and action items in a timely fashion.

- Divide (or subdivide) the five clauses of ISO 9001 among the committee members. Each should be responsible for those that are logically part of his or her job. The rest should be assigned to those who are interested in the topic or who have special talents (i.e., training might be assigned to someone who has teaching experience). The assignment of these elements does not necessarily mean the assigned individuals must write procedures. However, they are responsible for volunteering the help needed to get the procedures finished and audited.

- Meet with top management to establish the quality policy and quality objectives. If these elements already exist, ensure they are currently applicable and that the committee is empowered to implement them.

- Use ad-hoc committees to tackle particularly difficult areas. Documentation often requires a great deal of research and dissection to determine if your control systems are effective and compliant. Establishing customer satisfaction criteria may warrant another ad-hoc assignment.

- Expose the committee to as much training as they can absorb in every aspect of the QMS, as they will be the champions and spokespersons for the QMS and for ISO 9001 within their areas of influence. They may also grow to become permanent members of a quality improvement team.

- The leadership of the committee may not necessarily be just one person. A capable consultant may direct the meetings for the first few months, until everyone is comfortable with their assignments and roles. The quality representative may logically chair the committee. However, I have seen successful groups that rotated the leadership to keep the group dynamic and interested.

- Especially in the early stages, much of the planning work may be done behind closed doors, but the jobholders must be involved in the development process as much as possible. Have regular company meetings in which the steering committee shares their progress and milestones with everyone. Regularly reward the committee with appropriate expressions of appreciation, such as a luncheon or a field trip. Celebrate significant milestones with everyone.

SUCCESSFUL INTERNAL AUDITING

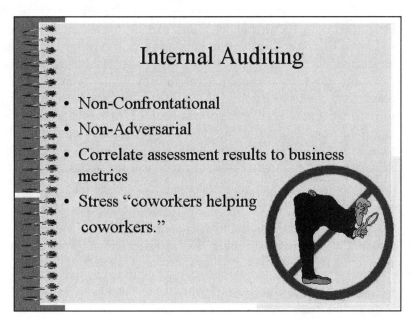

Having lived the evolution from quality control to quality assurance to problem avoidance, I'm not sure exactly when we discovered the need for innovative process conformance control. Because the release of ISO 9001 and the move away from punitive controls both blossomed in the last decade of the 20th Century, both deserve credit for the evolution of internal auditing.

As we have seen, the nonprescriptive verbiage contained within the five clauses of the ISO 9001 standard suggests that you document the processes that make you successful in some form that can be communicated to all of the process owners, operate within those process procedures, and then implement objective methods to ensure that those procedures are being followed. The key method that the standard suggests for compliance is a program of ongoing, nonconfrontational internal audits. The ISO 9001 internal auditing methodology is a proactive process of identifying whether the procedures you have documented are being followed and are effective. This approach is a dramatic departure from the detective and punitive auditing that classically trained quality professionals have used since the beginning of the Industrial Revolution. Internal auditing is coworkers helping coworkers to ensure process efficacy, as opposed to policemen "writing up and shooting down" violators. Internal auditing is the assessment of processes, not the criticism of people. Proponents of internal auditing are proving every day that fixing problems is much easier and more cost-effective than punishing people.

The other dramatic difference between internal auditing and most conventional methods of conformance monitoring is that internal auditing goes beyond providing statistical failure data and sets the stage for a culture of continual improvement. When performed properly, internal auditing can be one of the most efficacious tools for continual improvement available. I have facilitated many successful ISO 9000 implementations, trained scores of auditors, and audited hundreds of companies. The benefits of internal auditing are, without doubt, the most compelling reasons to implement an effective QMS in your company or for implementing internal auditing as a compliance tool.

ISO 9000:2000 (3.9.1) provides this definition of internal auditing:

A systematic independent and documented process for obtaining audit evidence and evaluating it objectively to determine the extent to which audit criteria are fulfilled.

The definition is somewhat convoluted, so let's dissect it to clarify its intent and meaning.

A Systematic, Independent, and Documented Process

Internal auditing must be conducted systematically: There must be an auditing schedule based on criticality of processes and previous experience about which areas are subject to process variability. Independence requires that the auditors be from areas other than those being audited. To ensure objectivity, there should be no conflicts of interest. The internal audit procedure must be documented. That documentation would typically include all steps of the audit process, the audit schedule, implementation, corrective action, follow-up, and criteria for training and certifying internal auditors.

Obtaining Audit Evidence

In the context of internal auditing, obtaining audit evidence is the methodical examination of a business process and the collection of data supporting the observations of the auditors. First, the process is examined by interviewing those who conduct the process on a regular basis for an explanation of how (in their own words) the process works. Their replies are compared to the written process procedures and deviations are noted. Next, the trail of paperwork or electronic data that the process generates is examined to determine if it matches the written procedures and if it is consistent with the verbal explanations given by the process operators. Again, any deviations are noted. Deviations are documented as "should be" and "is" conditions.

The following is an example of a deviation or finding:

> Procedure 5-01, Document Control, states that "All reproduction requests are approved by a supervisor before being presented for processing by the Document Clerk." Document Clerk stated that she sometimes signs the requests when a supervisor is busy. The Document Clerk examined 15 Documentation Requests and found four that were not signed, and three of those were approved.

In the example, the auditor read the procedure being audited, interviewed the person who usually operates the process, and searched for objective evidence that the process was being followed as it was documented. In performing the audit there was only an objective examination of the process. In the documentation of the audit, there is only a factual statement of the observations and the evidence. The root cause of the process variation is obviously critical to your business success. For this introduction, we need note only that the audit was conducted objectively, it focused on the process and documentation, and data was collected without accusation or condemnation of the individuals interviewed.

Evaluating It Objectively

After noting the "should be" and the "is" conditions, the auditor(s) form an expert opinion about the effectiveness of the process for the purpose stated in the written procedure. This evaluation forms the basis for the audit report and any required corrective action requests. These documents will be transmitted to the appropriate managers for explanation, resolution, and any root-cause analysis dictated by the complexity of the issues.

Determine the Extent to Which Audit Criteria Are Fulfilled

As we discuss the qualifications for an internal auditor, it becomes clear that a key attribute is an analytical personality. The most effective internal auditors have a little bit of Sherlock Holmes in their makeup; that is, they can follow a thread of a clue and develop a deductive analysis of any given situation. This trait is key to assessing the effectiveness of what was observed during an internal audit and to presenting an objective body of evidence and determining the extent to which audit criteria are fulfilled.

Let's look at what might be stated as the purpose of the example cited earlier.

Procedure 5-01: Document Control Purpose: This procedure controls the issuance of documents that are used to manufacture our products. Due to the critical nature of our products, precise document control is essential to ensure that our customers receive only the most current revisions of our product.

A well-trained internal auditor would analyze any noted deviations from procedure, read the purposes stated in the written procedure, and conclude that the gravity of the deviation is more significant than a few missed signatures. Precise document control is stated as essential to business success, not just a check-and-balance exercise. In this example, the generality of the procedure may not be effective enough for the stated intent, the process operators may not be trained sufficiently in the criticality of what they are doing, or the procedure may be so cumbersome that it does not lend itself to being followed each and every time it is used.

Determination of which of these options is truly the case will be made by root-cause analysis.[1] For the purpose of this definition, the internal auditor must provide an expert opinion of whether the process being audited meets its stated purpose to guide those who will examine the deviation and affect corrective action.

If we put all the pieces back together, internal auditing can be defined as a systematic, independent, documented process for obtaining audit evidence and evaluating it objectively to determine the extent to which audit criteria are fulfilled, or as the objective appraisal of business processes by analytical observers who are chartered only to uncover objective evidence of process effectiveness. We continually refer to the definitions of internal auditing as we reinforce the case for proactive modeling of the continual improvement process. We also refer to the definition when detailing methodology of internal auditing. In fact, we continue to refer to the definitions throughout the process so that we can keep the perspective of what internal auditing is and why we need to use it.

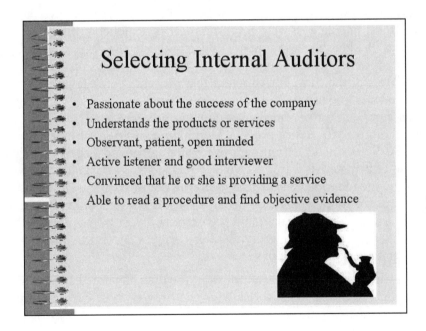

Selecting Internal Auditors

- Passionate about the success of the company
- Understands the products or services
- Observant, patient, open minded
- Active listener and good interviewer
- Convinced that he or she is providing a service
- Able to read a procedure and find objective evidence

1. *Root-cause analysis is a generic term for an investigation into the absolute fundamental cause of a problem, deviation, nonconformity, or other issue, until the true "root" cause is found. This process prevents repeatedly fixing the same symptomatic problem.*

Now that we have defined internal auditing, we will explore its practical applications and methods. As with every aspect of ISO 9001 implementation, there is no single approach that is prescribed or directed. Internal auditing must fit your company culture and make sense for your business size and environment. In very small companies, I have trained every employee to be an internal auditor. In some large companies, the culture requires a separate internal audit group, very much like financial auditors. Still other companies find it cost-effective to use consultants as paid "internal" auditors. The approach you use is unimportant to the training. An effective internal auditor should follow the same steps, regardless of his or her function within an organization.

However you plan to conduct internal audits, it cannot be overstated that their only purpose is to verify that you are following your own procedures. They are called *compliance audits* and they differ from classic financial and quality audits in that, when conducted correctly, they are nonconfrontational, are not "witch hunts," and are designed to objectively evaluate procedures rather than to discover and punish individuals who violate business rules. In nearly 30 years of auditing, I have discovered, over and over, that most people who were producing errors or nonconformities were not fully trained in their jobs, did not understand what was expected of them, or were presented with no risks for performing the process incorrectly.

Most of the time, I have found that process operators have no written procedures, the procedures are neither adequate nor correct, the operators have not been trained in the procedures, and there have been no objective evaluations of the actual process. Developing a QMS that meets the tenets of ISO 9001 will, by definition, drive your company to be process driven instead of being crisis driven. It will encourage you to train all process operators and to identify risks for those who will not own their own processes and rewards for those who are contributors to the continual improvement process. Internal auditing will, in a proactive and positive way, ensure that all the hard work you put into developing a viable QMS is not wasted in costly noncompliance and lack of execution.

The Audit Checklist

- Turn statements into questions.
  - If it is not a documented procedure or an ISO 9001 clause, it is not an auditable item.
- Decide where you need to be.
- List specific items to look for.
- Leave plenty of room for notes and comments.

Let's look at how to verify that you are doing it.

Assume that we have scheduled an internal audit of Uncle Gino's Pizza-to-Go pizza-making process. The first step is to define the process being audited. In this case, it is the entire process of making and delivering a pizza. We schedule the audit with the store owner and select a team of internal auditors. They contact the owner and arrange a mutually agreeable time for the audit. Because this is the first time the process is being audited, they will have to develop an audit checklist.

Based on the written process procedure, the first few items on the checklist should look something like the following:

- What is the first step taken when a customer calls?
- When the information is entered, what is the second step?
- What items should be verified with the customer?
- Audit 10 samples from the audit history from the last two weeks. Verify that all information is complete. Note the phone numbers of the records that were audited.
- What cleanliness step is taken next?

The employees being audited would be expected to describe, in their own words, the steps detailed in the written procedures. They should walk the auditors through the process and be able to provide the information requested. In a mature audit, we would probably just ask an experienced operator to describe the process of making and delivering a pizza and note any deviations in the checklist. Deviations from procedure are noted on the checklist and, after the audit, become nonconformities documented in an audit report. These nonconformities are then forwarded to the store owner in the form of CARs. The CARs describe the breakdown in the process and ask that the recipient respond to the following questions:

- What was the actual problem?
- Why did it occur?
- What steps will be taken to prevent recurrence?

At this point, auditing becomes profoundly different from traditional quality audits and inspections. First, we are asking the responsible manager to diagnose a problem with a process, not to find faults with his or her people. Once the root cause of the problem has been found, we do not close the books and move onto the next problem. Instead, we require that the process owner demonstrate that steps have been taken to preclude recurrence of the same or similar process problems. In a well-run audit, a closed-loop system of cause, effect, and corrective action is followed to its practical and cost-effective conclusion.

This brings closure to the three elements of ISO 9001: Write down what you do, do what you write down, and make sure you are doing it. For more in-depth help developing an internal auditing program, along with examples of mock audits, audit reports, corrective actions, and auditor certification programs, consult the author's book, *Successful Internal Auditing to ISO 9000* (Prentice Hall, 1999).

10

SELECTING A REGISTRAR

Forming a partnership with the organization that will perform your ISO 9001 certification and surveillance audits is a critical step for any company. Once the initial certification audit is performed, the certificate of compliance issued to your company is typically neither transferable nor assignable to another registrar.[1] There are wide variations in the credentials of registrars, their fee structures, and their abilities. A reputable registrar will be working for your success and to minimize the time spent at your facilities. A "bargain" registrar, or one who is not familiar with your industry, may give you a low price estimate and then have to spend extra days overcoming a lack of knowledge or incompetence. There are several key factors to consider when selecting a registrar.

Like your consultant, your registrar is your partner in success. Although registrars are ethically bound to only perform conformance audits,[2] as business people who are taking your money, they are also critically invested in

1. *In recent years, the competitive field of certification registration has led to marketing strategies in which a registrar will offer to accept the certification of a rival registrar. This practice is neither good nor bad. If the offer appears to be too good to be true, it probably is.*
2. *Registrars may not give consulting advice, although many reputable registrars provide suggested improvement data in their audit findings.*

ensuring your success. It makes no business sense for them to have to recommend that you cannot be certified. The difference between registrars is how diligent they are in ensuring your conformance.

Any registrar worthy of consideration performs conformance audits in accordance with the guidelines they are ethically bound to follow as dictated by the bodies that certify them. For instance, the Registrar Accreditation Board (RAB) in the United States, the Dutch Council (RvA), and the Brazilian INMETRO, among others, may certify a registrar. They may also hold credentials from automobile manufacturers to audit to QS9000 or from QuestForum to audit to TL 9000. Each of these bodies sets forth audit standards that the registrars must follow, and each of these bodies performs regular conformance audits of the registrars to determine if they are operating within their guidelines.[3]

Unfortunately, there has been a wide range of ethical commitment across registrars. The stiff competition, the profit motive, and the need to satisfy customers has caused a number of registrars to compromise their commitment to perform due diligence. Some use contract auditors who are not well trained. Some simply peddle certificates with little ethical commitment.

Europe is several years ahead of the rest of the world in the evolution of ISO 9001. There has been some corruption and fraud reported and a number of companies have dropped their certifications because there has been a decrease in overall integrity of audits in a few European countries. Hopefully, we are learning preventive lessons from these reports and not propagating mediocrity. The 2000 revision will also, hopefully, help curtail substandard compliance certifications.

Some registrars are sponsored by industry groups and have no ties to the EU or any recognized notified bodies. Some industries have "sector-specific" standards, such as TL 9000 and AS 9001. Registrars working with these standards are no more or less effective as auditors; they just have their own set of standards, which adds even more variation to the service you might receive from a registrar. If you are becoming certified to comply with a requirement of your industry, you may not have a choice in registrars.

I am a small businessperson and an entrepreneur and I do not want to stifle up-and-coming registrars, but I would perform extensive research on any small registrar before I would recommend them to a client. If you have no external input (consultant, support group, industry group), I would start by soliciting bids from the major registrars. They all advertise in industry

---

3. *ISO 19011 (ISO 10011) is the standard used to set criteria for auditors and registrars.*

trade journals such as *Quality Progress* and *Quality Digest*. Both ASQ (which publishes *Quality Progress*) and Quality Digest also have search engines on their Web sites to help you locate registrars. Once you have received your quotes, call the list of references that the potential registrars provide. Discuss the services that were provided, the compliance to schedule, the audit experience, the problems, and any anecdotes about the experience. The references will very often give you a great deal of useful information that may help you with your implementation and certification process.

Before you sign up with a registrar, also make sure that you have a working relationship that complements your business culture. If you are an open-collar, laid-back organization and your registrar is spit-and-polish with no sense of humor, you may be just as disappointed as if you would be if he or she did a poor job of auditing.

11

CUSTOMER FOCUS AND RESULTS MEASUREMENT

This chapter looks at the three dramatically positive additions to ISO 9001. First is the inclusion of requirements to determine the needs of the customer, act on them, and evaluate how effectively your organization has met those needs and expectations. The second addition is the focus on quality statistics as a factor that affects the company's bottom line. The third positive inclusion is the requirement for continual process improvement.

WHAT IS A CUSTOMER?

In one way or another, we all have customers. It is most often the end user of our product or service. It can also be an internal customer who is the next person in the line of process evolution in your organization. It may also be an obscure customer. For instance, in a public school, is the customer the student, the parents, industry, or society? ISO 9004 uses the term *interested parties* to indicate other organizations that are indirectly impacted by your business, such as regulatory agencies or your local community. These can also be considered customers. When building a system of customer focus, it is wise to identify all possible customers and deal with each in order of their importance to your business.

What Is ISO 9001's Customer Focus?

Once you know who your customer is, ISO 9001:2000, Clause 5.2 (Customer Focus), comes into play. It states, "Top management shall ensure that customer requirements are determined and are met with the aim of enhancing customer satisfaction." Subclause 5.5.2.c places on the management representative the duty of "ensuring the promotion of awareness of customer requirements throughout the organization." Subclause 5.6.2.b states that "customer feedback" should be a part of management review. Subclause 5.6.3.b states that "improvement of product related to customer requirements" should be part of management review output. Subclause 6.1.b states "the organization shall determine and provide resources to enhance customer satisfaction by meeting customer requirements." Subclause 7.2 is entirely about customer-related processes, including determination of requirements, review of requirements, and customer communication. A really key requirement in 7.2.2 is "Where the customer provides no documented statement of requirement, the customer requirements shall be confirmed by the organization before acceptance." Subclause 7.5.4 deals exclusively with customer property. Subclause 8.2.1 (Customer Satisfaction) states, "As one of the measurements of the performance of the quality management system the organization shall monitor information relating to customer perception as to whether the organization has met customer requirements. The methods for obtaining and using this information shall be determined." Subclause 8.4 (Analysis of Data) includes this: "The analysis of data shall provide information relating to a) customer satisfaction." Subclause 8.5.2 (Corrective Action) includes this: "A documented procedure shall be established to define requirements for a) reviewing nonconformities (including customer complaints)."

In all, in the 14 pages of ISO 9001, the word *customer* is used 48 times. That sends a loud, clear message that a company that is compliant with ISO 9001 should be customer focused.

What Does This Mean to My Organization?

First you need to determine if you have built an organization based on customer need or on a "field of dreams" (if you build it, they will come). If you are a distribution company, you most likely provide products that your customers have a stated demand for. If you are a computer manufacturer, you may believe that, as long as you design systems with more speed and functionality, you will have a never-ending demand for your product. If you are an insurance company, you might offer products designed by actuaries and presented as the only alternatives that your consumers may have.

The reason for first "typing" your company is not judgmental; it is a precursor to determining how much of a cultural shift you have in front of you to become customer focused. Companies that provide products that are in high demand often neglect to consider all issues of their customer base (until the market goes flat). Others that should be totally responsive to customer needs, like a contract manufacturing operation, may have already built customer focus into their infrastructure. The following content of an effective customer focus program is applied universally. The pain of implementation depends on how badly you want to grow and prosper.

- Determine customer needs. By some fact-finding methodology, determine exactly what your customer's and potential customers' stated needs are as they relate to the product or service you provide.

- Determine customer expectations. By some fact-finding methodology, determine exactly what your customer's and potential customers' expectations are as they relate to the product or service you provide. Expectations are often unstated, so it is up to you to find out what a customer needs but often does not communicate. For instance, if you are an automotive service center, you might give the best service in the world, but you may have never considered the market of customers that can only bring their cars in at night or on weekends.

- Communicate customers' stated and implied needs to everyone in the organization. This should not be a secret. If everyone is vested in meeting the stated and implied needs, there is a higher chance of them being met than if workers work in a vacuum.

- Communicate with the customer. Open channels of communication and make the customer a part of your organization. Too often, customers only get to speak with a salesperson, engineers talk to engineers, and quality people talk to quality people and there is no common communication. This leads to mixed messages and priorities driving your ability to supply products or services. Perhaps your customers want a single point of contact for all issues or maybe they need weekly meetings to track project status. Communication is always "the problem to the answer."

- Make it clear what is being sold. If your customers buy part number 1234 from you, it is incumbent on you to provide sufficient data to the customer so that they know exactly what they are buying. This could be a complete technical specification sheet for an electronics system or a list of expected outcomes provided by a consultant to his or her clients. Verbal and incomplete data are setups for unhappy customers and, perhaps, litigation.

- Gather results. Absence of complaints does not demonstrate customer satisfaction. No news can hurt much more than bad news. It is in your best interest to find some methodology to obtain continual and objective feedback from your clients. This might be in the form of customer feedback cards, direct telephone inquiries, market surveys, or customer feedback meetings. Customer complaints and returned goods are treasure chests of information for helping you improve processes and customer satisfaction.
- Turn the results into data. Build statistical databases and trend charts based on the feedback data. Use the information to make informed decisions about new products, services, product improvements, service improvements, training, and marketing.
- Act on the data. Take action based on factual data. Improve processes, initiate training, and give customers feedback on what you are doing to improve your products or services.
- Do it continually. This is not a one-time exercise. It must be continual and never ending.

MEASURING RESULTS

Previous revisions of ISO 9000 suggested that organizations use "statistical techniques" to determine process effectiveness. Here we look at how the 2000 revision has moved quality statistics from the inspection department to positively driving the bottom line.

A football game without statistics would be meaningless. If coaches do not keep track of first downs, yards gained, play effectiveness, and score, they cannot continually make the key corrections needed to implement the most effective strategies. Companies that do not collect and track data on their processes cannot know what to improve. As in football's final score, monthly financial reports do not tell the whole story, and they are published too late to make any changes that can affect the outcome. Here we deal with measuring the effectiveness of ISO 9001 implementation so that midcourse corrections can be taken when necessary, and so leaders can continually monitor the amount of value they are receiving from the ISO 9001 journey.

Developing an effective family of measures is a formidable task for any company. First, we may not want more information than we are willing to deal with. Many mangers are keyed only to monthly financial numbers and have developed a method for manipulating the process each month to keep them in good stead with their higher managers. Introducing more revealing measures might hinder their ability to jockey resources and painful corrective steps may have to be implemented (finally!). Also, although we can often understand statistics in sports, they are somehow an abstraction in business. I have facilitated many brainstorming sessions in which the room was dead quiet when I would challenge workers and managers to come up with meaningful measures for the processes they operate.

At the opposite extreme, a number of years ago I toured a large aerospace company that had challenged every group in every department to develop meaningful measures of their own performance and to post those measures every week outside their work area for all to see. I was most taken with the ladies in the copy center. They had developed methods to track the number of scrap pages, the number of minutes of machine downtime, and the response time from request to delivery of copies, and they had plotted graphs of their increased performance levels. They had evidence of how they had provided the copy machine manufacturer with downtime data that caused the manufacturer to speed up its service request response time and to store parts that often failed on site so the copy center could maintain a continually improving response time. What a concept: A copy center that focused on the needs of the internal customer and improved their processes through self-evaluation!

What to Measure

There is no simple answer about what you should measure to indicate performance. The answer depends on your ability to quantify the processes you perform and measure their outcome against some set of standards. The one certain answer is that the folks who operate the processes are the ones who know best what to measure and what the norms are. Often, they do not want to measure anything, again, because it impairs their ability to resolve problems practically. For very complex companies, a facilitator is almost a necessity to coach you through the process of developing a family of meaningful measures. For smaller companies, decide what key indicators you must know to ensure that your customers' needs are being met. For instance, your key business indicators may be the number of units shipped on time compared to promised dates, the number of service calls received versus number of products shipped, infant mortality versus number of components, and so on. Once these key business indicators are derived, you can then challenge the process owners to find their own measures that provide backup data to these key business indicators. As a warning, however, you must be prepared to take decisive corrective action when the indicators are negative and you must be prepared to reward those who drive results positively beyond stated expectations.

With the 2000 revision, the imperative to collect and use meaningful data has been dramatically expanded. There are requirements to measure customer satisfaction and to monitor and measure activities to run the QMS. Measurable quality objectives must be measured and action taken on the data. Training effectiveness must be evaluated. In other words, management by fact is no longer an option in the world of ISO 9001:2000.

When you start your strategic quality initiatives, you should benchmark current performance levels and then continually monitor how the implementation effort impacts the key business indicators. Use this data to make changes to your starting lineup, correct your playbook, and pat your star performers on the back before they suit up for the next game.

Make it Worthwhile

All efforts for collecting process metrics will be pointless if they are not tied directly to business performance measures. Collecting data without demonstrating how it directly relates to the key indicators that all levels of management use as business barometers is a waste of time. For instance, reporting incoming defect rates is just an exercise unless the reporting is tied to production schedule performance metrics. In other words, who cares if incoming parts are late or defective unless they impact planned production schedules? What is the point of collecting this data unless purchasing uses it to evaluate suppliers and take corrective actions? One of the key tenets of "Quality as a Profit Center" is using statistical data to drive process improvement which, in turn, drives increased profitability.

CONTINUAL PROCESS IMPROVEMENT

Never confuse motion with action.
—Benjamin Franklin

The third major change to ISO 9001 is the requirement to make continual process improvement a key element in any viable QMS. This section explores how such a "soft" requirement can be made into an enterprisewide success model.

It has always been my position that the internal auditing required by ISO 9000:1994 inevitably results in continual improvement and a well-implemented QMS. Many disagreed and, in the 2000 revision, Clause 8.5.1 was added, specifically requiring a continual improvement initiative. This must be manifested in continual improvement of the QMS, processes, and other external relationships.

There is no published road map to continual improvement. It is very much a series of processes individual and unique to your organization. It starts with the quality policy and quality objectives. What is the desire of top management in regard to continual improvement? Is it absolutely core to every fiber of their being or is it merely an acceptable by-product of quality management? The answers to these two questions determine how it is implemented in your organization and how effective it is. Once they are answered they need to become part of the strategic planning. Each business unit must examine what continual improvement means to them and how they will measure it. ("Management by fact" rears its ugly head again!)

Figure 11.1 illustrates the continual improvement model. It is used again in Chapter 13 as the process approach model. It is not an accident that the logic that is true for the process of building a product or delivering a service is the same one that is used to continually improve them. In fact, they should be inseparable.

Continual improvement always begins with data. That information is either an external input, such as a strategic plan element or a preventive action suggestion, or is the result of data collected from monitoring processes. In either case, that data must be acknowledged as viable information (as opposed to anecdotal or unsubstantiated information). It must be internalized and become knowledge, instead of tables of information. The true meaning of the data must be reached by consensus as the result of scientific discovery, mitigated by competence and experience. Before any action is taken, agreement must be reached on what the data means. Here's an example.

I was quality manager at a company that manufactured computers to measure temperature and pressure in petrochemical flow applications.

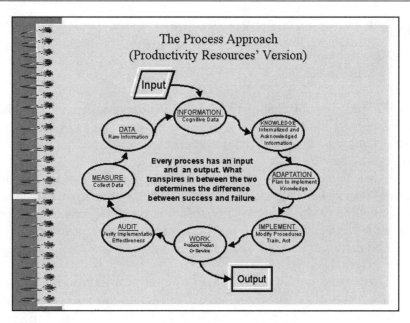

FIGURE 11.1. The continual improvement model.

There were repeated reports of field failures in the expensive memory chips of the computer. Manufacturing engineering was pulling their hair out trying to determine if it was a handling problem, a design problem, or a manufacturer's problem. They made the decision to discontinue using a particular manufacturer's memory chips, but the problem persisted. One day, as I was taking an objective look at the entire process, I discovered that the test technician had a drawer full of memory chips and when one failed, he would pull another from his collection and keep replacing them until he found one that worked. The others went back in the drawer. Because memory chips are sensitive to static and he was not using the proper protection procedures, the field failures were an inevitable result of his mishandling and his zeal to save money on memory chips. The moral of the story is that engineering was making decisions on the basis of anecdotal data instead of scientific discovery. Instead of turning data into knowledge, they turned it into wasted effort.

Once the data is internalized, it has to be adapted to the particular application. Essentially, it means that we now have valid data, but what are we going to do with it? In continual improvement, prioritization of need and resource availability should greatly determine the course of action. If an opportunity for improvement is found in an area such as the incident with the memory chips, an action plan would be immediately implemented. If it is a valid reason to build a new facility, a great deal more planning is necessary before action is taken. If it is a reinforcement of an already planned improvement, it might be integrated into the existing plan.

The next step is to implement the needed procedural changes, add needed resources, train the process owners, and then prepare to act. This implementation phase is the actionable result of continual improvement. Next comes the action that the process requires. This might be a pilot run or a beta test to validate the internalized knowledge used to develop the revised process. It may even be actual implementation if testing is not required. An audit or verification process follows implementation. As a result of auditing or verification, objective data is collected. That data then becomes the raw information to begin the continual improvement process anew.

Where, When, and How?

Continual improvement should be implemented in every process in the organization from management to customer satisfaction. It should be an ongoing event that is planned into every activity. It might be in the form of a formal preventive action program. It might be line items from the strategic plan. It could be the continual analysis of data regarding product, services, customers, suppliers, processes, analysis, trends, technology, or evolving cultural shifts. Above all, continual improvement must be tied directly to key business performance metrics. The outcome of continual improvement must be enhancement of strategic business objectives; otherwise it is a waste of time.

12

CONCURRENT AND INDUSTRY SEGMENT STANDARDS

The original ISO 9000 standard has spawned a number of guideline standards and a series of industry sector-specific standards based on the international standard. For instance, the automotive industry incorporated ISO 9000 into a seven-volume series of standards known as QS9000, which are mandatory for first-tier suppliers to the major automobile manufacturers. Also, many countries have released it in their own language or using a different numbering schema. In the United States, the American National Standards Institute (ANSI) and the ASQ have released ISO 9000 as Q9000. It differs only in the American and British spellings of words.

Each company must use diligence to determine if they are compelled by customer edict or by need for competitive position to become certified to any of these standards. This chapter lists many of the ISO 9000 series of standards and the industry spin-offs with a basic description of each. If you need more information about the ISO family of standards, you can look them up on the official ISO Web site at *www.iso.ch*. You can search by number for the remaining standards on any Internet search engine and find a host of data about each one.

Note that any ISO standard supporting ISO 9001 that is dated prior to 2001 is not current with the 2000 revision to ISO 9001. These supporting documents should not be used as implementation guidelines for ISO 9001:2000.

ISO 9000:2000	Quality Management Systems: Fundamentals and Vocabulary
ISO 9000:1994	(Superseded by ISO 9000:2000)
ISO 9001:2000	Quality Management Systems: Requirements
ISO 9001:1994	Quality Systems: Model for Quality Assurance in Design, Development, Production, Installation, and Servicing (coexists with ISO 9001:2000 through December 2003)
ISO 9002:1994	Quality Systems: Model for Quality Assurance in Production, Installation, and Servicing (coexists with ISO 9001:2000 through December 2003)
ISO 9003:1994	Quality Systems: Model for Quality Assurance in Final Inspection and Test (coexists with ISO 9001:2000 through December 2003)
ISO 9000-1:1994	Quality Management and Quality Assurance Standards – Part 1: Guidelines for selection and use
ISO 9000-2:1997	Quality Management and Quality Assurance Standards – Part 2: Generic guidelines for the application of ISO 9001, 9002, and 9003
ISO 9000-3:1997	Quality Management and Quality Assurance Standards – Part 3: Guidelines for the application of ISO 9001 to computer software
ISO 9000-4:1993	Quality management and Quality Assurance Standards – Part 4: Guidelines for reliability programs
ISO 9004-1:1994	(Replaced with ISO 9004:2000)
ISO 9004-2:1991	Quality Management and Quality System Elements – Part 2: Guidelines for services
ISO 9004-3:1993	Quality Management and Quality System Elements – Part 3: Guidelines for processed materials
ISO 9004-4:1993	Quality Management and Quality System Elements – Part 4: Guidelines for quality improvement
ISO 10005:1995	Quality Management: Guide for Quality Planning
ISO 10006:1997	Quality management: Guide for Project Management
ISO 10007:1995	Quality Management: Guide for Configuration Management

ISO 10011-1:1990	Guidelines for Auditing Quality Systems – Part 1: Auditing
ISO 10011-2:1991	Guidelines for Auditing Quality Systems – Part 2: Qualification criteria for auditors
ISO 10011-3:1991	Guidelines for Auditing Quality Systems – Part 3: Management of auditing programs
ISO 10012-1:1992	Quality Assurance Requirements for Measuring Equipment – Part 1: Metrology programs
ISO 10012-2:1997	Quality Assurance Requirements for Measuring Equipment – Part 2: Guidelines for control of measurement processes
ISO 10013:1995	Guidelines for Developing Quality Manuals
ISO 10014:1998	Guidelines for Managing the Economics of Quality
ISO 10015:1999	Quality Management: Guidelines for training
ISO 13485:1996	Quality Systems – Medical Devices: Particular requirements for ISO 9001
ISO 13488:1996	Quality Systems – Medical Devices: Particular requirements for ISO 9002
ISO/DIS 19011	(Planned replacement for ISO 10011 and the ISO 14000 series of auditing guidelines)
ISO 14000	Environmental Systems: Environmental Management Systems similar to the ISO 9000 series of standards
ISO 14969	Quality Systems – Medical Devices: Guidelines for the application of ISO 13485 and ISO 13488
AS9001	ISO 9001-based quality system for the aerospace industry
QS9000	ISO 9000-based quality system for the automotive industry
ISO 16949:1999	Quality Systems – Automotive Suppliers: Particular requirements for the application of ISO 9001:1994
TL9000	ISO 9000-based quality system for the telecommunications industry
TE9000	Special standard for tooling equipment for the QS9000 standards
SA8000	Social Accountability Standard: Social responsibilities in business practices

All of these standards are in constant revision. This list was accurate as of Spring 2001. The non-ISO standards are sponsored and controlled by various industry and governmental organizations. They may or may not follow and stay current with the ISO 9000 series of standards. ISO 14000 is the first spin-off that moved entirely out of the quality arena to cover environmental issues. SA8000 is the first industry standard to tackle the subjective topic of social accountability in business practices. You can find qualified registrars to certify your company in any of the ISO standards (ISO 9001, 9002, 9003, and 14001) and in the commercial spin-off standards (QS, AS, TE, SA, etc.).

13

KEY SUCCESS STRATEGIES

This chapter summarizes the key points made thus far in earlier chapters, highlights the critical success factors, and adds anecdotal and experiential information to help implementers make the process of ISO 9001 implementation as simple and rewarding as it can be.

It is critical at this point that you are intensely introspective about your company and your culture before drafting an initiative. You might not be able to separate fact from fiction without the help of a consultant. You might not be allowed to tamper with certain positions and processes. You might be able to devote a lot of time and resources to this effort or you might be forced to work on this after hours with minimum support. Each of these factors helps determine how the initiative is put together. You might wind up with a prioritized shopping list or a total re-engineering effort. You can't force change. Some issues will be within your providence to affect and some will not. Keep the following posted conspicuously for your implementation team:

The Consultant's Prayer
May I have the courage to change that which must be changed,
May I have the patience to accept that which I cannot change,
And may I have the wisdom to know the difference.

Let's start our review of the key success strategies by reviewing the first two steps of ISO 9001: Write down what you do, and do what you write down.

WRITE DOWN WHAT YOU DO

As with nebulous business terms such as quality and performance, the understanding of ISO 9001's definition of a process requires us to reach an agreement in meaning, context, and usage. In ISO 9001 parlance, business processes are the steps necessary to successfully operate the value delivery system. That is, for ISO 9001, each step from a customer's inquiry through delivery of the final product or service and determination of customer satisfaction is part of the business process approach. Some companies choose to exclude the actual sales and accounting functions and the human resources organization from their ISO 9001 QMS.

There are arguments that work either way for including everyone in an organization or for defining the support functions outside the QMS. Once you have chosen a path, the steps for identifying and documenting processes are the same. Previously, I presented the example of document reproduction as a process or process step. Other common processes include quotations, receiving and entering an order, control of test and measuring equipment, control of software revisions, and the actual steps of producing your particular product or service. You must clearly define the processes and their interactions within your company and document them. If you have not already taken the time to adequately define your business processes, you may be so invested in performing convoluted and redundant activities each day that you are unsure of what you are doing and why you are doing it. At this point, the assessment of the effectiveness of your processes might appear adequate. However, when you begin using internal auditing, you will likely find many opportunities for improvement.

The Process Approach

ISO 9001 makes reference to "the process approach" to managing an organization. There is a graphic representation in ISO 9001 that is based on the classic PDCA cycle.[1] Figure 13.1 moves a bit beyond PDCA and the one in ISO 9000 and offers some more food for thought as you ponder your key success strategies.

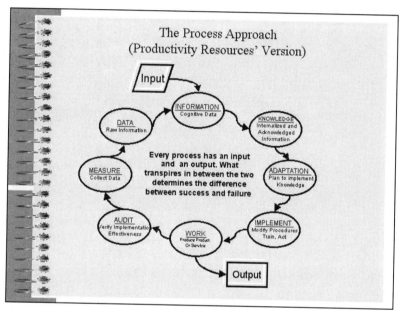

FIGURE 13.1. The process approach.

It starts with each process having an input, usually in the form of data (drawings, work instructions, procedures, etc.). The second step is to turn that cognitive data into knowledge. That is, someone must internalize the data to ensure all requirements are present before proceeding. This might include data from similar processes, standards, statutory issues, capacity, environment, and so on. Once all the data is collected and intellectualized, it can be adapted to an implementation plan. The plan is then integrated into the workflow, along with any necessary training or workflow modification.

---

1. *PDCA is an acronym for plan, do, check, and act, a classic process model.*

The work is accomplished and an output is produced. The result is then audited to verify effectiveness of the process and key measurements are taken. Data is collected as a result of the audit and that data becomes the input to the continual improvement of the process. It sounds relatively intuitive, but most of the more than 430 companies that I have worked with over the last 31 years had poorly defined business processes, regardless of the type of business or the size. Instead of using a PDCA model, cadres of "problem solvers" continually search for the answer to this question: How can we ensure that our processes produce the desired result, repeatedly and profitably? Without clear definition of the processes, no matter how mundane the operation or how critical the product, the search for the Holy Grail pales compared to the search for effective business process controls.

Once again, the simplicity of ISO 9001 enables us to confront problems and break their convoluted and inexplicable horror down into definable operations with measurable outcomes. ISO 9001 uses the term *process approach* to define each step in the value delivery system. It challenges us to look at that which makes us successful and document the steps that a trained process operator would follow to achieve the desired outcome. The concept that each task we do in our work environment is (or should be) an auditable process is critical, so let's take a look at some processes.

Process 1: Making an Uncle Gino's Pizza-to-Go Pizza

Mission: To deliver to the customer a delicious, hot pizza of consistent quality, with the exact ingredients specified by the customer, within 30 minutes of receiving the order.

A Typical Business Process

- Hire some high school students who will work for minimum wage.
- Show them how to make a pizza a couple of times. Yell at them when they screw up.
- Spend the rest of your career answering customers' complaints and interviewing new students to replace those who couldn't follow your simple rules.

A Well-Documented Business Process

- Receive telephone order and type information into the data entry terminal. Confirm ingredients, size, and style with customer. Verify address and delivery location. Confirm price with customer.
- Wash hands and put on a new pair of latex gloves.
- Referring to the data entry readout, select the size and style of crust.
- Brush two ounces of olive oil evenly across the crust.
- Apply five one-ounce ladles of tomato sauce evenly across the crust.
- Select toppings and amount from the data entry readout and apply evenly per the sample photos.
- Place on the bake oven conveyor.
- Print customer receipt and staple to a box for the size pizza ordered.
- Stage the box at the end of the bake oven conveyor.
- Fill the remaining orders and check for accuracy.
- Locate the customer's address in the map book and note the location on the delivery ticket.
- As soon as the conveyor delivers the pizza, cut into 16 sections and box. Place the box in the hot pouch for delivery.
- Check the order again for accuracy.
- Drive to the customer's location. Obey all traffic laws.
- Review the order with the customer to ensure accuracy. Verify the delivery time with the customer and note it in the travel log.
- Count the money received and change given. Return to the restaurant.
- Clean the hot pouch and return it to the delivery staging area.
- Follow up in two hours with a phone call to ensure that the customer was satisfied with the pizza.

Most businesses would take the approach defined as a typical business process; that is, most companies do not take the time to define processes so that the critical path of making a product or producing a service is clearly delineated. The business manager would typically assume that everyone understands what a pizza looks like and how one is put together. He or she would also assume that employees would "just know" about personal hygiene, cash control, driving a delivery vehicle, and customer satisfaction: "After all, we've all had pizza delivered, haven't we?" In 18 steps, the task of making and delivering a pizza to order has gone from a mindless act of associated events with variable outcomes to an auditable, repeatable, manufacturing process that, when followed, ensures that the customer receives the exact product ordered, on time, and at the agreed-on price. Documenting this rote procedure creates a process that sets the stage for repeatability, measuring results, and identification of the critical process steps. If the process operators are trained in the procedure and held accountable for its outcome, the little time it took to document the procedure can be paid for in consistency, productivity, and repeat customer business. When we know what steps we are taking, we can change them and improve on them.

Obviously, documenting the procedure alone does not motivate a minimum-wage worker to grasp your vision and deliver a perfect pie every time. You could enforce the procedure by standing over the employees and yelling at them every time they miss a process step. You could dock their pay each time a customer complaint is received. You could also use quality objectives followed by internal auditing to ensure our success. In the Gino's Pizza-to-Go example, coworkers would be trained in and then systematically audit the 18 steps of the procedure. That is, they would examine the process, step by step, find evidence of compliance, document the results, and use the audit findings for corrective action and continual improvement. Auditing is discussed in more detail later.

Understanding the concept of processes is so critical that I want to share one more example of how poorly most of us define and document processes and how we are constantly disappointed in their outcome. Anyone who has children or was a child can relate to this example of the benefits of a well-defined process.

Think about how many times you've told your children to mow the grass. Were the results you obtained exactly what you expected? If you do not have children, think about the same scenario with your parents telling you to mow the grass. How many times were there missed spots, clippings not bagged, the mower left in the driveway, or the edging not done? Who trained you and your children to mow the grass? Hasn't it mostly always been by assumed observation and some intuitive sense of what a properly manicured lawn looked like? What would the process of mowing the grass look like if it were properly documented?

Process 2:   Mowing the Grass

Mission: To maintain a consistent appearance in the vegetation surrounding the house and to ensure a safe home environment, free from pest and rodent infestation.

- Put on heavy boots and safety glasses.
- Inspect the mower. Verify the air filter is clean and the blade is tight.
- Be sure the level adjustment is set properly and all wheels are at the same height.
- Check the engine oil. Add as necessary.
- Fill the gas tank. Go get gas if there is none in the gas can.
- Start the mower and mow in a logical sequence.
- Be sure to cut all areas that you can reach with the mower.
- Inspect the edger. Add gasoline/oil mixture. Check to be sure there is enough cutting line in the edger and that it is properly wound.
- Run the edger around all perimeter areas. Be careful not to damage flowers, trees, or decorative trim.
- Rake up excessive grass clippings. Place clippings in compost bin.
- Inspect your work and verify the job was done correctly. Report any damage that occurred during mowing and edging.
- Clean the edger and mower and return them and all tools to their storage spaces. Report any observed problems with the mower or edger.
- Keep track of when the oil needs changing in the mower and check for any signs of blade wear.
- Report any observed problems in the flower beds, trees, and shrubbery or with insect infestations.

Do we communicate our processes, or do we assume that people understand what is expected of them? If we are to be held responsible for our actions, they must be clearly communicated. They should be no more complex than necessary to clearly communicate the expected outcome to a trained operator. If you can make your process procedures no wordier than the Ten Commandments, and as easily understood, you have an auditable process!

IMPLEMENTING THE PROCESSES

The second step is to operate your company using the process procedures that you have developed. Again, I am stating the obvious. However, my experience has been that after endless hours of hard work by committees of caring employees, people either ignore the process procedures they wrote or go out of their way to find work-arounds to them. Now isn't that a contradiction? If you documented what you do, why would you circumvent your written procedures?

There are two common reasons. The first is that procedure writers who have not had the benefit of a facilitator experienced in process procedures will write procedures that document how they wished things work instead of what is actually happening. This is a common pitfall in ISO 9001 implementation. By making procedures for a perfect world, they create a problem with the process operators who are not expecting to find redirection in the written word, especially if they were not part of developing the written procedures. They may feel as though new procedures have been sprung on them under the guise of ISO 9001 implementation, or the procedure writers may not have foreseen some pitfalls that modifying the process steps have caused.

The second reason for written procedures not being followed is that they are too cumbersome and the process operators have developed convoluted mechanisms for getting the job done, no matter what. I observed a mill operator in a machine shop who took his hat off every time he made an adjustment to the machine. When I confronted him, he said he had written a sheet of brief operational instructions on his hat, because the released procedures were too long and were located in the foreman's office on the other side of the shop. No matter how wonderful the operating procedures may have been, they did not help this process operator do his job. The procedures were written in a vacuum, without regard to those who had to follow them. Internal auditing would have meant endless hours of documenting nonconformities, causing nothing but heartache and grief.

When documenting what you do, make sure the process operators are directly involved in developing their own written procedures. When you have them documented, test them to see if they are adequate. Make sure a trained operator can follow the procedures to repeatedly produce the desired result. Then share them with others who feed the process and those who receive the outcome of the process (internal suppliers and internal customers).

By involving those who use the procedure, those who feed it, and those who benefit from it, you stand a pretty good chance of having an auditable process. By using this technique, you will likely wind up with a different (new and improved) process. That being the case, you will have to train the process operators on the procedure before you declare it operational. Again, it sounds redundant to train people in their own operating procedures, but it will avoid long lists of nonconformities, hurt feelings, frustration, and an endless process of procedure rewriting.

A Review of Other Key Strategies

Management Awareness

All managers must be aware of the options facing them in the future of your business. These options include every logical possibility from keeping the status quo to total process re-engineering to selling the company. Champions of this effort must use every tool available to them (seminars, videotapes, consultants, plant visits, retreats, books, presentations, etc.) to make the decision makers aware of the options facing them as they prepare for a leadership role in the new century. Please do not make the fatal mistake of choosing a single path and presenting it as the only option. Intelligent leaders need to make informed decisions based on consensus thinking from the best of the best.

Assessment of Readiness to Change

Before embarking on any new path, there must be an honest and cathartic assessment of the climate for change within your organization. Consider the following questions:

- Are there certain rules and traditions that are absolutely sacred?
- Are there certain individuals and job slots that will be in place through the end of time?

- Is change okay, as long as it doesn't affect key individuals?
- Do the decision makers spend most of their time in the trenches with the troops? Putting out grass fires? In planning and strategy sessions? With a business broker? Talking with customers? Monitoring their investments? On the golf course?
- To what degree will you be allowed to succeed in your strategic quality initiative?
- Who will be the champions, the nay-sayers, the passive followers, and the silent saboteurs?
- Is there too much turmoil right now to even begin to change the culture?
- Will this effort be allowed to grow and evolve or will it be discarded when the next program du jour comes along?

A force field analysis might be the appropriate tool to help you in your assessment. List all of the forces that are driving change on the left side of a page and all those opposing change on the right. Assign the forces relative values (i.e., "The CEO is a strict authoritarian" gets more opposing points than "lack of a training program"). At the end of the brainstorming session, add up the points and see if you are positive, negative, or in the middle. A high negative score will not bode well for starting any dynamic, human-based changes. If your company is willing to address the opposing forces, then overcoming them becomes part of the strategic plan and adds to the time required. If there is no willingness to change, your strategic initiative is doomed before you start.

Develop a Strategic Plan

In Chapter 8, I outlined the elements that should be included in a strategic plan. Because every company has a unique product, service, and culture, it would be presumptuous of me to suggest that you follow the outline exactly as written. Also, it would be unwise for you to follow the outline verbatim without questioning what is right for your culture. The outline is a good way to launch your initiative. It may even prove helpful in isolating key areas that you know need reworking or redesign. Using Chapter 8 as a guide, select the approach and tools that will best suit your culture, then develop an implementation plan. Even if the plan is no more than a list of expected outcomes, it must exist in some form to provide a road map for your journey. If it is too restrictive or constrictive, it will be counterproductive. If only a few at the top know what it is, it will never work. The strategic plan is the shared vision that must be communicated openly, effectively, and repeatedly.

Develop a Corporate Charter

Generate a quality policy and mission statement that will lead everyone in your organization into the future. Identify your quality objectives. They will continually evolve, but there must be a baseline. Develop a system to communicate this information regularly to everyone in the organization.

Develop a Family of Measures

Remember that a football game isn't much fun without a scoreboard. As the game is being played, you need statistics to know how to make corrections to your strategies before the outcome is certain. Keeping records from the beginning lets you know where you were and where you are headed.

Train Management in the Culture of Continual Improvement

The only way to obtain buy-in is to educate your leaders in the whats and whys of your strategic quality initiative. They must be walking and talking models of ISO 9001. If you are working toward self-directed work teams, they must be working diligently on converting the top-down management structure into a model of leadership.

Train at All Levels

The only way change works is if everyone sees the benefits to themselves and to the company. Every employee must become responsible for his or her own actions. The only way to pass an ISO 9001 audit is for everyone to be living the procedures as you wrote them.

Implement the Strategic Plan

Keep the plan visible and visit it regularly. Have meaningful milestones and celebrate their achievement.

Measure Results

Use the family of measures to give a complete picture of how the company is running. The jobholders should be the ones who generate most of the measures. The measures should be kept continually. Process performance metrics correlated to financial results will produce a true picture of how the company is performing and how well the continual improvement process is working.

Benchmark Against the Best in Class

Seize every opportunity to learn new and better methods. Implement those that make sense for your culture.

Make Midcourse Corrections Based on Measured Results

A strategic plan should be designed to be adaptable to change. Changes in technology, customer needs, jobholder culture, and financial considerations are all valid reasons to make objective corrections to the master plan.

Follow a Continual Process of Planning, Training, Implementation, Measurement, and Evaluation, Forever!

The measures should be kept continually and be a nonfinancial representation of results. They must, however, tie directly to the key business metrics of your organization.

Making It Last

We did not inherit this land from our forefathers, we are borrowing it from our children.
— Unknown

Nothing lasts forever. The last few decades of sweeping cultural changes and massive technological breakthroughs have proven that to be true. The bottom line is that we must constantly posture ourselves to proactively pioneer our future instead of letting the future drive us. We are on a journey without an end, but our nature is to want to arrive at one point, smell the flowers, and then start down another road. We have to learn to smell the flowers as they pass by. Our commitment to the future must be passion, not fashion. We have to make continual improvement habitual. We have to train and educate on a perpetual calendar. We have to modify the old requisite of "learning something new every day" and add to that "evaluate its impact and take appropriate action." We have to plan to leave a legacy of self-perpetuating growth, not one that the last one out should turn off the lights.

14

ISO 9001
AS A PROFIT CENTER

This chapter presents the key methodologies developed by Productivity Resources, LLC and implemented in companies such as Dell's ARB to turn ISO 9001 implementation from an overhead cost to a profit center.[1] These principles have been developed in the author's previous five books and proven over nearly a decade of implementations in a wide diversity of business sectors.

I have spent much of this book discussing each aspect of QMS implementation from the written requirements of ISO 9001:2000 to experiential implementation guidelines, anecdotal stories, and an implementation at Dell Computer. In the next chapter, I report the results of the implementation at Dell ARB and provide a look into the future of totally integrating quality management into business management. This chapter brings together all of the proven tools of process management discussed thus far in this book into a methodology of turning overhead expenses into profit opportunities that I call "ISO 9001 as a Profit Center," shown in Figure 14.1.

---

1. *Profit center is a euphemism for minimizing overhead burdens and, therefore, reducing operating costs, leading to enhanced profitability. It is not a reference to profit center as typically used in accounting terminology.*

Hopefully, you will find that we have successfully built the foundation for this model. You will be able to use it along with the results and future vision chronicled in Chapter 11 to build your own strategic plan for moving quality from an overhead cost to a positive driver of bottom-line profitability and business success.

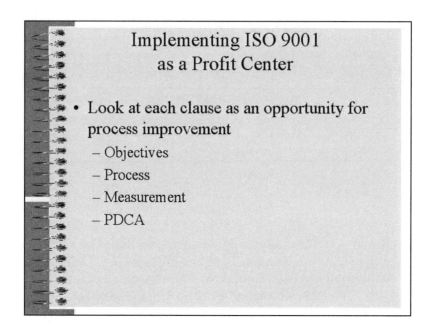

There is elegance in the simplicity of this model. ISO 9001 as a Profit Center is no more (and no less than):

- Determining the key objectives of each clause of ISO 9001 and analyzing how the stated requirements present an opportunity for minimizing process variability and maximizing productivity.
- Identifying and auditing every process in your organization to determine how the process approach described in ISO 9001 and ISO 9004 can streamline operations, reduce quality costs, and give ownership to all process operators.
- Measuring the outcome of every process against planned results and tying them directly to key business performance metrics.

- Dismantling overhead functions such as quality control, configuration control, document control, and so on, and integrating these functions into the value delivery system, providing an opportunity to make more profit instead of incurring overhead costs.
- Using the PDCA model to build a never-ending cycle of continual process improvement.

Let me frame it with an experience our company had in the financial services world. Transfer agents are companies that handle record keeping and investor services for issuers of securities. They are bound by Securities and Exchange Commission (SEC) regulations. As a matter of normal business practice, one would expect transfer agents to keep accurate records of investors so that dividends, annual reports, and other investor communications can be made promptly. Fairly regularly, however, investors move or die and these companies are not notified of address changes or the passing of a customer. Often, the first indication of a problem is undeliverable mail returned by the postal service. It is costly and time consuming to track down these lost investors, so many companies did nothing with lost assets until individual state statutes kicked in requiring them to remit the unclaimed funds to the appropriate states. This, too, is a costly process because each state has its own laws about how to deal with unclaimed assets. The states would then hold the funds indefinitely or until claimed by their rightful owner. To require transfer agents to track down lost investors, the SEC passed a new regulation in 1997 under which transfer agents had to perform at least two searches for their lost investors before declaring the assets unclaimed, and therefore eligible for disbursement to the state treasuries.

Because we are entrepreneurs, and driven by our knowledge of ISO 9000 as a Profit Center, we developed a software package to market to transfer agents. The software helped them to perform the necessary tracking of lost investors and to report the results to the SEC. Those who saw the regulation as an opportunity to refine their processes and perform a valuable service for their clients are now proactively using this software package to streamline their operations, find and distribute funds to security holders, reduce the state disbursement exercise, and meet the SEC regulation. Those with vision are viewing the regulation as an opportunity instead of a threat and they have made measurable process and client satisfaction improvements. Instead of allowing lost security holders' funds to wind up in a state treasury, the visionary companies are creating an opportunity (from a regulatory requirement) to delight clients who were unaware that they had lost assets!

So what are the steps of turning ISO 9001 into a profit center? The first step is to take a fresh look at each process in your organization from the following perspective. Ask these questions:

- Is the process defined as to input, methodology, and expected result?
- Are there metrics to ensure that planned outcomes are achieved?
- Are there resources and training in place to ensure that processes are capable of being implemented?
- Are operators currently trained and competent?
- Is there a clear map of how the process interrelates to the upstream and downstream processes?

If the answer to any of these questions is in the negative, you will enhance productivity and profitability just by evolving methods to bring your processes under control. Refer to the process model in Chapter 13.

The next step is to look at each clause of ISO 9001 and ask these questions:

- What is the purpose of the requirement in this clause?
- How does the requirement impact my organization?
- How can I use the requirement to enhance my process outcome?

Let's discuss some real examples to answer these questions.

Clause 4.1 states, "When an organization chooses to outsource any process that affects product conformity with requirements, the organization shall ensure control over such processes. Control of outsourced processes shall be identified within the quality management system." In performing a gap analysis (see Appendix D) to this clause, the question to be answered is what are outsourced processes and what are the controls for outsourced processes. The answers may run from "we don't have any outsourced processes" to "we will have to place a permanent quality representative at our supplier's company." Somewhere between these extremes is the cost-effective answer for your company.

First, what is an outsourced process? If you are a sheet metal company, it might be chrome plating. If you are a software manufacturer, it might be burning CDs. If you are an insurance company, it might be a call center. The sheet metal shop might send parts over to ABC's Plating with a purchase order that says "Chrome plate the parts." This is as foolhardy as asking your child to mow the grass.[2] Without specifying thickness, gloss level, permissible defects, and a host of other parameters, you are setting yourself up for failure, sooner or later, when you receive a part that you believe is unacceptable and you wind up in a dispute with your supplier because you have no acceptance criteria in place. This one very small example of how you can create a profit opportunity from an ISO 9001 requirement. The clause causes you to objectively look at your outsourcing procedures and you may discover that you have a problem waiting to happen or a scenario in place that has already cost you rework time, missed schedules, and unhappy customers. For the sake of argument, let's say that you have qualified the company, have established acceptance and rejection criteria, and clearly specify the processes you need. Have you considered using the guidelines of ISO 9001 and ISO 9004 to establish a partnership with the supplier through which you welcome them as extensions of your company and establish "just-in-time" or "most favored customer" relationships with them? Often when outsource suppliers become strategic partners, cost variations, schedule conflicts, and quality issues diminish because the adversarial supplier–customer relationship is dismantled.

Let's look at another profit center example. Subclause 4.2.3 (Control of Documents), says, "Documents required by the quality management system shall be controlled." This requirement will also run the range from "we don't have any controlled documents" to "we will have to hire a librarian and open a document control center." What currently exists at your company? Do sticky notes rule your company? Do you have a staffed document control center? Is either profitable for your organization? Have you ever looked at document control as an opportunity to increase profitability?

Documentation used in the QMS needs to be appropriate for your culture, organization, and industry. If you are manufacturing drugs, your documentation control system will likely be very comprehensive and may require strict forms control, backup of electronic files, and a librarian to handle product liability records. If you are a distributor of water filters, you may have a very simple system of orders, pick sheets, and shipping documents. If you have a highly complex organization, are you overdocumenting and keeping more records longer than your business and regulatory agencies require? Do you have a librarian just because you have always had one? Is that position an enormous overhead burden that could be eliminated if individual departments controlled their own documents? If you have a less

---

2. *See the metaphor in Chapter 13.*

sophisticated company, is your online system complemented by folks using yellow pads to track work orders because "the system" does not provide the functionality they need to do their jobs? Are you making customers unhappy because there is no clear way to provide the status of an order due to your failure to document past-due orders?

Rather than using the clauses of ISO 9001 as justification for building a compliance bureaucracy, answer the questions raised earlier in this chapter (Is the process defined as to input, methodology and expected result? Are there metrics to ensure that planned outcomes are achieved? Are there resources and training in place to ensure that processes are capable of being implemented by competent operators? Are operators currently trained and competent? Is there a clear map of how the process interacts with upstream and downstream processes?). Look for the process improvement motive attached to almost all of the requirements in the standard.

Implementing ISO 9001 as a Profit Center

- Identify key metrics for each element of the BMS
- Encourage every process operator to own their metrics
- Correlate internal audits to positive changes in the metrics
- Complete the family of measures by linking it to business performance

The next critical element to making ISO 9001 into a profit center is to attach a family of measures to every process: Measure everything. This is discussed at length in Chapter 11. Without a system of continually evaluating your processes for effectiveness, how can you objectively apply resources to the areas that are in need of improvement? Continual improvement can be effectively driven just by managing by fact instead of managing by instinct or by crises. The opposite scenario is to be data rich and information poor; that is, you may be wasting precious time and resources by collecting information that is not useful or not being used. Some organizations inhibit meaningful productivity by spending too much time collecting inappropriate or useless data.

Finally, when you have analyzed your processes, made them robust, tied the clauses of ISO 9001 to continual improvement motives, and implemented a family of measures, you are ready for the final (and most important) step. Miss this step, and all of the efforts you have put into quality management will be lost. None of this matters unless you tie performance metrics directly to key business indicators.

We all are aware that top management is driven by the bottom line. Just as you asked how clauses of ISO 9001 can be turned into a profit center, you must ask how each performance metric can demonstrate that it is an indicator of profitability or a warning sign of impending problems. In Chapter 3 you will see how the process metrics developed for the Dell BMIS have been used to tie directly to the key business measures. These can all be traced back to individual statistical controls used in each process step. If you can demonstrate that continual process improvement has an ongoing positive effect on profitability, senior management will become your biggest supporter. If you can show, through metrics, that you have successfully avoided a potential customer disaster through preventive action, your senior managers will gladly approve your next request for quality systems training. If you can provide input to your marketing efforts by furnishing information about customers' unstated needs through quality surveys, you may be invited to the next strategic planning meeting as a welcome guest.

The entire ISO 9001 as a Profit Center model is built on common sense, common purpose, and a shared vision of success. Implementation is not easy. Breaking old habits and "paradigm paralysis" can prevent success, even though all logic and documented success stories scream the need for change to proactive quality management and continual improvement. Seek out every chance to show success models (e.g., the Dell ARB story) to your senior managers. The Foreword to this book should somehow wind up in the senior management's next presentation on quality.

15

THE TEACHABLE
BUSINESS MODEL

THE TEACHABLE BUSINESS MODEL

Success is measured in moments and to achieve continual improvement, there must be a plan to build on ISO 9001 as a Profit Center. The proposed next phase is called the teachable business model.

From my experience auditing more than 430 companies in the last 31 years, I have found that Dell has one very distinctive attribute: All employees are trained in Dell's vision and business model. That training makes each employee an entrepreneur, guided by proven business models and responsible to all other Dell employees for the output of their work. Over the last four years, I have replicated this methodology in other organizations and it has become the teachable business model.

There are five components to the teachable business model. The first is to transform managers into leaders and to provide a shared vision. This is accomplished through a methodology called Business Management Stratagem (BMS).[1] The second component is to have the entrepreneurial leaders

---

1. *BMS is an entrepreneurial business development methodology facilitated exclusively by Productivity Resources, LLC.*

The Teachable Business Model

- Entrepreneurial Leadership
- The Healthy Learning Community
- The Tools
- Sharing the Rewards
- Replication

build a healthy learning community of employees who are also entrepreneurs and who are driven toward excellence. The third is to provide the tools for everyone to be able to execute the shared vision. The fourth is to build a compensation system of risks and rewards that is equitable to all and rewards everyone in the organization for their contributions to the success of the shared vision. Finally, there is a methodology to replicate this model at all levels and to build a system of self-regenerating and self-improving processes.

Be forewarned that the teachable business model is an advanced set of tools that cannot be successfully implemented based on the brief discussion this chapter, nor can it be implemented without skilled coaching in an environment that will support all of the principles. The information is provided to stimulate thought and promote curiosity about what is available beyond ISO 9001:2000 and ISO 9004:2000.

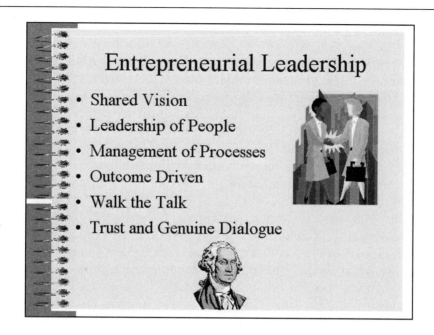

Entrepreneurial Leadership

The LASt model starts with identifying the true power in an organization; that is, the individual who can set policy and make it happen. This is almost always the president, chairman of the board, or CEO. Entrepreneurial leadership cannot start in middle management or at the grass-roots level. It must be driven from the top.

The secret to transforming managers into entrepreneurial leaders is as simply elegant as the natural healing of the body, but it is the most frightening and formidable of challenges for an individual to face. If top management would take time to put aside the technical issues and the fiscal constraints for a moment they would see the path to enlightenment.

We have met the enemy, and not only may he be ours, he may be us.
—Walt Kelly (Pogo)

The nonsecret panacea begins with the true power (the most senior leader) discovering who they are, what their vision is, and how they affect those around them. First they have to clarify and document their vision. Most entrepreneurs assume that those they employ understand their vision experientially or telepathically. In fact, most employees get snapshots and snippets of what the leader has in mind and then rely on their industry experience and personal values to guide their contribution. In time, this group unknowingly forms the personality and infrastructure of the organization while the leader is busy raising capital and selling his or her product. When there is no road map, travelers almost always wind up at unexpected destinations. As important as capital and marketable concepts is a clear vision of what the leader has in mind for realization of his or her dream. Once defined, it must be shared with those who are key to launching the business. In a strange twist to the leadership paradox, leaders often hire people to write clever mission and vision statements to go in a business plan, yet never internalize the true meaning of the message or realize its importance to success or failure.

Once the vision is clear, an environment of trust and genuine dialogue should evolve. The conundrum of "communication is the problem to the answer" is core to the fact that people need dialogue as compared to monologue. It means listening to and understanding one another instead of dictating or using condescending manipulation. It means ideas and opinions being expressed in an open, safe environment. It means discussion and participation in sharing the building of visions, creating strategies, implementing processes, and resolving problems (as well as avoiding them). It means knowing that each person is treated as an important part of the whole instead of being treated as a thing, a number, and a replaceable commodity. This does not imply robotic full agreement or consensus. It does mean that when an agreed-on strategy is reached, committed support, responsibility, and accountability are required from everyone. When everyone in senior management walks the talk of trust and genuine dialogue, the journey to success will have begun.

Drive thy business or it will drive thee.
—Benjamin Franklin

The Healthy Learning Community

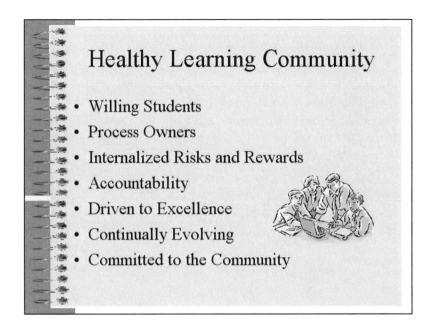

Healthy Learning Community

- Willing Students
- Process Owners
- Internalized Risks and Rewards
- Accountability
- Driven to Excellence
- Continually Evolving
- Committed to the Community

Today, most for-profit business leaders seek quick-fix answers to increasingly complex problems, in particular, those having to do with human relations. The behavioral machinations of the past 50 years have not resulted in healthier work communities, but increased alienation, indifference, and dysfunction. Talented people are not only at a premium, but they move from one firm to another as if playing musical chairs. Costly training programs are too often preparing people for other, greener fields of opportunity. Loyalty is a rare phenomenon in today's organization. Companies are so desperate to do the right things that they continually search business journals for the newest breakthrough in leading-edge business tools and best practices. For example, CEOs and presidents are replaced when they no longer fit the latest profile. Trendy consultants of the moment are enlisted to perform surgical re-engineering. Pay structures and benefits are manipulated while workout rooms and swimming pools are built, as is the latest remaking of corporate culture and image. In all too many cases, these "changes of the week" have little or no depth and serve only to further divide and confuse people.

The successful organizations of the new millennium will build communities that are so robust that workers will, above all, want to be an integral part of the team's success. Greener pastures will be redefined as "going to work tomorrow." The ingredients of the healthy learning community include the following:

- Willing students: A workforce of people who are always eager to learn new ideas and new concepts and be open to change.
- Process owners: Formerly "employees," who now take full responsibility for their work and its outcome.
- Internalized risks and rewards: The process owners in the healthy learning community will have clearly defined risks and rewards for their actions.
- Accountability: Process owners will be accountable to each other as well as the leadership and the customer.
- Driven to excellence: They will never settle for mediocrity or any goal that doesn't promote and further the mission and vision of the organization.
- Continually evolving: They will always be searching for a better way or a door to open paradigms.
- Committed to the community: Each member will grow personally stronger by contributing to the success of the healthy learning community.

The Tools

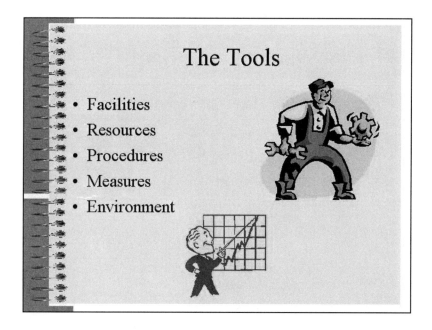

Clause 6 of ISO 9001:2000 deals with "tools" (resource management). They are also discussed frequently in other chapters of this book. Their role in the teachable business model is one of ensuring that resource planning is as integral to strategic planning as working capital. These tools not only include facilities and people, but process procedures, a family of measures, and an environment that encourages continual evolution.

Sharing the Rewards

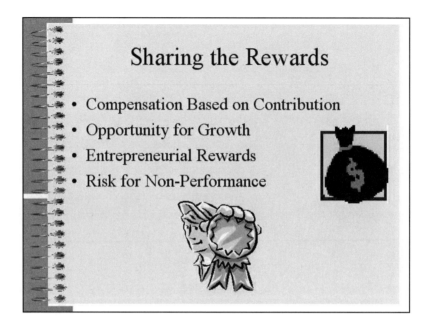

I have used the phrase *risk and rewards* a number of times in this book. Most organizations have traditional compensation systems based on seniority, bullying, inequitable profit sharing, and tenure. There is often little risk for nonperformance, especially for tenured employees. In the tight labor market of the recent past, mediocrity has become acceptable and "head hunting" has become a new sport. My observations and experience have shown that compensation that is totally based on contribution must replace traditional methods, so that base salary is only increased when a worker learns a new skill. Profit sharing is based not only on meeting overall business goals, but on team goals and individual contributions. There must also be rewards for new entrepreneurial ideas that lead to profitable innovation. None of this, however, is effective unless there is unambiguous risk for nonperformance. That risk must be clear, and individual team members must be first and foremost accountable to their team.

Replication

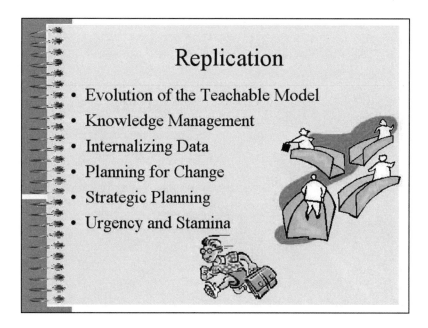

If you are still with me and have been able to realize the miracle of implementing the teachable business model, the greatest challenge is to replicate it throughout the organization and make it an integral part of your culture. The model must continually evolve and be redefined as it is driven by technology, customer needs, and human growth. There must be a clear methodology for handling the knowledge created by the healthy learning community and well-defined processes for internalizing the knowledge and turning it into future strategic objectives. Finally, the teachable business model must replace panic and exhaustion with a sense of urgency to drive results and a high degree of stamina driven by the adrenaline of mutual success.

Again, let me emphasize that these methods are only for those organizations, like Dell, that have the vision to challenge conventional wisdom and pioneer the future. As they say in extreme sports, "Don't try this at home without an experienced instructor."

ISO-BABBLE AND AUDIT-BABBLE: A GLOSSARY OF ISO 9000 TERMS

Activity   The state of being active; action.

Ambiguous   Using words with doubtful or double meaning.

Analysis   Breaking something complex into simple elements or components.

Appropriate   Specially suited for or fitting.

Approved supplier   A provider of services or products that has met minimum documented criteria established by the company for selling to the company.

Approved supplier list   A document listing those suppliers approved to sell to the company. This may also be a computerized system that does not allow purchase orders to be placed with suppliers not meeting the documented approval criteria.

Audit   The systematic review of a process, compared to its documented procedures or requirements to determine its effectiveness.

Audit checklist   Guides for auditors to follow during an audit to ensure that all procedural areas are audited.

Audit criteria   Documentation used as reference for an audit.

Auditee   Person or persons being audited.

Audit evidence   Records, information, or other statements of fact that are relevant to audit criteria.

Audit, external   Scheduled audits by independent certified auditors (third party) or other interested parties (second party) for the purpose of maintaining QMS certification.

Audit guide   A representative of the function being audited who can direct the auditors to the appropriate areas within the audit scope. Guides also help resolve misunderstandings and communications issues during an audit.

Audit, internal   A systematic, independent, and documented process for obtaining audit evidence and evaluating it objectively to determine the extent to which audit criteria are fulfilled.

Audit notes   Comments in an audit report noting observations of positive activities demonstrating exemplary continual improvement or activities worthy of praise.

Auditor, internal   An individual who has completed company-prescribed training and has witnessed the required number of audits to be certified by the company as an internal auditor.

Auditor-in-training   An individual who has completed the required classroom training for an internal auditor, but has not yet completed the required number of audit observations.

Auditor's notes   The completed audit checklist and notes kept by the auditor(s) during an internal audit. These notes are generally kept for reference and are not published.

Audit report   A summary of findings and observations resulting from an audit. All findings must refer to the procedure and paragraph that was contrary to the observed deviation. Major and minor findings are noted as such.

Audit schedule, internal   A published audit schedule that ensures all areas of a QMS are audited on a regular and systematic schedule to ensure ongoing effectiveness.

Audit team   One or more auditors conducting an audit. Teams are used to enhance the effectiveness of audits by giving different educated perspectives of the observed activities.

Authority   The power or right to enforce obedience.

Calibration   Verification that a measuring device is accurate and traceable to a known and accepted standard of accuracy.

Capability The ability to realize a product that will fulfill the requirements.

Comment A statement made in an internal audit report of an observed situation that did not qualify as a finding because a clear deviation from procedures was not in evidence, but is included as a potential problem or subject for continual improvement. Outside an audit, this would be documented on a preventive action request.

Competence Demonstrated ability to provide knowledge and skills

Compliance Meeting the stated and implied intent of a documented requirement, policy, or procedure.

Compliance matrix A cross-reference table that identifies procedures in a QMS and their relationship to the elements of ISO 9000.

Concession Gaining approval from a customer or internal authority to use as is or to regrade a nonconforming item or service.

Conformity Affirmative and documented evidence that a product or service is fit for use for its stated purpose.

Continual improvement Recurring activity to increase the ability to fulfill requirements.

Contract An agreement between the company and a customer.

Contract review The process of accepting a contract from a customer and gaining agreement on all terms and conditions before validating the contract.

Control, document, and data Positive control of documents, procedures, data, forms, and computer records used within the QMS.

Control, revision A system of dates, numbers, or letters indicating the revision level of a form, procedure, document, or computer record.

Corrective action Action to eliminate the cause of a detected nonconformity or other undesirable condition.

Corrective action, closed-loop A procedure that ensures that all requests for corrective and preventive action are handled in a timely manner, all follow-up is performed, the action taken is effective, and there is a scheduled follow-up to ensure continued effectiveness of the corrective action.

Corrective action procedure A procedure within the QMS for dealing with deviations from published policies and procedures. It includes reporting the symptoms, detailing the circumstances, suggesting possible causes, performing root-cause analysis, and ensuring a remedy is implemented to prevent recurrence.

Corrective action request (CAR)   A document generated resulting from all major findings in an audit or to eliminate the cause of a detected nonconformity.

Customer satisfaction   The customer's perception of the degree to which the customer's requirements have been fulfilled.

Customer-supplied product   Customer-owned product temporarily in the possession of the company for value-added or repair work.

Deductive reasoning   The ability to follow a procedure and methodically move through its steps until the evidence gathered and observed can determine effectiveness.

Defect   Not meeting the requirement relating to intended or specified use.

Dependability   A collective term used to describe the availability of performance and its influencing factors.

Design and development   A set of processes that transforms requirements into characteristics, or the specification of a process, product, or system.

Element (tenet)   A term used in the ISO 9000:1994 standard relating to sections of the document now known as clauses in the ISO 9001:2000 standard.

Exclusions   The action of excluding, leaving out.

Finding   Results of the evaluation of the collected audit evidence.

Finding, major   A finding that will jeopardize the effectiveness of the QMS. This can be absence of a required procedure, total breakdown of a policy or procedure, or multiple occurrences of minor findings in the same procedural area.

Finding, minor   A finding that can be classified as a single lapse in following a procedure or an observed incident that, on its own, cannot jeopardize the effectiveness of the QMS.

Findings, preliminary   A debriefing with the audit guide immediately after the audit is completed to ensure that the auditors have all of the necessary information to write an audit report and that the audit guide acknowledges any observed findings.

Framework   A structure made of joined parts.

Functional   Relating to activity rather than to structure or form.

Identification   Positive markings on a product or document that verify its identity and revision level.

Inspection (verification)   An activity placed at critical points within a process to positively determine conformance before a product or service can move to the next step or operation.

Management review   A formal review by the company leadership of the state of the QMS. This review is conducted at least annually.

Management system   Designed to establish and achieve policy and objectives. A management system of an organization can include different types such as a business, financial, or quality management system.

Measurable   Able to be measured.

Measurement process   A set of operations to determine the value of a quantity.

Methodology   The method of doing something.

Mission statement   A statement of truths and values that establish the moral and ethical makeup of a company.

Nonconformity   A defect in a product or service or not meeting a requirement.

Objective evidence   A trail of paper or data that demonstrates that procedures are followed in their logical sequence, producing the desired outcome.

Observation   An incident found during an audit that is outside the scope of the planned audit. It is usually a deviation observed in an unrelated area or in a procedure or standard not on the current audit agenda.

Obsolete document   A form, procedure, or document that is no longer current but is retained in a segregated area for historical and traceability purposes.

Operational procedures (operations procedures, standard operations procedures, etc.)   Documented procedures that describe a process in sufficient detail to train skilled operators and to audit the processes' outcome.

Order entry   Entering an approved contract into the value delivery system.

Preventive action request   Documented action taken to prevent a potential nonconformity or undesirable situation.

Procedure   The way an activity or process is performed.

Process   A set of interrelated or interacting activities that transform inputs into outputs.

Process approach　The systematic identification, interaction, and management of processes within an organization.

Process, special　A process the outcome of which cannot be readily verified by physical inspection or observation.

Product　The result of a process.

Project　A process that contains a set of managed activities with a start and finish.

Purchase order　An agreement between the company and a supplier or provider.

Quality　The degree to which permanent characteristics fulfill the requirements.

Quality management　Activities to direct and control an organization in regards to quality.

Quality management system (QMS)　A management system to direct and control an organization with regard to quality.

Quality objective　The planned, executed, and measured goals of the company pertaining to quality that support the quality policy.

Quality plan　A document specifying how a company plans to adhere to its written procedures, by whom, and when. For most companies, this is documented in the operational procedures.

Quality planning　The act of developing a quality plan and the ongoing effort to include quality requirements in business planning.

Quality policy　A concise statement issued by the company leadership declaring their intent as to the direction the company will follow in day-to-day business and their commitment to achieving their quality objectives. Sometimes used interchangeably with vision or mission statements.

Quality policy manual　A top-level document that sets policy for how a company is to be run, as it relates to the value delivery system. Also referred to as business management system or quality management system.

Quality records　Documents filled out or accumulated as part of the QMS (no longer defined in ISO 9001:2000; instead record is defined).

Record　A document stating results achieved or providing evidence of activities performed.

Registrar　An independent firm that has credentials authorizing them to perform audits to ISO 9000, Q9000, or other internationally recognized QMS standards.

Repair   Action on a nonconforming product that may change the parts but make them acceptable for the intended use.

Requirement   Need or expectation that is generally stated or implied.

Rework   Action on a nonconforming product to make it conform to the requirements.

Root-cause analysis   A methodical investigation of the underlying causes of a deviation from policy or procedure performed when there are repeated instances of the same deviation or when the cause of a deviation is not immediately apparent.

Service   Generally an intangible result of at least one activity between a customer and supplier. The service can be performed on tangible items or between people.

Shall   Defines a strict requirement from which no deviation is allowed.

Should   Defines something that is recommended but not necessarily required.

Specification   A document stating requirements.

Statistical techniques   Indicators or collected data used by a company to indicate performance against established measurable standards.

Suitable   Suited for or appropriate for a purpose.

System   Set of interrelated or interacting elements.

Test   Determination of one or more characteristics according to a procedure.

Top management   A person or group of people that directs an organization at its highest levels.

Traceability   The ability to determine the evolution of a product, service, or document back to its individual components, its history, or its previous steps. Degree of traceability is dependent on customer requirements and criticality of the item.

Training   Communication of necessary information to those responsible for operating the processes of the QMS. Training may be formal or on-the-job.

Training record   Written verification that required training was carried out appropriately and in a timely manner.

Validation   Confirmation, using objective evidence, that the requirements for a specified intended use have been met.

Value delivery system   Those actions performed within a company that directly benefit the customer.

Verification   Confirmation with objective evidence that specified requirements have been met.

Verification of purchased product   Predelivery inspection or test of a product or service, performed at a supplier's facility, by a representative of the company or the company's customer.

Vision   The strategic plan for the path a business plans to take to ensure its successful future.

Work instruction   Detailed, step-by-step instructions necessary for complex or critical processes to be completed and audited satisfactorily.

SAMPLE QUALITY MANUAL

The following sample quality manual is written for a service-oriented company. It is written to comply with the requirements of ISO 9001:2000. It is an actual working document for the company named and has been approved by ABS Quality Evaluations for conformance to ISO 9001:2000, Clause 4.2.2 (Revision EF, April 29, 2001).

Productivity Resources, LLC
Quality Policy Manual
Controlled Issue # _____
Issued to: _____
Revision EF
April 29, 2001
Authorized by:

_____

Tom Taormina, Managing Partner
George Wagner, Senior Partner

PRODUCTIVITY RESOURCES, LLC

QUALITY POLICY MANUAL

QUALITY MANAGEMENT SYSTEM

This manual defines Standard Policy for the Quality Management System (QMS) of Productivity Resources, LLC. The scope of this manual is from receipt of an inquiry for services to completion of a consulting implementation, project, or service. The manual includes all inputs and outputs for individual and interrelated processes.

The company is comprised of three business-consulting units, which are: Entrepreneurial Leadership (EL), Business Management Systems (BMS), and Financial Services (FS). Each of these units can operate independently or operate collectively on common projects.

Entrepreneurial Leadership

This unit consults in the area of communication and dialogue within organizations. It facilitates setting a solid foundation of trust, honesty, respect, and "genuine dialogue" within organizations. This program is often the precursor to BMS consulting in entrepreneurial companies.

Reference: SOP 101 - EL Quality Plan and Objectives

Business Management Systems

This unit consists of process evaluation and improvement consulting with the objective of helping organizations achieve their strategic quality and business goals. It utilizes ISO 9001 as a framework for a totally integrated business management system.

Reference: SOP 102 - BMS Quality Plan and Objectives

Financial Services

This unit provides consulting services in business management, quality, and information technology specifically to the financial services industries (banks, insurance companies, securities dealers, etc.). It uses many of the tools of the other two business units to provide services to targeted industries.

Reference: SOP 103 - FS Quality Plan and Objectives

Although we maintain "virtual" offices throughout the United States, all business units are operated from our headquarters in Virginia City, Nevada. Interaction between the business units is "virtual" and adapted to fit business opportunities. It is our intent to maintain certification to ISO 9001: 2000 within the scope of "providers of business process consulting services."

At Productivity Resources, LLC, our mission is to be the premier provider of business process consulting and organizational leadership development. We define premier as:

- Operating to the highest level of business and professional ethics
- Meeting our stated commitments
- Achieving customer satisfaction
- Being a profit center instead of an overhead expense

Our company is committed to supporting our QMS with documentation, implementation, and maintenance of processes that meet the requirements of the ISO/Q9001:2000 standard. This manual is numbered to coincide with the ISO/Q9001:2000 numbering system to facilitate auditing.

Reference Documents

ISO 9000:2000	Quality Management Systems – Fundamentals and Vocabulary
Q9000:2000	Quality Management Systems – Fundamentals and Vocabulary
ISO 9001:2000	Quality Management Systems – Requirements

Q9001:2000	Quality Management Systems – Requirements
ISO 9004:2000	Quality Management Systems – Guidelines for Performance Improvements
Q9004:2000	Quality Management Systems – Guidelines for Performance Improvements

The business processes, their application, sequences, interrelationships, and effectiveness, identified herein, are further detailed in lower level documents. Planning, monitoring, operation, control, measurement, and analysis of our services will be done through quality plans and objectives, strategic planning meetings, management reviews, internal audits, preventive action and corrective action, statistical process control, and continual improvement initiatives. Each of these functions is documented in operations procedures.

It is the responsibility of the Partners to provide adequate resources and information to support this QMS and they are also responsible for providing competent, qualified, and trained personnel in all areas for services offered to the customer. All Associates will receive an initial business model orientation that includes metrics for measuring the success and profitability of the Company. Furthermore, the Associates will be trained on all service modules applicable to their business unit to ensure the customer receives the required level of service. Development plans will be reviewed with each Associate at least annually to evaluate effectiveness and to define training needs so the Associates continue to improve their skills.

Business processes will be established for management, resource provision, product (service) delivery, and measurement of results. The business processes within the company will be validated upon inception, revalidated upon change, monitored and verified during operation, and continually improved as necessary to provide the customer and other interested parties with the requested and required services. The Associates within the Company have been given responsibility commensurate with their assigned tasks and empowered with the appropriate authority to ensure the quality policy and quality objectives are carried out at all times. Any services outsourced to other service providers will be controlled by the Company's QMS.

Reference: SOP 104 — Outsourcing of Services

The following organization chart and process flow represent the methodology for ensuring the tenets of our QMS and ISO 9001:2000 are met.

Productivity Resources, LLC
Organizational Chart

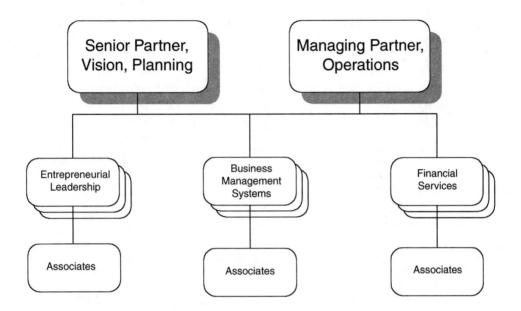

Note: The Managing Partner is the QMS management representative. The Senior Partner Chairs all management reviews.

Productivity Resources, LLC
Process Flow Chart

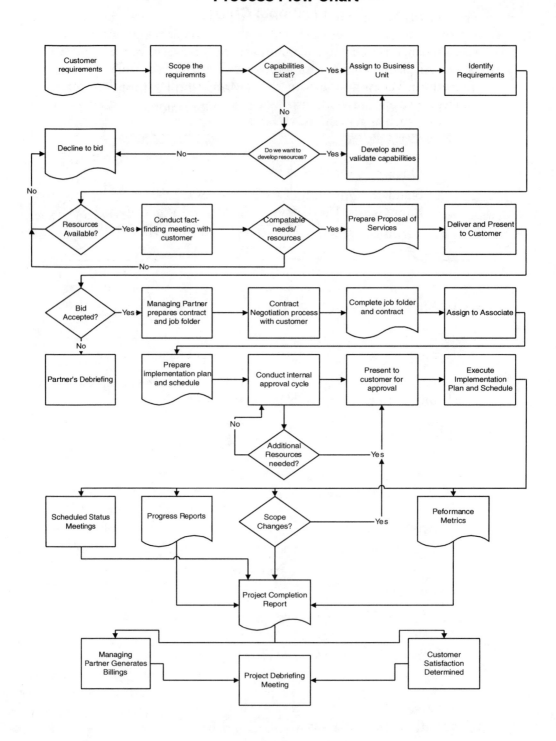

DOCUMENTATION REQUIREMENTS

Productivity Resources, LLC, has established a three-tier documentation system to ensure our services conform to customer requirements and provide guidance for effective planning, service delivery, and control of processes. All documentation for processes is established, implemented, and maintained. Where appropriate, the documentation will be in the form of a policy, procedure, or work instruction or other means to communicate information such as flowcharts, visual aids, software, or templates. The tiers are defined as follows:

1. Quality Policy Manual
2. Standard Operating Procedures (SOP), Training Curriculum, Flow Charts, Visual Aids, Software, and Work Instructions
3. Forms and Reference Documents

4.2.1 QUALITY POLICY

Productivity Resources helps organizations achieve their stated and implied goals through assessment, intervention, awareness, and training.

Quality Objectives

We will help our clients achieve short-term tactical solutions to priority business issues and long-range strategic plans to maximize the effectiveness of human and physical resources. Our methods include the following:

- Actively listening to client needs
- Identifying the business outcomes to be enhanced
- Assessing organizational readiness for change
- Analyzing the business processes
- Assessing the human factors
- Identifying cost-effective solutions
- Forming a partnership and an implementation strategy with the client

- Active engagement and commitment from the client
- Identifying metrics to evaluate effectiveness
- Facilitating implementation, assessment, and closure
- Following up to ensure business outcomes are achieved
- Knowledge transfer to the client to achieve self-sufficiency

Quality Records

Each representative of the Company will maintain client files. The representative in charge of the account will maintain the records. The records are readily accessible to any employee that will provide a service on the implementation or project via e-mail, fax, or through a reputable carrier on the Approved Suppliers List.

The Partners will maintain financial records pertaining to the Company. Independent consultants will maintain their own expense records.

4.2.2 QUALITY MANUAL

This Quality Policy Manual will be established, implemented, and maintained in accordance with this document. This manual includes all clauses of the ISO 9001:2000 standard except those listed here. Subclauses 7.5.1c & d, 7.5.2, and 7.6 — Monitoring and Measuring will be conducted via matrices and charts created for each client according to their needs. Productivity Resources will not use equipment that needs to be validated for suitability. Qualification of personnel will be covered in the training and certification section of the Company's documentation.

Reference: SOP 7.501 – Monitoring and Measuring

Documented procedures will be established and maintained for each function of the process flowchart and will be referenced herein. Where further detail is necessary to help train new Associates, the documented procedures will make reference to resource documents, training curriculum, software, and work instructions.

Control of Documents

Control of documents will be accomplished by using a database control system that includes revision level and dates. A custodian will be appointed with responsibility to ensure that proper review, approval, issuance, and updates are obtained at every stage of the document life. The review, approval, and update functions include determining adequacy of the documents prior to use. The custodian will be responsible for posting a list of revision changes and deletions of documents within the Company. The latest revision or update of the company documentation will be obtained upon request to the points of use. All documents will be legible and readily identifiable. Verification will be validated during internal audits. Obsolete documents will be identified and maintained to provide a history of changes.

Reference: SOP 4.201 – Document and Data Control

4.2.4 CONTROL OF RECORDS

Client information will be maintained indefinitely or as prescribed by the contract in status files to differentiate between open and closed projects. Records will be legible, identified by company name, and readily retrievable to the point of use.

Reference: SOP 4.202 - Identification, Storage, Protection, Retrieval, Retention and Disposition of Records

5.1 MANAGEMENT RESPONSIBILITY

The Productivity Resources, LLC, Partners, as managers of the Company, are committed to the policies set forth in this manual and supporting documentation. This commitment is demonstrated by continual use of the quality policy and quality objectives as guiding principles in the conduct of daily business, within and without. Management will communicate the importance of meeting the clients' stated and implied needs as well as any statutory and regulatory requirements for the services being provided by facilitating and overseeing projects to demonstrate the intended level of customer service. Management will assign resources commensurate with the scope of each project. Management will initiate management reviews at least once a year to ensure the policy and objectives are still valid and supported by each Associate.

Reference: SOP 5.301 – Internal Communication

Reference: SOP 5.601 – Management Review

5.2 CUSTOMER FOCUS

Prior to accepting an assignment, Partners, Associates, or an evaluation team will determine the stated and implied needs of the customer. As contract requirements evolve the contract will be reviewed and changes will be implemented. The implementation plan and resources will also be continually evaluated to ensure the customer derives maximum benefit from our services. At the completion of each project, management or a designee will review the customer contract to ensure any written or implied requirements were met. At this time a methodology for getting customer feedback will be identified and evidence of the feedback will be maintained in the client file. The client will be contacted immediately if issues or questions are detected. Clients will be contacted on a regular basis to see if there is ongoing satisfaction with the services provided. Further assistance will be communicated if the Associate sees other areas of opportunity that are provided by the Company. Clients will be informed when new services are designed that may enhance the processes already in place.

Reference: SOP 7.201 - Determination of Customer Requirements

Reference: SOP 7.202 – Customer Communication

Reference: SOP 8.201 – Customer Satisfaction

Reference: SOP 8.401 – Customer Satisfaction Data

5.3 QUALITY POLICY

The quality policy and objectives will be reviewed at least annually to ensure they reflect the management vision and company purpose. Management will ensure that the quality policy reflects commitment to the policy and objectives of the Company by modeling and mentoring. Management will ensure that when necessary, results of these reviews will result in continual improvement initiatives. It is management's responsibility to ensure all Associates of the company understand the intent of the policy and execute it in their daily work assignments.

5.4.1 QUALITY OBJECTIVES

Management is directly responsible to ensure that quality objectives are part of each year's strategic planning and that they are measurable and fit within the framework of the quality policy. The quality objectives will usually be contained in the quality plans for the three business units. Each Associate will be notified of his or her role in meeting the company's objectives and how performance and profit sharing will be related to accomplishment of assigned goals. The goals set to meet the objectives will be communicated and documented on each Associate's job development plan.

5.4.2 QUALITY MANAGEMENT SYSTEM PLANNING

Management is responsible to ensure that quality management planning is scheduled and carried out and that the integrity of the system is maintained. The following items will be considered as input to the planning:

- Quality policy and objectives
- Customer feedback
- Needs and expectations of the client
- Standards and requirements of the industry or business
- Projects quoted but not accepted
- Strengths and weaknesses of previous projects
- Corrective actions

- Customer suggestions and preventive action
- Perceived opportunities and threats
- Necessary assessments, measurements, verification, validation, and monitoring
- Changes affecting the QMS

A strategy plan will be documented as a result of the quality planning activities with goals and objectives that include:

- Further training and expertise needed
- Action items and timeframes to implement the plan
- Budgetary and personnel needs
- Measurement of progress
- Additional software or resource needs
- Need for process improvement
- Need for documentation and records

Reference: SOP 5.401 – Business Unit QMS Planning

5.5.1 Responsibility, Authority, and Communication

Responsibility and authority for processes and services will be clearly defined in the Company's documentation (see 4.2). Management will ensure that responsibility and authority is commensurate with the scope of each job title. Individuals who have direct responsibility to execute a process will be given the opportunity to review any documentation that relates to their function. Accountability from each Associate will be reviewed and discussed during yearly evaluations and will be directly tied to profitability and customer satisfaction measures.

5.5.2 Management Representative

The Managing Partner will serve as the representative to oversee the Quality Management System. The management representative will be responsible to ensure the system is established, documented, implemented, and maintained. Any concerns or needs for improvements will be communicated to management through the management representative. The management representative will ensure that QMS and customer requirements are communicated to all Associates who have the need to know. He or she will also communicate with external parties, partners, and clients on matters relating to the Quality Management System.

5.5.3 INTERNAL COMMUNICATIONS

It is management's responsibility to ensure that genuine dialogue occurs throughout the Company, especially regarding the QMS and customer. Management will ensure there is a forum available for all Associates to communicate. The forum can be in the form of e-mails, a Web site, conference calls, minutes, or company meetings.

5.6.1 MANAGEMENT REVIEW

Management reviews can take on any reasonable form as long as the objectives from the previous planning, management reviews, and input from Associates is considered. The main objective is continual improvement. Any deficiencies found will be reviewed and discussed to ensure they are not left out of future planning. Employees who make great strides in improvement of the QMS will be recognized. Minutes of the reviews will be maintained and will include action items and timeframes for completion. Action items can be completed by any means as long as documentation is kept for each item and everyone in the management review gets communication of the resolution. If necessary, any Associate with action items can reconvene the management review if input is needed from the whole group.

Reference: SOP 5.601 – Management Review Input, Output, and Meetings

6.1 PROVISION OF RESOURCES

Resource allocation and availability for consulting and for QMS execution will be continually reviewed and identified. The Company may discover during management reviews, customer input, or with new business review that further resources are needed. Management will maintain enough resources and staff to support the QMS objectives and client needs as monitored by internal audits and customer satisfaction measures.

6.2 HUMAN RESOURCES

The Company will continually assess Associates' competence based on their education, training, skills, and experience. For existing Associates, this assessment will be in the form of customer satisfaction measures, audits by the Partners, and the results of training. For potential Associates, selection criteria and experience needs will be determined. Included in all human resource assessment will be criteria for the following:

- Competence of personnel
- Assessment of training needs
- Evaluations of effectiveness
- Determination of awareness of relevance and importance
- QMS training needs
- Maintenance of human resources records

Reference: SOP 6.201 - Qualification, Education, Training, Competence Criteria, and Training Records

6.3 INFRASTRUCTURE

A list of available company software and resources will be provided to each Associate during orientation. It is most desirable for each Associate to use resources from this list so that everyone in the Company can download and access documentation if necessary.

Other tools, software, and equipment needed by the Associates will be obtained individually. The environment used to accomplish the Company's objectives and requirements of the customer will also be the responsibility of each Associate.

Reference: SOP 6.301 – Infrastructure Requirements

6.4 WORK ENVIRONMENT

Typically the work environment will be the client or customer site. Most or all of the paperwork done to support each project will be done from a home office or other area determined by the Associate.

7.1 PLANNING REALIZATION

Planning the services needed for each customer assignment is dependent on industry, demographics, and customer requirements. The Company will not pursue new endeavors unless they fit the scope of the current quality policy and objectives. The Company may use existing methodologies and processes, but tailor them to the client's needs as necessary. Whether tailoring current processes or creating new ones, the Company will consider the quality planning objectives discussed in Section 5.4.2 of this manual. When a large project utilizing cross-functional resources is necessary, a separate quality plan will be drafted, approved, and implemented. In all project planning, consideration will be given to resources, verification, validation, monitoring, and acceptance criteria. Records of planning will be maintained.

Reference: SOP 7.101 – Project Planning

7.2.1 Determination of Requirements Related to Product (Services)

The Company's representatives are required to ensure that all stated and implied needs are discussed with the customer prior to bidding any project. Associates of the Company are the process and subject matter experts and are tasked to match our services with the specifics of the client's business. It is our responsibility to ensure that the client is made aware of the details of a typical project and how their specific needs may affect the implementation and timeframes. We are also obligated to consider any regulatory or environmental requirements specific to the client's industry and ensure that knowledgeable resources are available to help incorporate those requirements into the implementation or project.

Reference: SOP 7.201 – Contract Review

7.2.2 Review of Requirements Related to the Product (Service)

Before accepting a contract the Company will ensure that the client's needs are understood and can be met within the framework of the three units defined in the scope of this manual. Furthermore, the Company is responsible to ensure that the client understands what will occur at every stage of the implementation. If the client would like to omit or change part of the implementation these omissions or changes will be added to the contract and signed by both parties before work is initiated.

Reference: SOP 7.201 – Contract Review

7.2.3 Customer Communication

During a project the Company will communicate with the client's representative on a periodic basis and give the status of the project. The frequency of the communication will be established in the contract. The communication may be done via weekly meetings and minutes, e-mail, fax, or phone. The responsible Associate will maintain daily notes of the work done on the project. Any requested or proposed changes to the scope of the project or implementation will be documented as an amendment to the contract. The customer will be kept informed as to changes in available processes and methods as they are discovered. At the completion of the implementation or project the customer will be contacted using a customer satisfaction form. Any issues or questions communicated on such form will be immediately addressed in person. If the issue was a complaint, it will be followed up with written correspondence to ensure the resolution is documented and the client receives the desired level of attention.

Reference: SOP 7.202 – Customer Communication

7.3 DESIGN AND DEVELOPMENT

The Partners in each of their areas of expertise accomplish the design of services, tools, documentation, and methodology. Once the initial design is in place, development is done by review and input by the other Associates. When a customer requests a new program, that customer will be included in the steps of design and development. Inputs are also taken from previous designs of service, customer feedback, emerging tools, and standards, quality plans, and strategic planning. During design and development it is paramount that all changes are tracked by using revisions and dates to avoid duplication and redundancy. Outputs will be in the form of documented theory, course outline, slide presentation, documentation, or software. Outputs will be reviewed for accuracy and clarity and verified against the input design.

During the review phase every Associate who has responsibility to deliver the product (service) will be given the opportunity to review and give written feedback. Conflicts will be resolved before the product is released. All feedback will be responded to and records of all the actions will be kept. Each person with the responsibility to deliver the final product or service will have a clear understanding of the product or service.

Verification will be done during the review stage and after each service or product is delivered to ensure that it still meets the input goals. If changes are necessary they will be accomplished and all responsible Associates will review the service or product before it is delivered again. Records of reviews and changes will be maintained.

When practical, test runs of the product or service will be done before delivery to the customer. When the customer is to receive the first issuance of a newly designed process, that customer will be made aware of the untested status of the product. Results of tests and changes will be recorded and maintained.

Changes will be tracked using revision and date. Records of changes will be maintained. Each product or service will be controlled at point of use and updates will be issued to other Associates on an as-needed basis. It is the responsibility of the person who designed the product or service to ensure that all Associates receive the latest revision. Evaluation of changes will be verified with customer evaluation or surveys.

Reference: SOP 7.301 – Design and Development

7.4.1 PURCHASING PROCESS

Productivity Resources, LLC, purchases only off-the-shelf items such as office supplies and computer equipment. The Company continually strives to obtain the best value. When shopping for supplies to be included in deliverables to customers or standardized products (business cards, letterhead, brochures, etc.), the Partners will specify products and sources. Items used for Associates' individual consumption will not be controlled. When new Associates are added to the company, they will be given a list of existing hardware and software so they can ensure they purchase compatible products. Purchasing of external services is handled and directed only by the Partners. No attempt is made to evaluate suppliers of off-the-shelf manufacturers' part numbers. The Partners will include their opinions of suitability of suppliers as necessary to ensure a level of performance commensurate with the needs of the customers' end product.

7.4.2 PURCHASING INFORMATION

It is up to each Associate to keep his or her own purchasing documents. Only the Partners have authority to write checks or issue purchase orders from Company funds. Purchase orders will contain a clear description of the item, part number, and price.

7.4.3 VERIFICATION OF PURCHASED PRODUCT

For catalog items, products will be inspected for damage, quantity, part number (if applicable), and type when they are received. Damaged goods and discrepancies in price will be resolved immediately.

Reference: SOP 7.401 - Purchasing

7.5.1 CONTROL OF PRODUCTION AND SERVICE PROVISION

Productivity Resources, LLC, is a service company. Documented procedures are available for Associates for all processes within the three business units and will be distributed to point of use or on a need-to-know basis. These procedures will include:

- Availability of information and instructions
- Use of suitable equipment and resources
- Availability of monitoring measures
- Implementation of monitoring and measuring methods
- Implementation of project delivery, completion, and follow-up activities

Reference: 7.501 – Control of Services

7.5.2 VALIDATION OF PROCESSES FOR PRODUCTION AND SERVICE PROVISION

An initial customer contract checklist will be reviewed at the end of each delivery of service along with information from customer evaluation forms and surveys. The objective will be reviewed and evaluated for delivery success. Length of time and cost of the project will be evaluated against projected targets. Any deficiencies in the process will be documented on corrective action forms along with suggested resolution and submitted to the Partner affected. Issues in regard to the customer will be reviewed for resolution and implementation. Immediate response will be submitted to the customer and a copy will be kept in the customer file. The Partners will review profit margins and adjustments to project or implementation timeframes and resources will be made available. Education or training for Associates will also be reviewed and arrangements made to correct issues before the next project.

7.5.3 IDENTIFICATION AND TRACEABILITY

All documents, software files, and presentations will be identified with a title related to the subject material. For software file acronyms, revision letters and dates can be used. An index of all available material will be kept on file by the head of each business unit.

7.5.4 CUSTOMER PROPERTY

For privacy and liability reasons, the Associate in charge of the implementation or project will track customer property. Customer property may be in the form of documents, software, training materials, specifications, or internal procedures. All copyright and trademark requirements will be followed. The customer will be asked if they require the property back at the completion of the implementation or project and the information will be recorded on the initial contact sheet. If the customer would like the information destroyed this will be accomplished, keeping the customer's privacy in mind. If customer property becomes damaged or lost during the implementation or project, the customer will be notified immediately. The details of the conversation or a copy of the correspondence will be kept in the customer file. Every attempt will be made to satisfy the customer's needs of replacement of the property.

Reference: 7.501 – Control of Customer Property

7.5.5 PRESERVATION OF PRODUCT

The only "product" produced by Productivity Resources, LLC, is intellectual property in written and computer format. All such media will be controlled, preserved, and protected from harm and from the elements.

8 MEASUREMENT, ANALYSIS, AND IMPROVEMENT

The Company's QMS and quality objectives' effectiveness will be evaluated with completion of an implementation or project, during company meetings and in management reviews. Deficiencies will be identified and corrected by affecting corrective action, updating applicable documentation, providing further training or education, or obtaining additional resources. The result of these assessments will lead to updating of quality plans and objectives with the purpose of continual improvement.

8.2.1 CUSTOMER SATISFACTION

Customer issues and conflicts will be immediately addressed and resolved. Feedback from these situations will be communicated to all Associates for education and growth. Information from customer evaluation forms and customer surveys will be distributed to all Associates. Periodic visits to active and past customers will be conducted as directed by the Partners to ensure the customer is satisfied or to determine if further assistance is needed.

8.2.2 INTERNAL AUDIT

Audits of the QMS, customer files, documents, customer satisfaction, applicability of service materials, and training needs will be accomplished on a scheduled basis by qualified personnel independent of the work being audited at least annually. These audits will be performed in accordance with the requirements of the QMS. Previous audit results will be reviewed when available. Audits will be scheduled and conducted according to status and importance of the process being audited. Auditors will be qualified through accredited training or a certified company auditor.

Reference: SOP 8.201 – Internal Auditing

8.2.4 Monitoring and Measurement of Process and Product

Audits will be used in conjunction with other measurements mentioned in section 8.1 to ensure that all processes and product comply with the Company's QMS, and ISO 9001:2000.

8.3 Control of Nonconforming Product

Nonconforming product will be handled according to the severity of the nonconformity. Questionable product will be evaluated against the customer's requirements, customer's contract, and implied needs. Nonconforming product can include product that is usable but does not meet the implied needs of the customer. If necessary, the customer will be contacted for permission to use product as is or clarification on the necessary action to make the product meet their expectations. Records of nonconformities will be maintained and used for historical data and trend analysis.

Reference: SOP 8.301 – Control of Nonconforming Product

8.4 Analysis of Data

Data gathered from process, product, customer, and supplier evaluation will be analyzed to identify trends. Negative trends will be evaluated for immediate reduction, root-cause analysis, and future elimination. Positive trends will be evaluated for replication in other areas to improve the QMS. Summary of such data and methods to correct and eliminate nonconformities will be included in inputs to management reviews and communication to other Associates.

8.5.1 CONTINUAL IMPROVEMENT

Productivity Resources, LLC, is committed to striving for excellence by evaluating all data and feedback for each business unit or product and incorporating improvements when feasible. Improvements will only be incorporated when they are beneficial to the Company and the customers. All feedback from customers will be responded to even if it doesn't warrant a change or improvement. In fact, whenever possible, the customer will be contacted to thank them for their input. When input is received via the corrective and preventive action process, the response will be processed using this vehicle.

8.5.2 CORRECTIVE ACTION AND
8.5.3 PREVENTIVE ACTION

The Company will implement and document a closed-loop corrective and preventive process that eliminates existing and potential causes of nonconformities. This process will be extended to all customers, suppliers, and partnerships. This process will utilize a form to record all issues and suggestions for review of trends. Initiators of issues will be tasked with providing a detailed description of the issue and recommended implementation. The planned implementation will include the root cause of the nonconformity and steps to eliminate its occurrence or recurrence.

Reference: SOP 8.501 – Corrective and Preventive Action Process

APPENDIX C

CROSSWALKS BETWEEN ISO 9001:1994 AND ISO 9001:2000

Paragraph	Title	Cross-Reference
	Correspondence Between ISO 9001:1994 and ISO 9001:2000	
4	Quality System Requirements (title only)	
4.1	Management Responsibility (title only)	
4.1.1	Quality Policy	5.1, 5.3, 5.4.1
4.1.2	Organization (title only)	
4.1.2.1	Responsibility and Authority	5.5.1
4.1.2.2	Resources	6.1, 6.2.1
4.1.2.3	Management Representative	5.5.2
4.1.3	Management Review	5.6.1, 8.5.1
4.2	Quality System (title only)	
4.2.1	General	4.1, 4.2.2
4.2.2	Quality System Procedures	4.2.1
4.2.3	Quality Planning	5.4.2, 7.1

Paragraph	Title	Cross-Reference
4.3	Contract Review (title only)	
4.3.1	General	
4.3.2	Review	5.2, 7.2.1, 7.2.2, 7.2.3
4.3.3	Amendment to a Contract	7.2.2
4.3.4	Records	7.2.2
4.4	Design Control (title only)	
4.4.1	General	
4.4.2	Design and Development Planning	7.3.1
4.4.3	Organizational and Technical Interfaces	7.3.1
4.4.4	Design Input	7.2.1, 7.3.2
4.4.5	Design Output	7.3.3
4.4.6	Design Review	7.3.4
4.4.7	Design Verification	7.3.5
4.4.8	Design Validation	7.3.6
4.4.9	Design Changes	7.3.7
4.5	Document and Data Control (title only)	
4.5.1	General	4.2.3
4.5.2	Document and Data Approval and Issue	4.2.3
4.5.3	Document and Data Changes	4.2.3
4.6	Purchasing (title only)	
4.6.1	General	
4.6.2	Evaluation of Subcontractors	7.4.1
4.6.3	Purchasing Data	7.4.2
4.6.4	Verification of Purchased Product	7.4.3
4.7	Control of Customer-Supplied Product	7.5.4
4.8	Product Identification and Traceability	7.5.3

Paragraph	Title	Cross-Reference
4.9	Process Control	6.3, 6.4, 7.5.1, 7.5.2
4.10	Inspection and Testing (title only)	
4.10.1	General	7.1, 8.1
4.10.2	Receiving Inspection and Testing	7.4.3, 8.2.4
4.10.3	In-Process Inspection and Testing	8.2.4
4.10.4	Final Inspection and Testing	8.2.4
4.10.5	Inspection and Test Records	7.5.3, 8.2.4
4.11	Control of Inspection, Measuring and Test Equipment (title only)	
4.11.1	General	7.6
4.11.2	Control Procedure	7.6
4.12	Inspection and Test Status	7.5.3
4.13	Control of Nonconforming Product (title only)	
4.13.1	General 8.3	
4.13.2	Review and Disposition of Nonconforming Product	8.3
4.14	Corrective and Preventive Action (title only)	
4.14.1	General	8.5.2, 8.5.3
4.14.2	Corrective Action	8.5.2
4.14.3	Preventive Action	8.5.3
4.15	Handling, Storage, Packaging, Preservation & Delivery (title only)	
4.15.1	General	
4.15.2	Handling	7.5.5
4.15.3	Storage	7.5.5
4.15.4	Packaging	7.5.5
4.15.5	Preservation	7.5.5
4.15.6	Delivery	7.5.1

Paragraph	Title	Cross-Reference
4.16	Control of Quality Records	4.2.4
4.17	Internal Quality Audits	8.2.2, 8.2.3
4.18	Training	6.2.2
4.19	Servicing	7.5.1
4.20	Statistical Techniques (title only)	
4.20.1	Identification of Need	8.1, 8.2.3, 8.2.4, 8.4
4.20.2	Procedures	8.1, 8.2.3, 8.2.4, 8.4

Correspondence Between ISO 9001:2000 and ISO 9001:1994

Paragraph	Title	Cross-Reference
4	Quality Management System (title only)	
4.1	General Requirements	4.2.1
4.2	Documentation Requirements (title only)	
4.2.1	General	4.2.2
4.2.2	Quality Manual	4.2.1
4.2.3	Control of Documents	4.5.1, 4.5.2, 4.5.3
4.2.4	Control of Records	4.16
5	Management Responsibility (title only)	
5.1	Management Commitment	4.1.1
5.2	Customer Focus	4.3.2
5.3	Quality Policy	4.1.1
5.4	Planning (title only)	
5.4.1	Quality Objectives	4.1.1
5.4.2	Quality Management System Planning	4.2.3
5.5	Responsibility, Authority, and Communication (title only)	
5.5.1	Responsibility and Authority	4.1.2.1
5.5.2	Management Representative	4.1.2.3
5.5.3	Internal Communication	

Paragraph	Title	Cross-Reference
5.6	Management Review (title only)	
5.6.1	General	4.1.3
5.6.2	Review Input	
5.6.3	Review Output	
6	Resource Management (title only)	
6.1	Provision of Resources	4.1.2.2
6.2	Human Resources (title only)	
6.2.1	General	4.1.2.2
6.2.2	Competence, Awareness, and Training	4.18
6.3	Infrastructure	4.9
6.4	Work Environment	4.9
7	Product Realization (title only)	
7.1	Planning of Product Realization	4.2.3, 4.10.1
7.2	Customer-Related Processes (title only)	
7.2.1	Determination of Requirements Related to the Product	4.3.2, 4.4.4
7.2.2	Review of Requirements Related to the Product	4.3.2, 4.3.3, 4.3.4
7.2.3	Customer Communication	4.3.2
7.3	Design and Development (title only)	
7.3.1	Design and Development Planning	4.4.2, 4.4.3
7.3.2	Design and Development Inputs	4.4.4
7.3.3	Design and Development Outputs	4.4.5
7.3.4	Design and Development Review	4.4.6
7.3.5	Design and Development Verification	4.4.7
7.3.6	Design and Development Validation	4.4.8
7.3.7	Control of Design and Development Changes	4.4.9
7.4	Purchasing (title only)	

Paragraph	Title	Cross-Reference
7.4.1	Purchasing Process	4.6.2
7.4.2	Purchasing Information	4.6.3
7.4.3	Verification of Purchased Product	4.6.4, 4.10.2
7.5	Production and Service Provision (title only)	
7.5.1	Control of Production and Service Provision	4.9, 4.15.6, 4.19
7.5.2	Validation of Processes for Production and Service Provision	4.9
7.5.3	Identification and Traceability	4.8, 4.10.5, 4.12
7.5.4	Customer Property	4.7
7.5.5	Preservation of Product	4.15.2, 4.15.3, 4.15.4, 4.15.5
7.6	Control of Monitoring and Measuring Devices	4.11.1, 4.11.2
8	Measurement, Analysis, and Improvement (title only)	
8.1	General	4.10.1, 4.20.1, 4.20.2
8.2	Monitoring and Measurement (title only)	
8.2.1	Customer Satisfaction	
8.2.2	Internal Audit	4.17
8.2.3	Monitoring and Measurement of Processes	4.17, 4.20.1, 4.20.2
8.2.4	Monitoring and Measurement of Product	4.10.2, 4.10.3, 4.10.4, 4.10.5, 4.20.1, 4.20.2
8.3	Control of Nonconforming Product	4.13.1, 4.13.2
8.4	Analysis of Data	4.20.1, 4.20.2
8.5	Improvement (title only)	
8.5.1	Continual Improvement	4.1.3
8.5.2	Corrective Action	4.14.1, 4.14.2
8.5.3	Preventive Action	4.14.1, 4.14.3

AN AUDIT CHECKLIST
FOR ISO 9001:2000

This appendix is a checklist that may be used to perform a gap analysis of your current QMS to the requirements of ISO 9001:2000. It can also be used as a preassessment tool prior to third-party registration audits. There are several caveats about its use, however.

There has not been sufficient time since the release of the revised standard for norms and conventions to have been developed and publicized. A comprehensive body of knowledge of common practices and interpretations will be some time in coming. Also, the ISO implementation guidelines place the burden of interpretation and applicability on the companies and their registrars. Therefore, you should use experienced consultants and registrars to help you in the implementation or transition process.

There are approximately 270 questions that are taken directly from the standard. Not all of them may be applicable to your organization. Many of them will require your company to take an interpretive position on exactly if and how each applies to your company, culture, and industry. You should start by clarifying the definition in the Comments column before determining if and how a question is applicable. Appendix A is a valuable tool for clarifying terminology.

Italicized text indicates that there is a qualifier attached to the question that will require a judgment call to be exercised. These qualifiers include *choose, appropriate, planned, adequate, applicable, needed, suitable, can be, may be, relevant, impractical, extent, dependent on, when necessary, intends, as required, readily determined, can include, undue delay,* and *satisfactorily.* You must define who can determine these qualifiers and when they may be used before each question is answered. For instance, when the standard says "as necessary," your organization must decide when and if it is necessary and which job function can make that determination.

All topic headings in Clause 7 are italicized because each is subject to exclusion by an organization if justifiably not applicable to that organization.

Also each reference where a process or procedure must be documented is shown in boldface.

Clause	Title	Gap Analysis Questions	Comments
4	Quality Management System (title only)		
4.1	General Requirements	1. Does the organization have a quality management system (QMS)?	Define what a QMS is
		2. Is the QMS a continual improvement model?	Define continual improvement
		3. *Are required processes identified?*	Define processes
		4. Is the application of the "processes" identified throughout the organization?	
		5. Is the sequence and interaction of the processes identified?	Define sequence and interaction
		6. Are there criteria and methods to ensure operation and control of processes?	Define operation and control
		7. Are resources available to support the operation and monitoring of processes?	Define resources and monitoring
		8. Are processes monitored, measured, and analyzed?	Define measurement and analysis
		9. Are actions implemented to continually improve processes?	

Clause	Title	Gap Analysis Questions	Comments
		10. Does the QMS meet the requirements of ISO 9001:2000?	
		11. Are there controls for outsourced processes?	Define outsourcing
		12. Are there processes for management activities?	Define management activities
		13. Are there processes for provision of resources?	
		14. Are there processes for product realization?	Define product realization
		15. Are there processes for measurement?	

4.2 Documentation Requirements (title only)

Clause	Title	Gap Analysis Questions	Comments
4.2.1	General	1. **Is there a documented quality policy?**	Define quality policy
		2. **Are there documented quality objectives?**	Define quality objectives
		3. **Is there a documented quality manual?**	Define quality manual
		4. **Are there documented procedures as required by ISO 9001:2000?**	
		5. *Do adequate documents exist to ensure effective planning?*	Define documents
		6. *Do adequate documents exist to ensure effective operations?*	
		7. *Do adequate documents exist to ensure control of processes?*	
		8. Are records kept as required by ISO 9001:2000?	Define records

Clause	Title	Gap Analysis Questions	Comments
		9. *Are required procedures documented?*	
		10. *Are required procedures established?*	Define established
		11. *Are required procedures implemented?*	Define implementation
		12. *Are required procedures maintained?*	Define maintenance
		13. *Is the QMS documentation appropriate to the size and activities of the organization?*	Define appropriate
		14. *Is the QMS documentation appropriate to the complexity and interaction of the processes?*	Define complexity
		15. *Is the QMS documentation appropriate to the competency of the personnel?*	Define competency
		16. *Is the medium of the documentation appropriate to the organization?*	Define medium
4.2.2	*Quality Manual*	1. *Is the QMS "scope" documented in the manual?*	Define scope
		2. *Are details and justification for exclusions included in the manual?*	Define exclusions
		3. **Are QMS procedures included in the manual or referenced?**	Define reference
		4. **Is there a description of the interaction between the processes in the manual?**	Define interaction
4.2.3	Control of Documents	1. *Are required documents controlled?*	
		2. Are records included in document control?	

Clause	Title	Gap Analysis Questions	Comments
		3. Is there a documented procedure for approval prior to use?	Define approval
		4. Is there a documented procedure for updates and reapproval?	Define reapproval
		5. Is there a documented procedure to ensure that changes are identified?	
		6. Is there a documented procedure to ensure that revision status is identified?	Define revision status
		7. Is there a documented procedure to ensure that relevant revisions are available where they are used?	Define relevance
		8. Is there a documented procedure to ensure that documents remain legible and identifiable?	Define legible and identifiable
		9. Is there a documented procedure to ensure that external documents are controlled and identified?	Define external documents
		10. Is there a documented procedure to identify and prevent unintended use of obsolete documents?	Define obsolete documents
4.2.4	Control of Records	1. Do records exist to prove evidence of conformity?	Define conformity
		2. Do records exist to validate the effectiveness of the QMS?	
		3. Are records legible, readily identifiable, and retrievable?	Define effectiveness
		4. Is there a documented procedure for identification of records?	
		5. Is there a documented procedure for storage of records?	

Clause	Title	*Gap Analysis Questions*	*Comments*
		6. **Is there a documented procedure for protection of records?**	
		7. **Is there a documented procedure for retrieval of records?**	
		8. **Is there a documented procedure for indicating retention time of records?**	
		9. **Is there a documented procedure for disposition of records?**	
5	Management Responsibility (title only)		
5.1	Management Commitment	1. Is there evidence that top management is committed to development and implementation of the QMS?	Define top management
		2. Is there evidence that top management is committed to continually improving the QMS?	Define commitment
		3. Does top management communicate the importance of meeting customer, statutory, and regulatory requirements?	Define communication
		4. Did top management create the quality policy?	
		5. Does top management ensure the establishment of quality objectives?	
		6. Does top management conduct management reviews?	Define management review
		7. Does top management ensure availability of resources?	
5.2	Customer Focus	1. *Does top management ensure that customer requirements are determined?*	Define customer requirements
		2. Does top management aim to enhance customer satisfaction?	Define customer satisfaction

Clause	Title	Gap Analysis Questions	Comments
5.3	Quality Policy	1. *Is the quality policy appropriate to the purpose of the organization?*	
		2. Is there a commitment by top management to comply with the quality policy?	
		3. Is there a commitment by top management to continually improve the QMS?	
		4. Does top management provide a framework for establishing and reviewing quality objectives?	
		5. Is the quality policy communicated and understood within the organization?	Define understanding
		6. Is the quality policy reviewed for continued suitability?	Define suitability
5.4	Planning (title only)		
5.4.1	Quality Objectives	1. *Are quality levels and objectives established for all relevant functions?*	
		2. Are the quality objectives measurable?	Define measurable
		3. Are the quality objectives consistent with the quality policy?	
5.4.2	Quality Management System Planning	1. Is there evidence of planning to carry out the requirements of 4.1?	Define planning
		2. Is there evidence of planning to carry out the quality objectives?	
		3. Do plans exist to maintain the integrity of the QMS when changes are planned and implemented?	

Clause	Title	Gap Analysis Questions	Comments
5.5	Responsibility, Authority, and Communication (title only)		
5.5.1	Responsibility and Authority	1. Are responsibilities and authorities defined?	Define responsibilities
		2. Are responsibilities and authorities communicated?	Define authority
5.5.2	Management Representative	1. Is there a management representative for the QMS?	Define management representative
		2. Is the management representative responsible for ensuring that required processes are established, implemented, and maintained?	
		3. Does the management representative report to top management on the performance of the QMS?	
		4. Does the management representative report to top management on improvement needs for the QMS?	
		5. Does the management representative ensure that awareness of customer requirements is promoted?	
		6. Does the management representative have liaison duties with external parties?	
5.5.3	Internal Communication	1. *Has top management established appropriate communication processes?*	Define communication
		2. Does communication take place regarding the effectiveness of the QMS?	
5.6	Management Review (title only)		
5.6.1	General	1. *Does top management review the QMS at planned intervals?*	Define planned intervals
		2. *Do these reviews cover continuing suitability, adequacy, and effectiveness of the QMS?*	

Clause	Title	Gap Analysis Questions	Comments
		3. Do these reviews cover assessing opportunities for change and improvement of the QMS?	
		4. Do these reviews look at assessing the need to change the quality policy or quality objectives?	
		5. Are records of management reviews maintained?	
5.6.2	Review Input	1. Do management review inputs contain the seven topics specified in 5.6.2?	See 5.6.2
5.6.3	Review Output	1. Do management review outputs contain the three topics specified in 5.6.3?	See 5.6.3
6	Resource Management (title only)		
6.1	Provision of Resources	1. *Does the organization determine and provide resources needed to implement and maintain the QMS?*	
		2. *Does the organization determine and provide resources needed to continually improve the effectiveness of the QMS?*	
		3. *Does the organization determine and provide resources needed to enhance customer satisfaction?*	
6.2	Human Resources (title only)		
6.2.1	General	1. *Are personnel working within the QMS competent on the basis of appropriate education, training, skills, and experience?*	
6.2.2	Competence, Awareness, and Training	1. Are competence levels established for all personnel working within the QMS?	

Clause	Title	Gap Analysis Questions	Comments
		2. *Is training or are other appropriate actions provided to satisfy any lacking needs?*	Define training
		3. Is training effectiveness evaluated?	
		4. *Are personnel made aware of the relevance and importance of their activities?*	
		5. Are personnel made aware of how they contribute to the achievement of quality objectives?	
		6. *Are appropriate records kept of training, skills, and experience?*	
6.3	Infrastructure	1. *Does the organization provide buildings, workspace, and utilities adequate to achieve product conformance requirements?*	Define infrastructure
		2. *Does the organization provide software and hardware equipment adequate to achieve product conformance requirements?*	
		3. *Does the organization provide supporting services adequate to achieve product conformance requirements?*	
6.4	Work Environment	1. *Does the organization provide a work environment needed to achieve product conformance requirements?*	Define work environment
7	Product Realization (title only)		
7.1	*Planning of Product Realization*	1. *Are the processes for product realization planned and in place?*	
		2. *Are the processes consistent with other processes of the QMS?*	
		3. *Were quality objectives and requirements determined?*	

Clause	Title	*Gap Analysis Questions*	*Comments*
		4. Were product-specific processes, documents, and resources determined?	
		5. Were verification, validation, monitoring, inspection, test, and product acceptance criteria determined?	
		6. Were requirements for evidence of meeting requirements determined?	
		7. Is the output of the planning in a suitable form?	
		8. Is the output referred to as a quality plan?	Define quality plan
		9. Was 7.3 used to plan the realization process?	
7.2	*Customer-Related Processes (title only)*		
7.2.1	*Determination of Requirements Related to the Product*	*1. Did the organization determine the requirements of the customer related to the product, including delivery and postdelivery activities?*	
		2. Did the organization determine the requirements of the customer, related to the product, that were not stated but necessary for intended use?	Define intended use
		3. Did the organization determine the requirements, related to the product, for statutory and regulatory compliance?	
		4. Did the organization determine any unstated requirements related to the product?	Define unstated requirements
7.2.2	*Review of Requirements Related to the Product*	*1. As a part of bidding, accepting, and changing customer orders, is a review conducted to determine if product requirements are defined?*	

Clause	Title	Gap Analysis Questions	Comments
		2. As a part of bidding, accepting, and changing customer orders, is a review conducted to determine if any changes from previous understandings were resolved?	Define resolution
		3. As a part of bidding, accepting, and changing customer orders, is a review conducted to determine if the organization has the ability to meet defined requirements?	Define organizational ability
		4. As a part of bidding, accepting, and changing customer orders, are review records maintained?	
		5. When customers provide no documented requirements, does the organization confirm Questions 1 through 3?	
		6. When requirements are changed, does the organization have a mechanism to ensure that all relevant personnel are made aware of the changes?	
		7. When it is impractical to formally review bid and orders, is catalog and advertising material utilized to accomplish Questions 1 through 3?	Define formal and informal review
7.2.3	Customer Communication	1. Has the organization determined and implemented effective communication with the customer relative to product information?	
		2. Has the organization determined and implemented effective communication with the customer relative to inquiries, contracts, order handling, and amendments?	
		3. Has the organization determined and implemented effective communication with the customer relative to feedback and complaints?	

Clause	Title	Gap Analysis Questions	Comments
7.3	*Design and Development* *(title only)*		Define design and development
7.3.1	*Design and Development Planning*	*1. Has the organization planned design and development in accordance with 7.3.1?*	
7.3.2	*Design and Development Inputs*	*1. Has the organization planned design and development inputs in accordance with 7.3.2?*	
7.3.3	*Design and Development Outputs*	*1. Has the organization planned design and development outputs in accordance with 7.3.3?*	
7.3.4	*Design and Development Review*	*1. Has the organization planned design and development review in accordance with 7.3.4?*	
7.3.5	*Design and Development Verification*	*1. Has the organization planned design and development verification in accordance with 7.3.5?*	
7.3.6	*Design and Development Validation*	*1. Has the organization planned design and development validation in accordance with 7.3.6?*	
7.3.7	*Control of Design and Development Changes*	*1. Has the organization planned design and development changes in accordance with 7.3.7?*	
7.4	*Purchasing (title only)*		
7.4.1	*Purchasing Process*	*1. Does the organization determine that purchased product conforms to purchase requirements?*	Define purchased product
		2. Does the organization determine the extent of controls placed on purchase requirements?	
		3. Do these controls depend on the effect of the purchased product on realization of the final product?	

Clause	Title	Gap Analysis Questions	Comments
		4. Does the organization evaluate and select suppliers?	Define suppliers
		5. Does the organization establish the criteria for selection, evaluation, and re-evaluation of suppliers?	
		6. Are records of evaluations and any necessary actions taken kept and maintained?	
7.4.2	Purchasing Information	1. In providing purchasing information, are requirements for approval of product, procedures, processes, and equipment specified?	Define purchasing information
		2. In providing purchasing information, are requirements for qualification of personnel specified?	
		3. In providing purchasing information, are requirements for quality management systems specified?	
		4. Does the organization ensure adequacy of purchase requirements prior to communication to the supplier?	
7.4.3	Verification of Purchased Product	1. Does the organization determine that purchased product conforms to purchase requirements?	See 7.4.1, Question 1
		2. Is there provision for the organization or its customers to perform verification at the supplier's facility when it is required?	
7.5	Production and Service Provision (title only)		
7.5.1	Control of Production and Service Provision	1. Is production and service carried out under controlled conditions?	Define production and service

Clause	Title	Gap Analysis Questions	Comments
		2. For production and service, is information available that describes the characteristics of the product?	
		3. For production and service, are work instructions available?	
		4. For production and service, is suitable equipment in use?	
		5. For production and service, are monitoring and measuring devices available?	
		6. For production and service, is monitoring and measurement implemented?	
		7. For production and service, are procedures in place for release, delivery, and postdelivery activities?	
7.5.2	*Validation of Processes for Production and Service Provision*	1. When the output of a process cannot be readily be determined by monitoring or measurement, is process validation conducted?	Define process validation
		2. When deficiencies may become apparent only after delivery of a product, is process validation conducted?	
		3. Do process validation procedures demonstrate the ability to achieve planned results?	
		4. For process validation, are there defined process review and approval criteria?	
		5. For process validation, is equipment determined to be approved?	
		6. For process validation, are personnel determined to be qualified?	

Clause	Title	Gap Analysis Questions	Comments
		7. For process validation, are methods and procedures specified?	Define methods and procedures
		8. For process validation, are records requirements specified?	
		9. For process validation, are revalidation requirements specified?	
7.5.3	Identification and Traceability	1. Are there appropriate identification and traceability procedures in place throughout the QMS?	Define identification and traceability
		2. Is monitoring and measurement status included in identification and traceability?	
		3. Is unique identification of the product assigned and recorded?	
		4. Is configuration management used to control identification and traceability?	Define configuration management
7.5.4	Customer Property	1. Does the organization exercise care when it has customer property in its control?	Define customer property
		2. Does the organization identify customer property?	
		3. Does the organization verify customer property?	
		4. Does the organization protect and safeguard customer property?	
		5. Does the organization notify the customer if their property is lost, damaged, or found unsuitable?	
		6. Does the organization maintain records on customer property?	

Clause	Title	Gap Analysis Questions	Comments
		7. Is intellectual property included in customer property?	
7.5.5	Preservation of Product	1. Does the organization preserve the conformity of the product and its constituent parts during internal processing and delivery?	Define preservation
		2. Does the organization employ material identification procedures?	
		3. Does the organization employ material handling procedures?	Identify handling
		4. Does the organization employ material packaging procedures?	Identify packaging
		5. Does the organization employ material storage procedures?	Identify storage
		6. Does the organization employ material protection procedures?	Identify protection
7.6	Control of Monitoring and Measuring Devices	1. Does the organization have a methodology to determine required measurement and monitoring?	
		2. Does the organization have a methodology to determine required measurement and monitoring equipment?	
		3. Does the organization have processes to carry out required measurement and monitoring per the determined requirements?	
		4. Is measuring and monitoring equipment calibrated prior to use or at specified intervals to known standards?	Define calibration
		5. Where no standards of calibration exist, is the basis for calibration or verification recorded?	

Clause	Title	Gap Analysis Questions	Comments
		6. Is measuring and monitoring equipment adjusted or readjusted as necessary?	
		7. Is measuring and monitoring equipment identified as to calibration status?	
		8. Is measuring and monitoring equipment safeguarded from adjustments that would invalidate results?	
		9. Is measuring and monitoring equipment protected from damage during handling, maintenance, and storage?	
		10. Is there a process in place to assess validity of previous measurements when equipment is found to be out of calibration?	
		11. Is there a process in place to take appropriate action on any product affected by out of calibration equipment?	
		12. Are calibration records kept and maintained?	
		13. Are there procedures to validate computer software used for monitoring or measurement?	Define test software
		14. Is software validation conducted prior to use and reconfirmed as necessary?	
8	Measurement, Analysis, and Improvement (title only)		
8.1	General	1. Is there a plan in place for monitoring, measurement, analysis, and improvement of the QMS?	
		2. Are there plans in place to demonstrate conformity of product?	

Clause	Title	Gap Analysis Questions	Comments
		3. Are there plans in place to ensure conformity of the QMS?	
		4. Are there plans in place to continually improve the QMS?	
		5. Are applicable methods and statistical techniques employed?	
8.2	Monitoring and Measurement (title only)		
8.2.1	Customer Satisfaction	*1. Does the organization monitor information relating to the customers' perceptions as to whether their requirements have been met?*	
		2. Are applicable methods determined to gather this information?	
8.2.2	Internal Audit	*1. Are internal audits conducted at planned intervals?*	Define internal audits
		2. Do these audits determine conformance to planned arrangements?	Define planned arrangements
		3. Do these audits determine conformance to ISO 9001:2000?	
		4. Do these audits determine conformance to QMS requirements?	
		5. Do these audits determine if the QMS is effectively implemented and maintained?	
		6. Are internal audits planned taking into consideration the status and importance of the processes and areas to be audited?	
		7. Are internal audits planned taking into consideration the results of previous audits?	
		8. Are internal audit criteria, scope, frequency, and methods defined?	

Clause	Title	Gap Analysis Questions	Comments
		9. Is selection of auditors and conduct of audits performed objectively and impartially?	
		10. Are auditors prohibited from auditing their own work?	
		11. Is there a documented procedure for planning and conducting audits?	
		12. Is there a documented procedure for reporting results and maintaining audit records?	
		13. *When nonconformities are detected during audits, does management for the responsible area take action without undue delay?*	Define undue delay
		14. Is follow-up performed to ensure verification of the actions and are verification results reported?	
8.2.3	Monitoring and Measurement of Processes	1. *Are there suitable methods in place to monitor and measure the processes within the QMS?*	
		2. Do these methods demonstrate the ability of the processes to achieve planned results?	
		3. *When planned results are not achieved, is appropriate corrective action taken to ensure product conformity?*	Define corrective action
8.2.4	Monitoring and Measurement of Product	1. *Are there suitable methods in place to monitor and measure product characteristics to ensure that all requirements are met?*	
		2. *Is this monitoring and measuring conducted at appropriate stages of production in accordance with planned arrangements?*	

Clause	Title	Gap Analysis Questions	Comments
		3. Is evidence of conformity with acceptance criteria maintained?	
		4. Do records indicate the person(s) authorizing product release?	
		5. *Does product release and service delivery proceed only after planned arrangements have been satisfactorily completed?*	
		6. *If not, have approvals been received from relevant authorities and the customer?*	
8.3	Control of Nonconforming Product	1. *Is nonconforming product identified and controlled to prevent unintended use or delivery?*	Define nonconforming product
		2. Is there a documented procedure related to the responsibilities and authorities for dealing with nonconforming product?	
		3. Does the organization have provisions to take action to eliminate the detected nonconformity?	
		4. *Does the organization have provisions for use of nonconforming product when concessions are granted by a relevant authority and by the customer?*	
		5. *Does the organization have provisions to preclude the use of nonconforming product for its original intent?*	
		6. Are records maintained of the nature of the nonconformities and the actions described in Questions 1 through 5?	
		7. When nonconforming material is corrected, is reverification performed to demonstrate conformity?	

Clause	Title	Gap Analysis Questions	Comments
		8. When nonconforming product is detected after delivery, is action taken appropriate to the effects or potential effects of the nonconformity?	
8.4	Analysis of Data	1. *Does the organization collect and analyze appropriate data to demonstrate the suitability of the QMS?*	Define appropriate data
		2. *Does the organization collect and analyze appropriate data to determine where continual improvement of QMS effectiveness can be made?*	Define data analysis
		3. Is the data generated as a result of monitoring and measurement?	
		4. *Is the data generated as from other relevant sources?*	Define relevant sources
		5. Does the data provide information relating to customer satisfaction?	
		6. Does the data provide information relating to conformity to product requirements?	
		7. Does the data provide information relating to characteristics of trends of processes and products?	Define trends
		8. Does the data provide information relating to opportunities for preventive action?	
		9. Does the data provide information relating to suppliers?	
8.5	Improvement (title only)		
8.5.1	Continual Improvement	1. Does the organization continually improve the QMS?	

Clause	Title	Gap Analysis Questions	Comments
		2. Is continual improvement accomplished through the use of the quality policy?	
		3. Is continual improvement accomplished through the use of the quality objectives?	
		4. Is continual improvement accomplished through the use of audit results?	
		5. Is continual improvement accomplished through the use of data analysis?	
		6. Is continual improvement accomplished through the use of corrective actions?	
		7. Is continual improvement accomplished through the use of preventive actions?	
		8. Is continual improvement accomplished through the use of management reviews?	
8.5.2	Corrective Action	1. Are actions taken to eliminate the cause of nonconformities in order to prevent their recurrence?	
		2. *Are corrective actions appropriate to the effects of the nonconformities?*	
		3. **Is there a documented procedure for reviewing nonconformities?**	
		4. **Is there a documented procedure for reviewing customer complaints?**	
		5. **Is there a documented procedure for determining the cause of nonconformities?**	

<table>
<tr><td></td><td></td><td>

6. **Is there a documented procedure for evaluating the need for action to ensure that nonconformities do not recur?**

7. **Is there a documented procedure for determining and implementing needed action?**

8. **Is there a documented procedure for recording the results of actions taken?**

9. **Is there a documented procedure for reviewing corrective actions taken?**

</td><td></td></tr>
<tr><td>8.5.3</td><td>Preventive Action</td><td>

1. Are actions taken to eliminate the cause of potential nonconformities in order to prevent their occurrence?

2. *Are preventive actions appropriate to the effects of the potential problems?*

3. **Is there a documented procedure for determining potential nonconformities and their causes?**

4. **Is there a documented procedure for evaluating the need for action to prevent occurrence of nonconformities?**

5. **Is there a documented procedure for determining and implementing needed action?**

6. **Is there a documented procedure for recording the results of actions taken?**

7. **Is there a documented procedure for reviewing preventive actions taken?**

</td><td></td></tr>
</table>

FUNCTIONS WITHIN A QUALITY MANAGEMENT SYSTEM

Within a compliant QMS, there are certain functions that must be performed. This appendix looks at each clause of ISO 9001:2000, attempts to define the function that would deal with the issues of running a compliant QMS, and makes suggestions of which departments, in typical organizations, might perform those functions. Depending on your organizational size, complexity, product, or service, you will need to assess if the functions are required and from which job position they will be covered.

Function	*Department(s)*	*Clause(s)*	*Comments*
QMS	Continual Improvement Committee, Quality, Management	4.1	Management representative leads a standing committee
Document control system	Management Representative, Engineering, Document Control Department, Administration	4.2.1	A comprehensive system for control of all documents and records within the QMS
Quality manual control	Management Representative, Quality Manager	4.2.2	Writing, controlling, and maintaining

(continued)

311

Function	Department(s)	Clause(s)	Comments
Document control	Management Representative, Engineering, Document Control Department, individual departments	4.2.3	Formal control of all documents, records, and computer media used in the QMS
Records control	Management Representative, Finance, Administration, individual departments	4.2.4	Control and disposition of organizational records
Management	President, CEO, COO, top management, Continual Improvement Committee	5.1, 5.3, 5.4, 5.5, 5.6	Establishment of the QMS and its policies and objectives and their communication; appoint management representative and conduct management reviews
Customer liaison	Management Representative, Sales, top management, Customer Service	5.2, 7.2.3	Ensure that customer's needs are determined, planned for, and met
QMS administration	Management Representative, Quality Manager	5.5.2	No need to have a formal quality assurance department
Resource management	Top management, Plant Manager, Management Representative, Quality Manager, Operations Manager, HR Manager	6.1, 6.2, 6.3, 6.4	Determine resource needs, provide appropriate awareness, training, infrastructure, and work environment
Training	Management Representative, Quality Manager, HR, Training Department	6.2.2	Establish competence, awareness, and training requirements and implement them
Product planning	Production Engineering, Planning, Production, Quality, Management, Sales, Safety Officer, Compliance Officer	7.1, 7.2.1	Planning for the processes necessary to realize the product or service outcome and to meet customer's needs and regulatory requirements
Contract review	Sales, Order Administration, Management	7.2.2, 7.2.3	Ensure that complete agreement is reached in regard to customer's orders for products or services, changes, and amendments and that capability exists to deliver

(continued)

Function	Department(s)	Clause(s)	Comments
Design control	Engineering, Planning, Production, Quality, Management, Sales, Safety Officer, Compliance Officer	7.3	Control and coordination of design and development planning, inputs, outputs, review, verification, validation, and design change control
Purchasing	Purchasing, Receiving, Quality	7.4	Supplier selection and control, purchasing and receipt of purchased products
Process planning	Production Planning, Production Control, Manufacturing, Order Fulfillment, Quality, Testing	7.5.1	Planning and scheduling of products and services, including resource availability and postsale service
Production	Manufacturing, Order Fulfillment, Inspection, Testing, Evaluation	7.5.1, 7.5.2	The processes related to delivering the products or services, including process control, validation, measurement, and inspection
Production control	Manufacturing, Order Fulfillment	7.5.3, 7.5.4	Identification, traceability, and control of customer property
Inventory	Inventory, Manufacturing	7.5.5	Integrity of the product at all times, from raw material to finished product
Metrology	Quality, Manufacturing, Engineering	7.6	Control of monitoring, measuring, and test equipment
Fulfillment	Continual Improvement Committee, Management Representative, Management	8.1, 8.2, 8.2.3	Ensure that conformity is monitored, customer satisfaction is determined, the QMS is validated, and processes are continually improved
Internal auditing	Continual Improvement Committee, Management Representative, Audit Group	8.2.2	Continual assessment of conformance and of the effectiveness of the QMS
Product inspection	Quality, Manufacturing	8.2.4	Product conformance verification steps (inspection, test, monitoring)

(continued)

Function	Department(s)	Clause(s)	Comments
Material review board	Quality, Manufacturing	8.3	Analysis and disposition of nonconforming product and material
Metrics	Engineering, Purchasing, Planning, Production, Quality, Management, Sales, Safety Officer, Compliance Officer	8.4	All functions in the value delivery system must collect and analyze process and product data and then take action based on that data
Continual improvement	All	8.5	Use the tools of corrective and preventive action along with metrics, internal auditing, inspection, and fulfillment to continually improve all processes and products

© 2001, Productivity Resources, LLC

INDEX

1987, xii, xiv, 1, 28, 47, 177
1994, xii, xiii, xiv, 1, 29, 47, 49, 50, 169, 177, 178, 179, 209, 214, 215, 252, 281, 284

A

activity, 249
analysis, 12, 56, 160, 161, 179, 204, 226, 249, 278, 286, 288, 308, 314
applicable documents, 74
approved Supplier, 249
approved Supplier List, 249
ARB, xv, xvii, 315
Asset Recovery Business, 315
audit, 62, 193, 197, 249, 277, 287, 313
audit checklist, 62, 249, 287
auditors, xii, 25, 56, 66, 150, 151, 176, 192, 193, 194, 196, 197, 198, 200, 215, 249, 250, 252, 306
availability, 66, 78, 83, 108, 112, 135, 136, 210, 252, 270, 292, 313

B

BMS, 57, 258, 315

C

calibration, 55, 143, 144, 250, 303, 304
CAR, 164, 252

certified, xii, 1, 15, 16, 17, 19, 20, 22, 23, 24, 169, 172, 177, 178, 180, 200, 213, 250, 278
competence, 50, 52, 71, 92, 102, 104, 105, 106, 107, 118, 128, 159, 160, 209, 251, 270, 285, 295, 312
competency, 49, 71, 72, 103, 104, 105, 290
compliance, xiii, xvi, 2, 3, 4, 8, 12, 13, 15, 63, 65, 67, 71, 82, 85, 109, 120, 131, 136, 139, 146, 157, 175, 176, 178, 185, 192, 196, 199, 200, 201, 222, 251, 297, 312, 313, 314
concession, 251
conformance, xi, xii, xiii, xv, xvi, 3, 21, 52, 56, 62, 65, 66, 72, 138, 155, 175, 178, 185, 192, 199, 200, 253, 257, 296, 305, 313
conformity, 55, 67, 68, 75, 83, 97, 107, 109, 112, 119, 135, 138, 142, 143, 145, 149, 153, 155, 157, 158, 159, 160, 291, 303, 304, 305, 306, 307, 308, 313
continual improvement, xiii, xiv, xvii, 2, 11, 17, 19, 49, 56, 60, 61, 62, 64, 66, 67, 69, 70, 71, 78, 79, 80, 81, 87, 93, 100, 102, 111, 115, 116, 145, 150, 152, 159, 160, 161, 162, 163, 164, 167, 168, 172, 176, 178, 180, 192, 195, 196, 209, 210, 211, 220, 222, 228, 229, 239, 250, 251, 267, 269, 277, 286, 288, 308, 309
continual process improvement, 2
control of nonconforming product, 56, 158, 283, 286, 307
corrective action, 56, 163, 164, 204, 251, 283, 286, 309

customer
    communication, 53, 122, 285, 298
    focus, 51, 59, 82, 100, 204, 284, 292
    property, 55, 140, 141, 286, 302
    requirements, 5, 49, 51, 59, 66, 82, 93,
        96, 98, 100, 101, 121, 148, 149,
        155, 159, 204, 255, 263, 269, 271,
        292, 294
    satisfaction, 13, 55, 148, 204, 252, 266,
        277, 286, 305
customer-related processes, 53, 120, 285,
    297

D

data analysis, 49, 81, 161, 162, 165, 167,
    308, 309
defect, 252
Dell Computer, xvii, 315
dependability, 83, 117, 126, 154, 164, 252
design and development, 53, 54, 124, 125,
    126, 127, 129, 130, 252, 282, 285,
    299
do what you documented, 2
document what you do, 2
documentation, 7, 18, 50, 61, 64, 68, 70,
    71, 72, 73, 75, 76, 77, 91, 103, 113,
    114, 118, 135, 156, 164, 178, 179, 183,
    184, 193, 249, 259, 263, 264, 265, 268,
    269, 270, 273, 277, 290

E

EU, 14, 15, 16, 28, 29, 200
exclude, 48, 62, 125, 134, 141, 142, 144,
    218
exclusion, 5, 62, 125, 142, 144, 146, 288
exclusions, xv, 50, 72, 73, 177, 252, 290
experience, xiii, 4, 8, 10, 15, 52, 63, 91,
    103, 104, 105, 106, 116, 128, 131, 135,
    161, 167, 168, 172, 177, 190, 193, 201,

209, 224, 239, 242, 246, 270, 295, 296,
    315
external parties, 93, 117, 269, 294

F

factual approach, 60, 100
functional, 182, 252
functionality, 77, 205

H

human resources, 52, 103, 285, 295

I

identifiable, 50, 74, 75, 265, 291
identification, 49, 55, 139, 140, 185, 253,
    265, 276, 284, 286, 302, 313
infrastructure, 52, 107, 108, 182, 270, 271,
    285, 296
inspection, 253, 283, 313
interaction of processes, 50, 73, 81
interested parties, 63, 69, 77, 79, 80, 81, 82,
    83, 85, 87, 89, 90, 94, 97, 98, 99, 100,
    102, 106, 108, 109, 115, 116, 118, 119,
    123, 124, 125, 126, 127, 130, 131, 134,
    136, 139, 141, 143, 145, 146, 147, 148,
    152, 154, 156, 157, 160, 161, 162, 164,
    166, 167, 168, 203, 250, 260
internal audit, 56, 150, 151, 152, 153, 165,
    179, 180, 190, 193, 194, 196, 197, 286,
    305
internal communication, 51, 94, 95, 284,
    294
internal communications, 49
internal customer, 10, 203, 207
International Organization for Standardi-
    zation, 28, 177
involvement of people, 60, 100, 103

ISO 9000, xii, xiii, xiv, xv, 1, 14, 15, 21, 27, 28, 29, 47, 48, 57, 59, 60, 61, 65, 138, 178, 192, 198, 206, 209, 213, 214, 215, 216, 219, 249, 251, 252, 254, 259

as a Profit Center, xv, 314

ISO 9001, xii, xiv, xv, xvi, 1, 2, 3, 4, 5, 7, 8, 9, 10, 11, 13, 14, 15, 16, 17, 18, 19, 20, 21, 22, 23, 24, 25, 29, 48, 50, 59, 60, 61, 62, 63, 65, 67, 73, 79, 87, 99, 110, 113, 125, 148, 150, 164, 169, 170, 172, 173, 174, 175, 176, 177, 178, 179, 180, 181, 182, 184, 189, 190, 191, 192, 196, 198, 199, 200, 203, 204, 206, 208, 209, 213, 214, 215, 216, 217, 218, 219, 220, 224, 227, 231, 239, 240, 245, 252, 257, 258, 259, 260, 264, 278, 281, 284, 287, 289, 305, 311

ISO 9002, xii, 48, 214, 215

ISO 9003, xii, 48, 214

ISO 9004, 48, 59, 60, 62, 63, 69, 70, 76, 79, 82, 87, 89, 90, 92, 94, 95, 96, 97, 98, 99, 102, 103, 105, 108, 110, 115, 123, 125, 127, 130, 132, 134, 139, 140, 141, 142, 144, 146, 147, 148, 151, 153, 154, 156, 159, 161, 163, 164, 166, 168, 178, 203, 214, 240, 260

L

leadership, xv, 60, 79, 100, 182, 241, 258, 316

legible, 50, 74, 75, 265, 291

M

Malcolm Baldrige, xiii, 19, 62, 315

management representative, 51, 92, 93, 94, 182, 281, 284, 294

management review, 51, 95, 96, 253, 281, 285, 294

management reviews, 51, 52, 78, 89, 96, 97, 112, 180, 269, 292, 295, 309

measurement

analysis and improvement, 55, 145, 147, 277, 286, 304

monitoring, 55, 56, 148, 153, 154, 286, 305, 306

measuring, 49, 55, 67, 136, 143, 144, 145, 148, 149, 154, 157, 175, 185, 206, 215, 218, 222, 250, 260, 275, 283, 286, 301, 303, 304, 306, 313

metrics, 24, 64, 78, 91, 94, 146, 154, 174, 186, 211, 228, 260, 264, 314

military standards, xi

monitoring, 49, 55, 65, 66, 67, 68, 81, 90, 111, 113, 118, 136, 137, 138, 139, 143, 144, 145, 148, 149, 153, 154, 156, 157, 160, 192, 209, 260, 268, 271, 275, 286, 288, 297, 301, 302, 303, 304, 306, 308, 313

N

natural resources, 112

needs and expectations, 49, 77, 81, 82, 83, 84, 87, 90, 106, 108, 109, 118, 119, 124, 125, 127, 128, 130, 148, 149, 154, 156, 157, 167, 203

nonconforming product, 158, 159, 255, 283, 307, 308, 314

nonconformities, 56, 98, 118, 131, 135, 150, 158, 159, 160, 163, 165, 204, 278, 279, 306, 307, 309, 310

nonconformity, 160, 253

O

obsolete documents, 74, 291

operations procedures, 253

outsourced, 50, 67, 68, 260, 289

P

partners, 13, 83, 84, 87, 102, 111, 135, 142, 157, 158, 184, 264, 269, 274

performance data, 90, 140, 147, 168

performance Improvement Guidelines, 63, 69, 76, 79, 82, 87, 89, 90, 92, 94, 95, 96, 97, 98, 99, 102, 103, 105, 108, 110, 115, 123, 125, 127, 130, 134, 139, 140, 141, 142, 144, 146, 148, 151, 154, 156, 159, 161, 163, 164, 166

performance improvements, 48, 60, 62

preservation of product, 55, 142, 286, 303

preventive action, 57, 165, 253, 283, 286, 310

process, xiv, xvi, 48, 60, 65, 100, 113, 115, 117, 118, 119, 138, 178, 180, 185, 209, 219, 220, 221, 223, 228, 244, 253, 260, 264, 274, 278, 279, 283, 313

process approach, 254

process control, 11, 52, 70, 72, 75, 313

product, 48, 52, 113, 118, 128, 155, 161, 184, 254, 272, 275, 277, 278, 282, 285, 296, 312, 313

product life cycle, 119

product realization, 53, 68, 69, 80, 81, 91, 108, 113, 114, 117, 131, 139, 155, 160, 285, 289, 296

purchasing, 15, 53, 54, 68, 91, 111, 127, 131, 132, 133, 134, 135, 157, 159, 274, 275, 282, 285, 286, 299, 300, 313, 314

Q

QMS, 49, 64, 254, 258, 288, 311

QS 9000, xiii, 215

quality, 5, 17, 48, 50, 51, 53, 59, 60, 62, 64, 72, 73, 85, 86, 87, 88, 89, 90, 172, 176, 180, 182, 183, 185, 192, 201, 214, 215, 227, 254, 257, 258, 259, 260, 263, 264, 267, 268, 271, 273, 277, 281, 284, 288, 290, 293, 311, 312, 313, 314, 315, 316

management, xii, xiv, xv, xvii, 1, 2, 4, 5, 10, 12, 15, 17, 20, 21, 28, 48, 59, 60, 61, 64, 65, 67, 68, 69, 70, 71, 72, 73, 75, 77, 78, 79, 80, 85, 89, 92, 93, 94, 95, 96, 97, 98, 99, 100, 101, 102, 103, 112, 113, 114, 115, 132, 145, 147, 148, 150, 151, 153, 156, 160, 162, 163, 164, 165, 167, 176, 178, 204, 209, 214, 253, 254, 258, 259, 260, 267, 268, 288, 300, 311

management system, 50, 51, 64, 89, 254, 284, 288, 293

objectives, 2, 49, 51, 52, 61, 70, 78, 79, 85, 86, 87, 88, 89, 90, 92, 94, 95, 96, 97, 101, 104, 105, 107, 108, 109, 113, 114, 162, 180, 190, 208, 209, 222, 227, 254, 260, 265, 267, 289, 292, 293, 295, 296, 309

planning, 90, 91, 96, 114, 214, 254, 268, 271

policy, xiv, 61, 70, 78, 79, 85, 86, 87, 88, 89, 90, 91, 93, 95, 96, 118, 162, 164, 174, 176, 190, 209, 254, 260, 265, 289, 292, 293, 295, 309

records, 254, 264

Quality Policy Manual, 60, 64, 254, 257, 258, 263, 264

R

RAB, 19, 29, 200

re-approve, 74

records, 50, 73, 75, 96, 99, 121, 129, 130, 132, 144, 155, 158, 265, 271, 273, 274, 278, 282, 312

registrar, 29, 199, 200, 254

regulatory, 50, 53, 63, 66, 71, 76, 77, 78, 79, 84, 85, 90, 98, 106, 108, 120, 124, 125, 126, 127, 136, 140, 156, 168, 178, 203, 265, 272, 292, 297, 312

relevance, 52, 104, 270, 291, 296

repair, 255

requirement, 51, 52, 53, 55, 255

resource management, 52, 101, 112, 285, 295

retention time, 75, 76, 292

retrievable, 50, 75, 265, 291

rework, 255

root-cause-analysis, 255

S

scope, xii, 61, 64, 68, 72, 73, 125, 150, 182, 250, 253, 258, 259, 266, 268, 271, 272, 273, 290, 305

self-assessment, 62, 70, 89, 98, 147, 149, 152, 153, 165, 167, 168

sequence & interaction, 50

service, xi, xii, 4, 15, 53, 54, 55, 68, 72, 82, 86, 93, 113, 114, 117, 120, 123, 125, 127, 132, 133, 134, 136, 137, 138, 139, 141, 143, 145, 148, 149, 155, 159, 168, 180, 182, 185, 200, 203, 205, 206, 207, 208, 209, 218, 221, 226, 251, 253, 255, 256, 257, 258, 260, 263, 264, 266, 272, 273, 274, 275, 277, 286, 300, 301, 307, 311, 312, 313

skills, 5, 10, 52, 72, 91, 93, 102, 103, 104, 105, 106, 116, 156, 183, 251, 260, 270, 295, 296, 315

software, xiv, 48, 55, 74, 75, 79, 107, 131, 134, 137, 139, 141, 142, 143, 144, 156, 183, 214, 218, 263, 264, 268, 270, 271, 273, 274, 276, 296, 304

specification, 255

standard operations procedures, 253

statistical techniques, 49, 61, 145, 152, 161, 206, 255, 284, 305

statutory, 50, 53, 66, 71, 76, 77, 78, 84, 85, 90, 98, 106, 108, 120, 124, 126, 127, 136, 140, 156, 168, 219, 265, 292, 297

suitable methods, 69, 153, 255, 306

system, 48, 50, 57, 60, 62, 100, 183, 255, 258, 263, 267, 268, 311

    approach, 61

T

tenders, 121

test, 255

The Process Approach, xiv

top management, 51, 59, 61, 69, 78, 79, 80, 81, 82, 85, 87, 88, 89, 91, 92, 93, 94, 95, 96, 97, 98, 99, 102, 115, 125, 130, 134, 139, 146, 148, 151, 152, 159, 164, 167, 168, 174, 179, 190, 204, 209, 241, 255, 292, 293, 294

traceability, 55, 99, 135, 139, 140, 184, 253, 255, 276, 282, 286, 302, 313

training, 10, 93, 103, 107, 179, 190, 208, 255, 263, 264, 284, 312

    effectiveness, 2, 49, 296

    record, 255

V

validated, xv, 53, 119, 128, 129, 138, 173, 180, 260, 264, 265, 313

validation, 54, 55, 79, 105, 111, 113, 115, 117, 118, 119, 124, 125, 128, 129, 130, 131, 133, 137, 138, 144, 146, 155, 156, 168, 255, 268, 271, 275, 282, 285, 286, 297, 299, 301, 302, 304, 313

verification, 54, 55, 68, 72, 96, 98, 109, 113, 115, 117, 118, 119, 124, 127, 128, 129, 130, 131, 133, 134, 135, 138, 143, 144, 145, 150, 154, 156, 157, 158, 211, 250,

verification, (*continued*)
253, 255, 256, 265, 268, 271, 273, 275,
282, 285, 286, 297, 299, 300, 303, 306,
307, 313
Verify that you are doing it, 2, 8

W

work environment, 2, 49, 52, 102, 107, 109,
110, 118, 220, 271, 285, 296, 312
Work instruction, 256

ABOUT THE AUTHORS

Tom Taormina

Certified Quality Manager;
Certified Management Consultant;
Certified Professional Consultant to Management.

Tom Taormina has been a quality professional for 31 years. For 14 years, he was a member of the Project Apollo team at the Johnson Space Center, including 10 years as a Quality Control Engineer with Ford Aerospace. In that time, he performed quality management system audits at more than 150 companies.

Taormina is the Managing Partner of Productivity Resources, LLC. He is a consultant in strategic quality improvement. He has developed seminars on ISO 9000 for Productivity, Inc., and for the American Productivity and Quality Center (APQC). For three years, he served as a subject matter expert on ISO 9000 for APQC. He has also developed and delivered seminars on self directed work teams for The University of Houston – Clear Lake and on conflict resolution for the National Aeronautics and Space Administration (NASA) at the Johnson Space Center.

He attended the University of Houston and has received additional training from Texas A&M, San Jacinto College, and APQC. Tom received his professional certifications from the American Society for Quality (ASQ) as a Certified Quality Manger, from the Institute of Management Consultants as a Certified Management Consultant, and from the National Bureau of Certified Consultants as a Certified Professional Consultant to Management. He is currently an adjunct to The Nevada University and Community College System and the State Manufacturing Assistance Partnership (MAP).

For more than a decade, Tom has facilitated many successful ISO 9000 implementations in a wide variety of business environments. He specializes in helping companies enhance their strategic quality initiatives through "ISO 9000 as a Profit Center." He is the author of *Virtual Leadership and the ISO 9000 Imperative* (English and Spanish editions) and *Successful Internal*

Auditing to ISO 9000 published by Prentice Hall. He has also written *Assessing ISO 9000 for Your Business: Key Elements and Strategies* published by ABS Government Institutes. His professional magazine articles have been published on four continents.

Keith A. Brewer

Certified Quality Manager.

Keith A. Brewer, ASQ Certified Quality Manager, joined Dell Computer Corporation in April, 1999. He is currently Project Strategist, Dell Americas Manufacturing Quality. From November 1, 1999 until February 1, 2001 he was responsible for all aspects of product quality in ARB and for the development, implementation, and deployment of ARB's Business Management System (BMS).

Brewer retired in 1998 after a 33-year career with IBM Corporation. During his tenure at IBM, Brewer's proven leadership in quality improvement, quality assessment, and business process management resulted in his selection for key roles in implementing pioneering programs and achieving aggressive results. He was an early leader in IBM's implementation of the Malcolm Baldrige National Quality Award program. He later served as program manager of re-engineering operations, for the IBM Server Group. In this position, Brewer was heavily involved in the restructuring of IBM's core business processes. He is highly respected for his leadership abilities, integrity, team-building skills, and analytical and communication skills.

Brewer is a seasoned manager and leader, having held senior management positions in finance, site operations, and branch office management. His management experience also includes accounting, application programming development, and business controls organizations. He was assigned to numerous senior staff leadership positions in division, group, and corporate functions, with significant roles in national and international operations.

As a senior examiner, Brewer led assessment teams evaluating a wide range of local, national, and international operations of IBM Corporation, including business units in the United States, South America, and Europe. He also taught many classes, including courses in process improvement, Malcolm Baldrige examiner training, leadership, and management philosophy and practice.

His experience and expertise in the areas of quality, process management, and re-engineering have resulted in invitations to speak on these topics to students at the University of Texas, St. Edwards University, the Texas

Adjutant General's Leadership Conference, numerous state and federal organizations, and in private industry.

Keith is a graduate of St. Edwards University, in Austin, Texas, a member of the AQ, and is an ASQ Certified Quality Manager. He has also been an active member of the Greater Austin Quality Council since 1991, serving as an examiner, instructor, and chair of the award, examiner, and nominating committees and the 1999 Panel of Judges. He currently is a member of the Board of Directors, Executive Committee, and Panel of Judges.

To interact with the authors, please follow the links at *www.ConsultPR.com.*

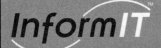

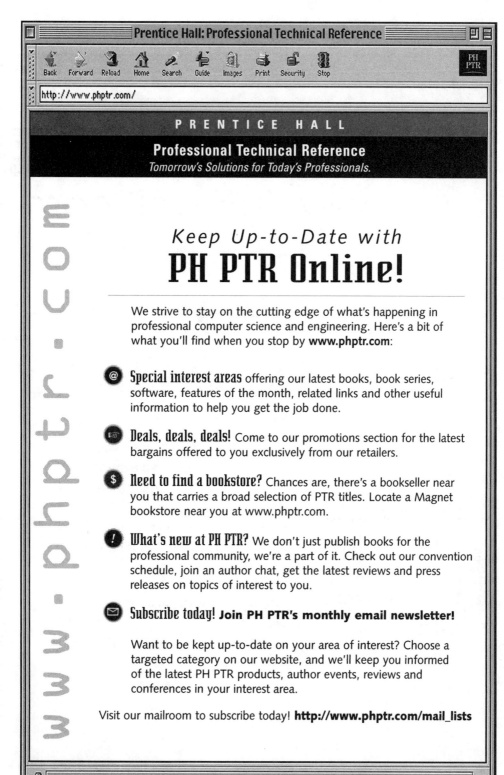